Local Authorities and the Human Rights Act 1998

Local Authorities and the Human Rights Act 1998

Michael Supperstone QC
James Goudie QC
and Jason Coppel

Butterworths
London, Dublin, Edinburgh
1999

United Kingdom	Butterworths, a Division of Reed Elsevier (UK) Ltd, Halsbury House, 35 Chancery Lane, LONDON WC2A 1EL and 4 Hill Street, EDINBURGH EH2 3JZ
Australia	Butterworths, a Division of Reed International Books Australia Pty Ltd, CHATSWOOD, New South Wales
Canada	Butterworths Canada Ltd, MARKHAM, Ontario
Hong Kong	Burterworths Asia (Hong Kong), HONG KONG
India	Butterworths India, NEW DELHI
Ireland	Butterworth (Ireland) Ltd, DUBLIN
Malaysia	Malayan Law Journal Sdn Bhd, KUALA LUMPUR
New Zealand	Butterworths of New Zealand Ltd, WELLINGTON
Singapore	Butterworths Asia, SINGAPORE
South Africa	Butterworths Publishers (Pty) Ltd, DURBAN
USA	Lexis Law Publishing, CHARLOTTESVILLE, Virginia

A CIP Catalogue record for this book is available from the British Library.

ISBN 0 406 92674 3

Typeset by Connell Publishing Services, Thame Oxfordshire
Printed by Redwood Books, Trowbridge, Wiltshire

Foreword

The Human Rights Act is the most important constitutional change in the UK since the European Communities Act 1972. Both pieces of legislation have had the effect of imposing significant controls on Parliamentary Sovereignty. The Human Rights Act gives effect in a subtle way to the European Convention on Human Rights. Rights derived from the Convention must be respected and public bodies, including local authorities will, wherever possible, have to exercise their powers in a way which is compatible with the Convention. Even where legislation compels a body to act inconsistently with the Convention, because it is impossible to construe it consistently, a court can grant a declaration that the Act contravenes the Convention, and a disappointed litigant may well secure before the European Court of Human Rights the remedy denied to him under national law,

The Convention will spread its tentacles into all areas of English law. Virtually all aspects of local authorities' operations will in principle potentially engage some provision of the Convention. No doubt in most cases authorities will already be acting in conformity with it, but there will inevitably be some areas where breaches will arise, albeit unwittingly.

The aim of this book is to describe the way in which the Act operates and to anticipate the areas where challenges to local authority decisions are most likely to arise. The book has been written by members of my former Chambers. The contributions are from barristers very well versed in the local government field. The analysis of the impact of the Act is excellent, and I am proud to be associated with the book. Local government lawyers would be well advised to have regard to the wisdom accumulated in this book. If they do, they can embrace the new law without trepidation!

Sir Patrick Elias
High Court Judge (Queen's Bench Division)

Royal Courts of Justice
London
October 1999

Preface

The Human Rights Act 1998 is already having an impact on the way Local Authorities take decisions. It is too early to judge the full effect of the Act on substantive local authority law. What is plain, however, is that local authorities should lose no time in reviewing their procedures to ensure that they best protect themselves from challenge when the Act comes into force on 2 October 2000.

The origins of this book lie in a conference given by 11 King's Bench Walk Chambers in January 1999. Conference papers have been updated and expanded and new chapters added. It has been prepared largely by contributors to *Butterworths Local Government Law.*

This book is a 'team effort' and we are very grateful to all those who have contributed to its production and publication, encouraging and assisting us to bring this work to fruition so speedily.

The Law is stated as at 4 October 1999.

Michael Supperstone QC
James Goudie QC
Jason Coppel

11, King's Bench Walk Chambers
Temple
London
EC4Y 7EQ

October 1999

Michael Supperstone QC,

Deputy High Court Judge; Recorder; Bencher, Middle Temple; Past Chairman, Administrative Law Bar Association; Principal Editor of Administrative Law Title of *Halsbury's Laws of England*; Co-editor of *Supperstone and Goudie on Judicial Review* (2nd edn); member of the Editorial Board of *Public Law*; Consultant Editor of *Butterworths Local Government Reports*.

James Goudie QC,

Deputy High Court Judge; Recorder; Bencher, Inner Temple; Joint Head, 11 King's Bench Walk Chambers; Past Chairman, Administrative Law Bar Association; Co-editor of *Supperstone and Goudie on Judicial Review* (2nd edn); Co-editor of *Butterworths Local Government Law*; Advisory Board, 'Judicial Review'; Consultant Editor of *Butterworths Local Government Reports*.

Jason Coppel,

Barrister; Author of *The Human Rights Act 1998: Enforcing the European Convention in the Domestic Courts (1999)*; Co-author of Butterworths *EC Law for UK Lawyers*.

Gillian Morris,

Professor of Law at Brunel University and undertaking advisory work in employment, public and human rights law at 11 King's Bench Walk Chambers. Author or Co-author of numerous books on employment and public law, including *Labour Law*; *The State as Employer: Labour Law in the Public Services* and *Trade Unions, Employers and the Law*.

Stephen Tromans,

Recently joined 11 King's Bench Walk Chambers from the City law firm Simmons & Simmons, where he was Head of Environmental Law. Amongst numerous other publications, he is Co-editor of *The Encyclopedia of Environmental Law* and author of *Contaminated Land*. He is a former Chairman of the UK Environmental Law Association.

John Cavanagh, MA (Oxon), LLM (Cantab),

Barrister; Treasurer, Employment Law Bar Association.

Akhlaq Choudhury, BSc (Glasgow), LLB (London),

Barrister.

Nigel Giffin, MA (Oxon),

Barrister; Committee Member, Administrative Law Bar Association.

Andrew Hillier, BA (Dublin),

Barrister.

Cecilia Ivimy, BA (Oxon),

Barrister.

Elisabeth Laing, BA (Cantab),
Barrister; Assistant Recorder.

Richard Leiper, LLB (Birmingham), MJur (Oxon),
Barrister.

Paul Nicholls, LLB (Sheffield), BCL (Oxon),
Barrister.

Peter Oldham, MA (Oxon),
Barrister.

Tom Restrick, BA (Oxon),
Barrister.

Clive Sheldon, BA (Cantab), LLM (UPenn),
Barrister.

Daniel Stilitz, BA (Oxon), MA (City),
Barrister; Consultant Editor of *Butterworths Local Government Reports.*

Jonathan Swift, BA (Oxon), LLM (Cantab),
Barrister.

Peter Wallington, MA, LLM,
Barrister; Sometime Professor of Law at the University of Lancaster and Brunel University.

Siobhan Ward, BA, LLM (Cantab),
Barrister.

Contents

Table of European & International Legislation

References in the right hand column are to page number. Where a page number is set in **bold**, this indicates that the legislation is set outin part or in full.

EUROPE

INTERNATIONAL

Table of Statutes

References in the right hand column are to page number. Where a page number is set in **bold**, this indicates that a statute is set out in part or in full.

Table of Statutory Instruments

References in the right hand column are to page number. Where a page number is set in **bold**, this indicates that a statutory instrument is set out in part or in full.

Table of Cases

Chapter 1

The Mechanics of the Human Rights Act 1998

INTRODUCTION

The Human Rights Act 1998 ('HRA 1998') is one of the cornerstones of the Labour government's programme of constitutional reform and one of the most important constitutional developments of recent years. It will have a profound effect on the decision making of all public bodies. Local authorities, however, have particular cause for concern since they are the primary decision makers in a range of fields in which HRA 1998 confers important new rights on individuals: child protection, planning, licensing and education, to name but a few.

HRA 1998 gives 'further effect' in domestic law to the rights enshrined in the European Convention on Human Rights ('ECHR'). ECHR is an international treaty signed in 1950 under the auspices of the Council of Europe. It requires its signatories to secure to individuals certain fundamental rights to individuals within their jurisdiction. The UK played a central role in drafting it and was one of the original signatories, but declined to incorporate the rights conferred by the Convention into domestic law. Convention rights could not, therefore, be directly invoked in the domestic courts, and public decision-makers, including local authorities, had no enforceable duty to comply with Convention rights. The UK did, however, accept the right of individuals to complain about any breach of their Convention rights before the Commission and Court of Human Rights in Strasbourg. The result was a catalogue of defeats for the UK government in Strasbourg, many of which involved decisions by local authorities.

Although HRA 1998 is commonly referred to as incorporating the Convention into domestic law, it does not in fact have that effect. It enables individuals to invoke Convention rights in the domestic courts for limited purposes and to limited effect. Crucially, however, it imposes an express duty on public authorities, including local authorities, to comply with Convention rights,[1] and many local authority decisions will be open to challenge if they do not so comply.

The new rights, contained in ECHR and conferred by HRA 1998 (which refers to them as 'Convention rights') are as follows:

The right to life (Art 2)
Prohibition on inhuman and degrading treatment (Art 3)
No slavery or forced labour (Art 4)

1 Section 6(1).

No unjustified detention (Art 5)
The right to a fair hearing (Art 6)
No retrospective penalties for criminal offences (Art 7)
Right to respect for private and family life, the home and correspondence (Art 8)
Freedom of thought, conscience and religion (Art 9)
Freedom of expression (Art 10)
Freedom of assembly and association (Art 11)
The right to marry (Art 12)
No discrimination (Art 14)
Right to property (Art 1 of Protocol No 1)
Right to education (Art 2 of Protocol No 1)
Right to free elections (Art 3 of Protocol No 1)
No capital punishment (Fourth Protocol)

The only substantive right within the Convention itself which is not given further effect by HRA 1998 is the right to an effective remedy (Art 13).

Virtually every decision taken by local authorities is potentially affected by Convention rights. In particular, the right to a fair hearing under Art 6 can be invoked in respect of a very wide range of administrative decisions. Aside from Art 6, certain areas of local authority activity will be directly affected by particular rights, for example education (the right to education, to respect for private and family life and to freedom of thought, conscience and religion), planning and environmental regulation (the right to property and to respect for the home), child wardship and care decisions (the right to family life), licensing (the right to property and to freedom of expression) and employment (the right to respect for private life, to freedom of association, and against discrimination).

The main provisions of HRA 1998 will not be brought into force until 2 October 2000. The reason for the lapse of time is the need to give judges and public authorities a breathing space in which to adjust to the new demands of Convention rights. However, even during this breathing space, local authorities must ensure that their decisions comply with Convention rights as once HRA 1998 comes into force, individuals will be able to make collateral (although not direct) challenges to local authority decisions which were made before HRA 1998 came into force. That is the effect of ss 7 and 22(4) of HRA 1998.

> 7. – (1) a person who claims that a public authority has acted (or proposes to act) in a way which is made unlawful by s 6(1) may-
>
> (a) bring proceedings against the authority under this Act in the appropriate court or tribunal; or
>
> (b) rely on the Convention right or rights concerned in any legal proceedings,
>
> but only if he is (or would be) a victim of the unlawful act.
>
> ....
>
> 22(4) Paragraph (b) of subsection (1) of section 7 applies to proceedings brought by or at the instigation of a public authority whenever the act in question took place; but otherwise that subsection does not apply to an act taking place before the coming into force of that section.

These provisions also apply to appeals from proceedings other than direct challenges to local authority decisions. For example, a gypsy or traveller who was the subject of enforcement proceedings before 2 October 2000 could rely on HRA 1998 in any appeal heard after that date.[2] Aside from the question of collateral challenge, local authorities ought to ensure that their current decisions comply with the Convention, since policies made and decisions taken now may remain in force and open to direct challenge after HRA 1998 comes into force.

STATUTORY INTERPRETATION IN CONVENTION CASES

The key to understanding the legal effect of the Convention rights is s 3 of HRA 1998. It provides:

> (1) so far as it is possible to do so, primary legislation and subordinate legislation must be read and given effect in a way which is compatible with the Convention rights;
> (2) this section-
> (a) applies to primary legislation and subordinate legislation whenever enacted;
> (b) does not affect the validity, continuing operation or enforcement of any incompatible primary legislation; and
> (c) does not affect the validity, continuing operation or enforcement of any incompatible subordinate legislation if (disregarding any possibility of revocation) primary legislation prevents removal of the incompatibility.

Section 3 has two central features. First, Convention rights cannot override primary legislation.[3] To allow Convention rights to take precedence over primary legislation passed subsequent to the Act would have involved a further erosion of the sovereignty of Parliament. However, s 3 goes further than would have been required by the sovereignty doctrine. The usual position is that an Act of Parliament has the effect of repealing (expressly or impliedly) *previous* inconsistent legislation. By virtue of s 3(2)(b), however, HRA 1998 cannot have the effect of expressly or impliedly repealing previous primary legislation. Secondary legislation and administrative acts do not attract protection pursuant to the doctrine of sovereignty of Parliament and cannot in themselves prevail over Convention rights. However, they may be authorised or required by legislation in which case the Convention right at issue must again give way.[4]

Second, and more important in practical terms, s 3(1) imposes on the courts a new duty to strive to interpret domestic legislation consistently with Convention rights. It is expected that in most cases any potential conflict between statute and Convention right will be capable of resolution by creative interpretation of the statute.

The current position is that the courts will only resort to the Convention as an aid to interpretation where a statutory provision is genuinely ambiguous, with at least one meaning which is consistent with the Convention and one which is

2 See *R v DPP, ex pKebilene*, [1999] 3 WLR 175.
3 Section 3(2)(b).
4 Sections 3(2)(c) and 6(2).

inconsistent with it.[5] Ambiguous provisions will continue to be given the Convention-friendly meaning. On the other hand, there will be a small minority of statutory provisions which are plainly in conflict with Convention rights and no amount of 'interpretation' can remove the effect of their clear wording. It will not be 'possible' to interpret them in accordance with Convention rights and the courts will be obliged to give effect to the statute rather than to the Convention right.

The real effect of s 3(1) is on the great mass of statutory provisions which confer powers or duties in general terms and say nothing expressly about Convention rights. For example, a local education authority shall ensure that there are sufficient schools in its area, a local authority shall provide leisure facilities, a local authority shall have power to employ officers and so on. They are not genuinely ambiguous in the *Brind* sense. In *Brind*, the relevant provisions were to the effect that the Home Secretary shall have power to give directions to broadcasting organisations. They were held not to be ambiguous. Under s 3, however, in the absence of compelling language to the contrary, the courts will imply words such that the provision at issue does not authorise breach of Convention rights. A simple example would be 'The Home Secretary shall have power to give directions to broadcasting organisations *provided that such directions are in accordance with the right to freedom of expression under Art 10 of the Convention*.'

The technique of adding words to prevent a breach of the Convention is analogous to that employed under EC law. Domestic courts are already under an obligation to interpret domestic law as far as possible in accordance with provisions of EC law, and may imply additional clauses into the domestic legislation if necessary.[6]

An alternative approach can be gleaned from cases where the courts deal at present with fundamental rights conferred by the common law. In such cases the courts start from the position that statute must contain clear words authorising a breach of those rights, otherwise they will assume that Parliament intended to comply with them. Generally worded provisions will not do. For example, 'The Home Secretary shall make rules governing the running of prisons'.[7]

The presumption that Parliament intended to comply with Convention rights will be all the stronger where the legislation in question was passed subsequent to HRA 1998. That is because s 19 requires any future Bill to be accompanied by a statement that the Government considers it to be compatible with Convention rights, or that it wishes Parliament to pass it notwithstanding that it is incompatible with Convention rights. It is not hard to predict that the latter option will be used only rarely. The Government has already adopted a practice of making statements of compatibility.

CHALLENGING ACTS OF LOCAL AUTHORITIES

The duty

The duty of local authorities to comply with Convention rights is contained in s 6 of HRA 1998.

5 *R v Secretary of State for the Home Department, ex p Brind* [1991] 1 AC 696.
6 See, for example, *Litster v Forth Dry Dock and Engineering Co Ltd* [1990] 1 AC 546.
7 *R v Secretary for State for the Home Department, ex p Leech* [1994] QB 198; *R v Lord Chancellor, ex p Witham* [1998] QB 575.

> 6. – (1) It is unlawful for a public authority to act in a way which is incompatible with a Convention right.
> (2) Subsection (1) does not apply to an act if–
> (a) as the result of one or more provisions of primary legislation, the authority could not have acted differently; or
> (b) in the case of one or more provisions of, or made under, primary legislation which cannot be read or given effect in a way which is compatible with the Convention rights, the authority was acting so as to give effect to or enforce those provisions.
> (3) In this section 'public authority' includes-
> (a) a court or tribunal, and
> (b) any person certain of whose functions are functions of a public nature,
> but does not include either House of Parliament or a person exercising functions in connection with proceedings in Parliament.
> .....
> (5) In relation to a particular act, a person is not a public authority by virtue only of subsection (3)(b) if the nature of the act is private.

The case law of ECHR indicates that a public authority may be held responsible for breaching Convention rights both directly and indirectly. Therefore:

> (1) a local authority must not take decisions which themselves directly breach Convention rights (for example, a decision to remove a child into care in breach of the right to respect for family life);
> (2) a local authority must not act in a way which contributes indirectly towards, or facilitates, a breach of Convention rights (for example, by providing land for, and subsidising an industrial plant which causes pollution in breach of the right to respect for the home):[8]
> (3) in certain circumstances, local authorities must fulfil positive obligations to intervene in relationships between individuals (for example, a local authority may have a positive obligation under Art 3 of the Convention to remove into care a child who is suffering domestic violence at the hands of his parents.[9]

Which decisions can be challenged?

There is no restriction on the types of act which may be challenged. Decisions, policies, bye-laws and so on, are all potentially open to review on Convention grounds. Not only local authorities themselves, but also related bodies, such as companies or charitable trusts set up by local authorities and at least some schools will be fixed with the obligation to respect Convention rights. It was explained in Parliament that the duty to respect Convention rights fell on two categories of public authority: obvious public authorities (such as local authorities) and bodies which are only public authorities by virtue of the fact that certain of their functions are of a public nature.[10] The latter category is

8 *López-Ostra v Spain* A/303-C (1994) 20 EHRR 277.
9 *A v United Kingdom* A/991 (1999) 27 EHRR 611.
10 Section 6(3)(b).

potentially very broad, although bodies within it are not subject to the Convention in respect of their 'private acts'.[11]

Standing to challenge local authority decisions

Section 7 of HRA 1998, set out above, provides that the s 6 duty to respect Convention rights can be enforced by way of direct challenge (by bringing proceedings against the authority in the appropriate court or tribunal) or by way of collateral challenge (by relying on the Convention rights concerned in any legal proceedings). In each case, however, there is a requirement that the person mounting the challenge 'is (or would be) a victim of the unlawful act'. Section 7(7) provides:

> (7) For the purposes of this section, a person is a victim of an unlawful act only if he would be a victim for the purposes of Article 34 of the Convention if proceedings were brought in the European Court of Human Rights in respect of that act.

Therefore, s 7 of HRA 1998 expressly incorporates the Strasbourg test of standing to rely on Convention rights (and so goes beyond the 'take account of' formulation in s 2(1)). A person must be a 'victim' of a violation of the Convention, which is a narrower test than that of sufficient interest under RSC Order 53. Section 7(3) states:

> If the proceedings are brought on an application for judicial review, the applicant is to be taken to have a sufficient interest in relation to the unlawful act only if he is, or would be, a victim of that act.

This makes clear that in judicial review cases, the test of sufficient interest can be no wider than the Convention's own test of standing.

A 'victim' of a violation of the Convention is a person who is directly affected by the act or omission at issue. There are a number of important points of distinction between the victim test and the test of sufficient interest:

> (1) save in very limited circumstances, the Convention does not permit representative actions by interested parties. The complainant must actually be a victim and cannot simply represent others who are victims. The effect is to rule out most actions by pressure groups. By analogy, Art 34 ECHR rarely permits trade unions to bring claims in their own right on the basis that they are the victims of measures taken against their members. The disputed measures must actually be aimed at the rights of the union. Hence in *Ahmed v United Kingdom*, the recent unsuccessful challenge to political restrictions on local government officers, the Commission held that the various individual applicants were victims of the restrictions and had standing to challenge them, but their union, Unison, did not;[12]
>
> (2) to be a victim, you must be a 'person, non-governmental organisation

11 Section 6(5).
12 Application 22954/93 (1995) 20 EHRR CD72.

or group of individuals'. Governmental organisations, such as local authorities, are excluded;[13]
(3) a person ceases to be a victim if the wrong done to him has been rectified (a matter which in domestic judicial review would normally be treated as relevant to the issue of remedy only).

The enactment of the Strasbourg victim test was one of the most contentious features of HRA 1998. It is, however, quite possible that the courts will be able to avoid or circumvent its requirements in appropriate cases. For example:

(1) it is likely that the standing requirements of s 7(1) do not affect the ability of parties to rely on the Convention in the same circumstances, and for the same purposes, as they could do prior to the passing of HRA 1998. They would not be able to invoke Convention rights as conferred by HRA 1998, but could argue that the requirements of the Convention are relevant, for example, to the interpretation of legislation and the development of the common law just as they were relevant before HRA 1998. The outcome would be anomalous but would at least avoid the perverse conclusion that the strengthening of the status of the Convention in domestic law has removed the pre-existing scope for certain parties to rely on it;
(2) existing mechanisms for enforcing fundamental rights through the common law, and through EC law, remain and will frequently confer a level of protection at least equivalent to that of the Convention rights;
(3) it is at least arguable that the duty of the courts under s 3 to seek to interpret legislation in a manner which is compatible with Convention rights is a freestanding duty which applies notwithstanding whether or not the person who will benefit from such an interpretation is a victim, on the basis that statutory provisions can only have one meaning, rather than alternative meanings depending on the identity of the parties before the court.

METHODOLOGY IN CONVENTION CHALLENGES

Once it has been established that the measure under challenge is an act of a public authority within s 6(1), and that the person challenging it has standing within s 7(1), three further stages ensue. First, it must be ascertained whether or not the measure under challenge does indeed disclose a breach of Convention rights. This will involve an examination of the substantive requirements of the Convention, and frequently, the application of the Convention principle of proportionality. The analysis must also account for the margin of appreciation or legitimate area of discretion which local authorities must be allowed in taking their decisions.

If no potential breach of Convention rights arises, the challenge fails. If, conversely, the measure does threaten a breach of Convention rights, the next issue is whether or not the measure is saved by the existence of incompatible legislation. Usually, this will turn on the application of s 6(2), which provides two potential lines of defence to local authorities:

13 Application 15090/89 *Ayuntamiento de M v Spain* 68 DR 209 (1991).

(1) s 6(2)(a) provides a defence where, as a result of incompatible primary legislation, the authority could not have acted any differently. That probably only applies in the limited circumstances where an authority was bound to act, and bound to act in a particular way, but not where the authority could legitimately have decided not to act at all. An example would be where Parliament enacts a tax which is in breach of a Convention right, and imposes a duty on local authorities to collect it;
(2) s 6(2)(b) is broader, absolving an authority from liability where it is acting pursuant to incompatible primary or secondary legislation.

Both defences, while ostensibly broad, are subject to the pre-condition that the governing legislation be shown to be incompatible with Convention rights. As noted above, that will rarely be the case since most statutory provisions will be capable of an interpretation which is consistent with the Convention, by the implication of additional words if necessary. In particular, generally worded powers in primary legislation will not be of any assistance under s 6.

In certain cases, s 3(2)(c) will be relevant, namely where:

(1) the measure under challenge falls within the definition of subordinate legislation (for example, a bye-law); or
(2) the legislative basis for an impugned decision is contained in subordinate legislation.

Section 3(2)(c) saves incompatible subordinate legislation where primary legislation prevents removal of the incompatibility (that is, where it is *intra vires* its enabling power). However, it would be a wholly exceptional case in which primary legislation would be interpreted as authorising the breach of Convention rights in subordinate legislation.[14]

Both ss 6 and 3(2)(c) require, in essence, a test of *vires*. If the decision of a local authority is in breach of Convention rights, it can be saved from challenge provided that it is *intra vires* a provision of primary legislation (or secondary legislation, in the case of s 6(2)(b)).

If a measure is held to be in breach of Convention rights and is not saved by primary legislation which is incompatible with the Convention, the court will proceed to the question of remedy under s 8.

THE EFFECT ON LOCAL AUTHORITIES

HRA 1998 is likely to have a profound effect on the process of local authority decision making, albeit that it may not, in the long term, produce major substantive reforms:

(1) it confers a variety of broadly-defined, new rights, at least one of which could be relied on (even if erroneously) in virtually every case;
(2) HRA 1998 demands a change in the culture of local authority decision making. New considerations must be taken into account, new reasoning processes adopted and authorities must be prepared for more intensive scrutiny of the merits of their decisions;

14 See *ex p Leech, above n 7.*

(3) inevitably, there will be an increase in successful legal challenges, although this will probably not be substantial in the medium to long term. Perhaps more importantly, many defeats will be once and for all defeats, in that it will not be open to the authority to go back and re-take a decision after adopting a different process.

Interpretation of the Convention

GENERAL PRINCIPLES OF INTERNATIONAL LAW

International law governing treaties was codified in 1969 in the Vienna Convention on the Law of Treaties (VCLT).[1] Although this post-dates the Convention, the court has stated that it considers itself bound by it.[2] VCLT Pt III s 3 provides the code on the interpretation of treaties and provides in part:

> *Article 31*
> *General rule of interpretation*
> 1. A treaty shall be interpreted in good faith in accordance with the ordinary meaning to be given to the terms of the treaty in their context and in the light of its object and purpose.
> 2. The context for the purpose of the interpretation of a treaty shall comprise, in addition to the text, including its preamble and annexes:
> (a) any agreement relating to the treaty which was made between all the parties in connexion with the conclusion of the treaty;
> (b) any instrument which was made by one or more parties in connection with the conclusion of the treaty and accepted by the other parties as an instrument relating to the treaty.
> 3. There shall be taken into account, together with the context:
> (a) any subsequent agreement between the parties regarding the interpretation of the treaty or the application of its provisions;
> (b) any subsequent practice in the application of the treaty which establishes the agreement of the parties regarding its interpretation;
> (c) any relevant rules of international law applicable in the relations between the parties.
> 4. A special meaning shall be given to a term if it is established that the parties so intended.
>
> *Article 32*
> *Supplementary means of interpretation*
> Recourse may be had to supplementary means of interpretation including

1 UKTS 58 (1980), Cmnd 7964. It is included in Brownlie, *Basic Documents in International Law.*
2 *Golder v United Kingdom* A/18 (1975) 1 EHRR 524, 532

the preparatory work of the treaty and the circumstances of its conclusion, in order to confirm the meaning resulting from the application of Art 31, or to determine the meaning when the interpretation according to Art 31:

(a) leaves the meaning ambiguous or obscure; or
(b) leads to a result which is manifestly absurd or unreasonable.

Article 33
Interpretation of treaties authenticated in two or more languages
4.... when a comparison of the authentic texts discloses a difference of meaning which the application of Arts 31 and 32 does not remove, the meaning which best reconciles the texts, having regard to the object and purpose of the treaty, shall be adopted.

APPLICATION OF THESE PRINCIPLES BY THE COURT

Purposive approach

While the emphasis of VCLT Art 31(1) would appear to be on the ordinary meaning of the treaty provision, the court has emphasised the purpose of the Convention. It relies on the somewhat nebulous teleological approach. As we shall see, the ordinary meaning of the words is used as a limitation on how far the purpose of the Convention can be pursued. The teleological approach is one adopted by the European Court of Justice.[3] Pursuing the stated purpose of the signatory states has allowed both of these supra-national courts to assert a broad jurisdiction.[4]

What is the purpose of the Convention?

The preamble to the Convention refers to the Universal Declaration and to the 'maintenance and further realisation of Human Rights and Fundamental Freedoms', those freedoms being 'best maintained on the one hand by an effective political democracy and on the other by a common understanding and observance of the Human Rights on which they depend'.[5] The court has said that democracy presupposes 'pluralism, tolerance and broadmindedness'.[6]

Examples of the purposive approach

Golder itself provides a clear example. The right of access to a court was determined to be part of the Art 6 right to a fair hearing, even though no such right is expressly provided for in the Convention. In *Soering* the court stated that Art 3 covered inhuman and degrading treatment where the applicant was liable to receive that treatment if he was extradited, even though the country to which he would be extradited was a non-Convention state. There is no express basis in the Convention in conferring that protection.

3 An early and vivid example is *Costa v ENEL* [1964] ECR 585.
4 Cf the separate opinion of (the British) Judge Fitzmaurice in *Golder*, at pp 548 ff.
5 See also *Soering v United Kingdom* A/161 para 87 (1989) 11 EHRR 439 and *Kjeldsen, Busk Madsen and Pedersen Denmark* A/23 para 53 (1976) 1 EHRR 711.
6 *Handyside v United Kingdom* A/24para 49 (1976) 1 EHRR 737.

Contrast with English law
In certain circumstances, the English courts will have regard to the circumstances in which legislation was introduced and the purpose for which it was introduced. However, they do so only to resolve an ambiguity in the meaning of the legislation. Where the meaning is clear, there can be no recourse to extrinsic sources.[7] There is no requirement for any ambiguity in the Convention text before its purpose is considered.

Effective interpretation

In pursuing the object and purpose of the Convention, the court will interpret the provision so as to ensure that the rights are effectively guaranteed. The rights are practical and effective, not merely theoretical.[8] One reason for the extra-territorial extension of Art 3 in *Soering* was to ensure that the Convention was effective.

Limitation: ordinary meaning

In pursuing the purpose of the Convention, the court will not, normally, disregard the ordinary meaning of the text. In *Wemhoff v Germany*[9] the court held that the wording of Art 5(1)(a) meant that Art 5(3) does not apply to appeal proceedings. The right to marry (Art 12) does not include the right to divorce.[10] An exceptional case was *Preto v Italy*[11] in which the court held that, whilst Art 6(1) requires that judgments be 'pronounced publicly', this did not apply to a (civil) court of cassation. It relied on a long-standing tradition to this effect amongst contracting states.

Reliance on domestic law

The *Preto* case shows that the court does refer to the domestic law of the contracting states in considering the interpretation of the Convention rights. Often, a divergence of practice is said to militate against there being a right, or at least to militate in favour of a considerable margin of appreciation. In *H v Norway*[12] the Commission had to grapple with the issue of abortion. It concluded that 'national laws on abortion differ considerably' and accordingly 'in such a delicate area the contracting states must have a certain discretion'.

However, diverse practices do not necessarily preclude a firm interpretation. The role of the court is to control national law; it is not subservient to it and has sometimes had to take the bull by the horns. A practice which is widespread is not necessarily compatible with the Convention. Thus, the court has taken a firm

7 For reference to international treaties to resolve ambiguity in domestic law see *Salamon v Customs and Excise Comrs* [1967] 2 QB 116; cf *Garland v British Rail Engineering Ltd* [1983] 2 AC 751; and see generally Hunt *Using Human Rights Law in English Courts* (1997) pp 13 to 18. For reference to *Hansard* to resolve ambiguity see *Pepper v Hart* [1993] AC 593.

8 *Artico v Italy* A/37 para 33 (1980) 3 EHRR 1; *Airey v Ireland* A/32 (1979) 2 EHRR 305.

9 A/7 (1968) 1 EHRR 55.

10 *Johnston v Ireland* A/112 (1986) 9 EHRR 203.

11 A/71 (1983) 6 EHRR 182.

12 Application 17004/90 (1992) unreported.

view in its interpretation of the requirement for an impartial tribunal under Art 6(1).[13]

On the other hand, the existence of a consensus among the contracting states may fortify the court in its approach. There appears, for example, to be a consensus as to the importance of freedom of the press within a democratic society.[14] It remains to be seen what effect the accession of Central and Eastern European states (and judges) will have on the court's jurisprudence.

A living instrument

The search in some cases for a consensus in domestic law as an aid to the interpretation of the Convention rights reflects the concept that the Convention is a living instrument. It is interpreted in the light of moral and philosophical attitudes at the time of the decision. This is in contrast with English law in which legislation is interpreted as at the time of enactment.

In *Tyrer v United Kingdom*[15] the court declared that the Convention is 'a living instrument which ... must be interpreted in the light of present day conditions'. This approach can be seen in the court's approach to homosexuals,[16] illegitimate children[17] and to transsexuals.[18] There are also practical examples. Thus, the concept of a private life must develop in accordance with technological developments.

Free-standing interpretation

It is an important principle, concomitant with that of the Convention as a living instrument, that terms used in the Convention are free-standing. They do not depend on any domestic law meaning, even if that was the origin of the term.[19] This necessarily reflects the supra-national nature of the Convention. For example, the words 'civil rights and obligations' in Art 6(1) have had to be interpreted in a manner which has meaning for both civil and common law jurisdictions. The independent classification of such terms means that the court does not have to defer to the meaning within the particular state before it.

Travaux préparatoires

Under VCLT Art 32, recourse may be had to the preparatory work of a treaty in order to confirm the meaning resulting from the application of the general rule

13 See for example *Hauschildt v Denmark* A/154 (1989) 12 EHRR 266.

14 See *Lingens v Austria* A/103 (1986) 8 EHRR 407.

15 A/26 2 EHRR 1..

16 *Dudgeon v United Kingdom* A/45 (1981) 4 EHRR 149; Lustig-Prean v *United Kingdom* (judgment of 27 September 1999).

17 *Marckx v Belgium* A/31 (1979) 2 EHRR 330..

18 *X, Y and Z v United Kingdom* A/753 (1997) 24 EHRR 143 – on this question the court did not accept the Commission's opinion (para 67) that there was a clear trend in contracting states towards the legal acknowledgement of gender re-assignment and that departure from that required justification. The court said that there was no shared approach amongst the contracting states (para 52). This approach was recently approved by the court (a decision of the Grand Chamber) in *Sheffield and Horsham v United Kingdom* (1998) 27 EHRR 163.

19 The origins of a term may not be entirely irrelevant, but they merely indicate a possible interpretation; they do not in any way dictate an interpretation. In *Adolf v Austria* A/49 para 30 (1982) 4 EHRR 313 the court stated that 'The legislation of the state concerned is certainly relevant, but it provides no more than a starting-point ...'

of interpretation (Art 31) or to determine the meaning where such application leaves the meaning ambiguous or manifestly absurd. In practice, reference is rarely made by the court or the Commission since they are often not helpful.[20] Furthermore, they date from the late 1940s and excessive reliance on them would be inconsistent with the principle that the Convention is to be interpreted as a living instrument.

Other international sources

The court has relied on (though it is not bound by) other agreements concluded within the Council of Europe.[21] Reliance has also been placed on the Universal Declaration of Human Rights, a text specifically referred to in the Preamble to the Convention,[22] and to the International Covenant on Civil and Political Rights.[23] The court occasionally refers to rights jurisprudence from other jurisdictions.[24]

Authentic texts

The two official texts of the Convention are in French and English, and each is equally authentic. In the rare event that there is a conflict in the texts, even following the application of the principles set out above, then VCLT Art 33(4) provides that the meaning 'which best reconciles the texts, having regard to the object and purpose of the treaty' should be adopted.[25] If the texts cannot be reconciled then the object and purpose of the Convention becomes decisive.[26]

Precedent

The court is not bound by its own, or the Commission's, previous interpretations of the Convention. In *Cossey v United Kingdom*[27] the court stated that it would usually apply its own precedents, in the interests of legal certainty 'and the orderly development of the Convention case law', but that it would depart from its earlier decisions if there were cogent reasons for doing so. In particular, this might occur where conditions within society had changed, in line with the principle of the Convention as a living instrument.

There is no strict distinction between *ratio decidendi* and *obiter dicta*. The weight to be attributed to an interpretative statement will depend on its generality and the context in which it was made.

20 In *Lawless v Ireland (No 2)* A/2 (1961) 1 EHRR 13 para 14 the court refused to look at preparatory work since it considered that the provision in question was sufficiently clear.
21 See for example *Gustafsson v Sweden* A/618 (1996) 22 EHRR 409 in which the Court referred to the European Social Charter.
22 For example *Kosiek v Germany* A/105 (1987) 9 EHRR 328.
23 For example *Müller v Switzerland* A/133 (1988) 13 EHRR 212, 225.
24 Reference to a decision of the US Supreme Court was made in *James v United Kingdom* A/98 (1986) 8 EHRR 123, 141.
25 See *James v United Kingdom* A/98 (1986) 8 EHRR 123 para 42.
26 See *Brogan v United Kingdom* A/145-B (1988) at p 134.
27 A/184 para 35 (1990) 13 EHRR 622.

The Principle of Proportionality

The principle of proportionality is a key element of the judicial application of the European Court of Human Rights ('ECHR'). Proportionality can be colloquially defined as 'the end must justify the means'. Lord Diplock once described proportionality as the principle that a public authority should not 'use a steam-hammer to crack a nut, if a nut-cracker would do'.[1] Restrictions which might, on the face of it, appear to be justified by the language of the relevant Article of ECHR may nevertheless be held by a court to be unlawful because the effects of the restriction are not strictly in proportion to its legitimate aims and objectives.

Few of the rights protected by ECHR are absolute (an example of an absolute right is Art 3 the prohibition of torture and inhuman or degrading treatment or punishment. The rights protected by Arts 8-11 of ECHR (respectively, the right to privacy and family life; freedom of religion; freedom of expression; and freedom of association) are subject to express limitations which permit restrictions on the rights for certain specified reasons. As regards the rights protected by these Articles, ECHR states that public authorities may interfere with the exercise of the rights concerned provided that the interference is prescribed by law and is necessary in a democratic society in the interests of matters specified in the Article concerned, such as public safety, the protection of public order, health or morals, or the protection of the rights or freedoms of others. In deciding whether the justification advanced for a measure restricting a right protected by Arts 8-11 is necessary in a democratic society, ECHR decides whether the measure is proportionate to its aims and objectives.

Other Articles are subject to express limitations which permit restrictions on the rights concerned in certain specified circumstances. So, for example, Art 5 which protects the right to liberty and security of the person, sets out specific circumstances in which a person may be deprived of his liberty in accordance with a procedure prescribed by law. This could be the detention of a minor by lawful order for the purposes of legal educational supervision. The right to a public hearing, protected by Art 6, is also subject to limitations, and the press and public may be excluded from all or part of a trial. The interests of morals, public order or national security in a democratic society, where the interests of juveniles or the protection of the private life of the parties so require, or to the extent strictly necessary in the opinion of the court in special

1 In *R v Goldstein* [1983] 1 All ER 434, at 436.

circumstances where publicity would prejudice the interests of justice are reasons for exclusion. The right to marry and found a family, protected by Art 12, is a right to do so 'according to national laws governing the exercise of this right.' Any restrictions on the rights granted by Art 5, 6, and 12 are scrutinised by the court to determine whether they are proportionate.

The principle of proportionality is extremely important because its practical effect is that it gives to the court the power to exercise a value judgment as to whether a particular restrictive measure is justified in all the circumstances. Many defeats suffered by states before EHCR are on the basis that the measure at issue is disproportionate.

It is impossible to predict how UK courts and tribunals will deal with the principle of proportionality once the Human Rights Act 1998 ('HRA 1998') is in force. The whole concept of proportionality is unfamiliar to the common law system of jurisprudence although a few judges have had to consider proportionality in the context of EC law issues.[2] In particular, until now the decision as to whether the end justifies the means in relation to a legislative measure has been left entirely to Parliament. The function of courts is only to interpret legislation, not to make judgments on it. Once HRA 1998 comes into force, however, judges of the High Court and appellate courts will be placed in the position of having to decide whether to make a declaration of incompatibility in respect of primary or secondary legislation, pursuant to HRA 1998 s 4, on the basis that the justification given for a restriction on a Convention right is, in the court's view, not good enough.

It is likely that in the first few years, the courts will be reluctant to rule against a legislative measure on the basis that it does not pass the test of proportionality, at least in circumstances where the decision would not also be open to review on the grounds of *Wednesbury* unreasonableness. Judges will be sensitive to criticism that they are interfering too much or are subverting the democratic process, and will no doubt be very keen to avoid any risk that their decision making is, or is seen to be, affected by their own subjective political or social views. An example of this concern may be found in the speech of Lord Lowry in *R v Secretary of State for the Home Department, ex p Brind.* Lord Lowry said that the application of the principle of proportionality would 'be an abuse of the court's supervisory jurisdiction'.[3]

Regarding the acts of public authorities, a few judges of the High Court are accustomed to deciding whether they should be quashed on the grounds that they are *Wednesbury* unreasonable, but the majority of High Court judges, and all county court judges and tribunal chairmen have no such experience. In any event, the scope for interference provided by the principle of proportionality is significantly greater than that permitted by the *Wednesbury* principle. This is considered when dealing with the Margin of Appreciation, below.

The problem for courts and tribunals is compounded by the vagueness of the principle. It is not susceptible to the precise and specific definitions beloved of

2 *Stoke-on-Trent City Council v B and Q plc* [1991] Ch 48.

3 [1991] 1 AC 696, at 766-7. Tasker Watkins LJ, in the Divisional Court, when rejecting the proportionality argument, said, 'The court will not arrogate to themselves executive or administrative decisions which should be taken by executive or administrative bodies': [1991] 1 AC 696 at 722A-B. Lords Bridge and Roskill, on the other hand, viewed with equanimity the possibilty that proportionality might one day be adopted as a free-standing ground of judicial review: 749G-H and 750C-F.

the common law courts, and, indeed, ECHR has not attempted to provide a comprehensive definition of the test of proportionality.

In the circumstances, it is likely that courts and tribunals will look for guidance to decisions of ECHR. Unfortunately, these are of only limited assistance. As stated above, the court has not set out a working test for proportionality but deals with the principle on a case-by-case basis and tends to focus on the facts of the case under consideration. Moreover, the issue of proportionality must be viewed in light of the margin of appreciation which the court grants to states, that is an area of discretion within which the court will not intervene to overturn a state's legislative judgment (see below).

Notwithstanding the lack of clear guidance from ECHR, it is possible to identify from the cases five tests which should be applied by a court or tribunal when deciding whether a particular restriction is proportionate.

The balancing test

The importance of the objective to be attained by the restriction must be balanced against the infringement of the individuals' rights as a result of the restriction.

So, for example, the court has held that a measure was disproportionate because the objective concerned was not sufficiently important. In *F v Switzerland*,[4] the court held that a Swiss court's order banning the applicant from remarrying within one year of his divorce failed the proportionality test because the court's motives, namely to protect those who might want to marry the applicant in the future, and to protect the applicant from himself, were not of sufficient weight to justify the imposition of a restraint on a fully competent adult.

Again, the court has held that a measure was disproportionate because the effect of the restriction on the applicant was too severe. In *Nasri v France*,[5] the court held that it would be disproportionate to deport an illegal immigrant because he was deaf and dumb and and dependent on his family for social development. Also, in *Dudgeon v United Kingdom*,[6] the court held that the application of criminal law to homosexuality in Northern Ireland pursued aims which were legitimate aims for the purposes of Art 8 of ECHR, but nevertheless held that the law contravened the Convention, because the justifications were outweighed by the serious detrimental effects caused to homosexuals.

In carrying out the balancing exercise, the court is prepared to undertake a wide-ranging survey of relevant evidence. For example, in *Young, James and Webster v UK*,[7] concerning the dismissals of British Rail employees for refusing to join a union, the court took account of the conclusions of a Royal Commission and other surveys of industrial relations practice. The court decided on the basis of the evidence that the objective relied on to defend the dismissals, namely to enable unions to protect their members' interests, would not have been adversely affected if unwilling employees had not been compelled to join the union. Indeed, the court will even compare the way things are done in other countries to decide whether a state's restrictive measure is unnecessarily draconian. The case of *Tinnelly & Sons Ltd and McElduff v United Kingdom*,[8] concerned the rule set out in s 42 of the Northern Ireland Fair Employment Act 1976 that a certificate issued

4 A/128 (1987) 10 EHRR 411, 420-422.
5 A/324 (1995) 21 EHRR 458.
6 A/45 (1981) 4 ELRR 149, 167.
7 A/44 (1981) 4 EHRR 38.
8 Judgment of 10 July 1998 (1998) 27 EHRR 249.

by the Secretary of State to the effect that certain steps had been taken on national security grounds could not be challenged in legal proceedings. The court held that s 42 was a disproportionate infringement of the right to a fair and public trial on the basis, inter alia, that other countries had found ways of dealing with the problems of reconciling national security and public justice in a way which enabled individuals to challenge the state's assertion that actions had been taken on national security grounds.

The 'relevant and sufficent reasons' test

A measure will not be proportionate if it is not supported by 'relevant and sufficient reasons'. In *Goodwin v United Kingdom*,[9] the court held that the reasons given for a mandatory injunction requiring a journalist to disclose his source were relevant but not sufficient to justify the infringement of the right of freedom of expression set out in Art 10, where the company which obtained the injunction had already obtained an injunction restraining publication of the confidential material which had been disclosed to the journalist. Accordingly, the court held that the injunction was disproportionate.

The test of careful design

The court will hold a restriction to be disproportionate if it is 'over-broad'. In *Open Door Counselling and Dublin Well Woman v Ireland*,[10] the court held that an injunction which imposed a permanent and perpetual prohibition on counselling centres providing information about the availability of abortion facilities abroad, regardless of the age or state of health of the pregnant woman or her reasons for seeking information was over-broad and, for that reason alone, disproportionate.

The 'essence of the right test'

The greater the extent to which the restriction impairs the very essence of the right protected by the Article concerned, the more likely it is that the restriction will be disproportionate. In *F v Switzerland,* the court considered that the temporary ban on remarriage impaired the essence of the right to marry under Art 12.

The evidential test

If the state is unable to produce evidence of the pressing social need which is the alleged justification for the restriction, the court will hold that the restriction is disproportionate. So, for example, in *Kokkinakis v Greece*,[11] the court held that a conviction and fine for a Jehovah's Witness who had been invited into a woman's house and engaged in a religious discussion with her was disproportionate, because there was no evidence that his actions had resulted in any improper pressure. It followed that there was no evidence that the restriction had advanced the legitimate aim of protecting the religious rights and freedoms of others.

9 Application 17488/90 (1996) 22 EHRR 123.
10 A/26 (1992) 15 EHRR 244, 266.
11 A/260A (1993) 17 EHRR 397, 421-422.

The new methods of scrutiny of the actions of public authorities are likely to have a knock-on effect on the way in which decisions are taken in the future. It is likely that public authorities will take more elaborate steps to record the decision-making process than is currently the case, at least where the decisions cover matters which relate to Convention rights, so that the objects of the measures can be identified, and the fact that the measures are proportionate to their objectives can be demonstrated.

The Margin of Appreciation

WHAT IS THE MARGIN OF APPRECIATION?

The 'margin of appreciation' is the legitimate area of discretion allowed by the European Court of Human Rights in Strasbourg ('ECHR') to national institutions in human rights cases. It is perhaps best viewed as the Convention equivalent of the *Wednesbury* doctrine in English law: a recognition of the limitations of the judicial role in questioning the decisions which are challenged before them. ECHR recognises that it has a restricted role, in part because it is an international court which is remote from the local conditions within which challenged decisions are taken. However, its self-restraint is also premised on deference to administrative and legislative bodies which have a greater expertise and day-to-day knowledge of the matters within their remit, and also a greater democratic legitimacy.

Not all Convention rights involve a margin of appreciation.[1] However, a significant proportion of Convention cases, notably those under Arts 8 and 10, raise, and indeed turn on, that issue. In most cases on private life and freedom of expression, the applicant will be able to establish that the basic Convention right has been restricted and the issue is then whether the authorities can justify the restriction as one which is 'necessary in a democratic society'. This requires an application of the proportionality test, and and in each case the authorities have an area of discretion within which they may legitimately consider a restriction to be necessary.

There are two central issues so far as the Human Rights Act 1998 ('HRA 1998') is concerned. Is the margin of appreciation doctrine going to be relevant in the domestic courts, and if so, to what extent does it differ from the conventional *Wednesbury* doctrine?

IS THE ECHR MARGIN OF APPRECIATION RELEVANT?

A widely-held view is that the margin of appreciation doctrine should not apply at all in cases brought under HRA 1998. It is nowhere express in the Convention but has been invented and developed in the case law of ECHR as a means of delimiting the supervisory role of an international court. Hence, it is argued that the doctrine is suitable for application only by ECHR and not by the domestic courts.

1 For example, Arts 2–4 confer absolute rights.

It is submitted, however, that the margin of appreciation doctrine, as it is applied by ECHR, is highly relevant to Convention claims brought in the domestic courts, at least indirectly. Although *the margin of appreciation* as applied by ECHR is likely to be rejected as inappropriate,[2] it is inescapable that *a margin of appreciation* must be allowed where the decisions of public authorities are challenged in the courts. The idea that public authorities have a certain area of discretion within which they may safely take decisions is fundamental to English public law. If it is accepted that an area of discretion should be allowed to the decision maker in Convention claims, ECHR's margin of appreciation is perhaps the most obvious source of authority on how that area of discretion ought to be delimited. First, the domestic courts must be aware of the extent of the discretion which would be allowed in ECHR in a particular case, so as not to allow any wider discretion (and so invite successful proceedings in ECHR). Second, as noted above, the ECHR margin of appreciation is founded on considerations such as respect for the greater democratic legitimacy and technical expertise of other decision-making bodies which are directly applicable in the domestic context and currently foster judicial restraint in the review of local authority decisions.

THE MARGIN OF APPRECIATION IN HRA 1998 CASES

However, the Convention test of necessity together with its margin of appreciation doctrine, is an altogether different and more stringent test compared with the *Wednesbury* approach to limitations on fundamental rights. It requires the exercise of a primary rather than a secondary judgment by the court, it is more flexible, and it will come down on the side of the applicant in far more cases than will a test of irrationality. More specifically:

(1) the threshold for review is lower under the ECHR margin of appreciation test. ECHR frequently reiterates that it is not sufficient for the purposes of compliance with the Convention that the decision maker has acted reasonably, carefully and in good faith.[3] Conversely, a reasonable and careful decision taken in good faith will always suffice under the *Wednesbury* test.

(2) the margin of appreciation test requires a different hierarchy of values. There is no question of balancing two competing values but rather of justifying a departure from one fundamental value by reference to other, strictly defined values.[4]

(3) assessment of the margin of appreciation may involve a genuine and searching review of the facts behind a decision. The evidence to be put before the court will therefore differ from that required in a domestic public law challenge.[5]

(4) the burden of proof is very much on the state to justify a derogation from a Convention right. Justifications must be 'convincingly established'.[6]

2 See, for example, *R v Stratford Justices, ex p Imbert* (1999) Times, 25 February.
3 See, for example, *Vogt v Germany* A/323 (1995) 21 EHRR 205, 235.
4 See, for example, *Sunday Times v United Kingdom* A/30 (1979) 2 EHRR 245.
5 See, for example, *Autronic AG v Switzerland* A/178 (1990) 12 EHRR 485.
6 See, for example, *Barthold v Germany* A/90 (1985) 7 EHRR 383.

Recently, in the cases brought by service personnel dismissed by reason of their homosexuality, ECHR held that the threshold for success under a Wednesbury challenge is set so high as to preclude any meaningful consideration by the domestic courts of the applicants' Convention claims to respect for their private lives.[7]

Perhaps the most important aspect of ECHR margin of appreciation, and the aspect which makes the outcome of Convention cases so difficult to predict, is that is a highly variable standard. The court has stated that 'the scope of the margin of appreciation is not identical in respect of each of the aims justifying restrictions of a right enshrined in the Convention'[8] and 'the scope of the margin of appreciation will vary according to the circumstances, the subject matter and its background'.[9] There is, in practice, a broad spectrum ranging from extreme reluctance to intervene at one end, to substituting the court's opinion for that of the decision maker at the other.

The following matters, among others, are relevant to the extent of ECHR margin of appreciation and may influence the domestic courts as well:

(1) the area of legal regulation involved. The court has regarded certain areas as being firmly within the discretion of the decision maker, for example planning law, which is dependent on an assessment of local circumstances by local bodies who are best placed to do so.[10] Environmental regulation is another, related area where a broad measure of discretion is accorded to national authorities.[11] Any area where broad choices of economic or social policy are involved will attract a broad margin of appreciation.

(2) freedom of political speech, including freedom of the press, is regarded by the court as particularly important and the margin of appreciation is virtually non-existent in such cases.[12]

(3) decisions on questions of morality, such as obscenity, attract a wide margin of appreciation.[13] Decisions on the licensing of sex shops by a democratically elected local authority would similarly be difficult to challenge.

(4) states enjoy a broad margin of appreciation in deciding how to meet the demands of positive obligations to protect Convention rights, and in particular, to protect them from the actions of non-state bodies in society. The domestic courts are likely to continue to be deferential on questions of allocation of scarce resources by public bodies.

(5) where two Convention rights clash, for example, the right to privacy from press intrusion (Arts 8 and 10), states have a broad margin of appreciation in deciding where to draw the line between them.

7 *Smith and Grady v United Kingdom*; *Lustig-Prean and Beckett v United Kingdom*, judgments of 27 September 1999.
8 See *Sunday Times v United Kingdom* A/87 at 276.
9 See *Rasmussen v Denmark*, A/87 (1984) 7 EHRR 371, 380.
10 See, for example, *Buckley v United Kingdom* (1996) 23 EHRR 101.
11 See, for example, *Fredin v Sweden* (1991) 13 EHRR 784.
12 See, for example, *Goodwin v United Kingdom* A/133 (1996) 22 EHRR 123; *Bowman v UK* (1998) 26 EHRR 1.
13 See, for example, *Müller v Switzerland* (1991) 13 EHRR 212, 228–229.

Remedies

INTRODUCTION

It is unlawful for local authorities, as 'public authorities' within the meaning of s 6 of the Human Rights Act 1998 ('HRA 1998'), to act in a way which is incompatible with a Convention right.[1] Accordingly, local authorities are liable to have proceedings brought against them for having acted unlawfully within the meaning of s 6(1) by persons who are the victims of such unlawful acts.[2]

Such proceedings must be brought in 'the appropriate court or tribunal' within the meaning of s 7(2) of HRA 1998, which provides that such court or tribunal may be determined 'in accordance with rules'. No relevant rules have yet been made. However, since no distinct human rights court is established by HRA 1998, it is likely that claims will be brought in the forum where the most closely analogous existing claims are already brought. Thus, it is probable that claims against local authorities will be brought by way of judicial review where public law issues are at stake, by way of civil action in the High Court and county court where the issue is one of private law, by way of an application to the Employment Tribunal where the issue relates to employment rights, and so on.

There is a general time limit of one year for bringing proceedings for breach of a Convention right.[3] This is overridden by any pre-existing shorter time limit, for example, the requirement in judicial review proceedings, under RSC Order 53 rule 4(1), that an application for leave has to be made 'promptly and in any event within three months of when the grounds for the application first arose'. However, the court or tribunal hearing a claim has the power to extend the one-year time limit where it considers it is 'equitable' to do so.[4] This test is similar to the 'just and equitable' test used for extension of time in the discrimination legislation.[5] It would appear that the discretion to extend the time limit does not apply where the general one-year limit is overridden by an existing stricter limit.

Article 13 of the Convention, which provides a guarantee of an effective remedy for violation of Convention rights, is the only substantive Article not to be

1 See HRA 1998 s 6(1).
2 See s 7(1).
3 See s 7(5)(a).
4 See s 7(5)(b).
5 See Sex Discrimination Act 1975, s 76(5), Race Relations Act 1976, s 68(6) and Disability Discrimination Act 1995, Sch 3 para 3(2).

incorporated by the 1998 Act.[6] However, the availability of remedies for breach of Convention rights is expressly provided for in HRA 1998, particularly in s 8:

> '(1) In relation to any act (or proposed act) of a public authority which the court finds is (or would be) unlawful, it may grant such relief or remedy, or make such order, within its powers as it considers just and appropriate.
>
> (2) But damages may be awarded only by a court which has power to award damages, or to order the payment of compensation, in civil proceedings.
>
> (3) No award of damages is to be made unless, taking account of all the circumstances of the case, including:
> (a) any other relief or remedy granted, or order made, in relation to the act in question (by that or any other court), and
> (b) the consequences of any decision (of that or any other court) in respect of that act),
> the court is satisfied that the award is necessary to afford just satisfaction to the person in whose favour it is made.
>
> (4) In determining:
> (a) whether to award damages, or
> (b) the amount of an award,
> the court must take into account the principles applied by the European Court of Human Rights in relation to the award of compensation under Article 41 of the Convention.'

In summary, (i) a court or tribunal may grant such remedies as are within its powers and which it considers just and appropriate; (ii) damages may be awarded only by a court or tribunal which has power to award damages or compensation in civil proceedings; (iii) an award of damages must not be made unless necessary to afford just satisfaction to the person in whose favour it is made; and (iv) the jurisprudence of the European Court of Human Rights ('ECHR') must be taken into account in deciding whether to award damages, and the amount of any award.

In addition, pursuant to s 4 of HRA 1998, the High Court (and higher appellate courts) may make a 'declaration of incompatibility' where it determines that a provision of primary legislation is incompatible with a Convention right. Since such a declaration is not binding on the parties to the proceedings in which it is made,[7] it is not a remedy in the conventional sense, but it may lead to subsequent redress (as to which see below).

The general principles which apply to remedies available for breach of Convention rights are considered below under the following headings:

(1) damages;
(2) remedies other than damages;
(3) declarations of incompatibility.

DAMAGES

As has already been noted, only those courts and tribunals which have jurisdiction to award damages or compensation in civil proceedings may award damages for

6 See s 1(1)(a).
7 See s 4(6).

breach of a Convention right.[8] It follows that two sets of proceedings will sometimes be necessary; one to establish that a Convention right has been breached, and a second to obtain damages. This will be the case where the breach of a Convention right is established in a criminal court, since the criminal courts cannot award damages. It is conceivable, though unlikely, that this would also be the case in judicial review proceedings. The Divisional Court has the power to award damages in such proceedings only where the respondent has committed the tort of breach of statutory duty and in the very limited circumstances where there has been misfeasance in public office (and exceptionally where the *ultra vires* act is in breach of EC law). It is therefore arguable that damages for breach of a Convention right not amounting to such misfeasance could not be awarded in judicial review proceedings. The more likely position, however, is that damages could be awarded in such cases, since the Divisional Court does have the power to award damages in an application for judicial review, albeit in limited circumstances. In a literal sense, therefore, the requirement of s 8(2) is met. Moreover, it is likely the courts would be reluctant to require multiple proceedings to be brought unless this was unavoidable within the terms of HRA 1998.

The central question in respect of the availability of damages for breach of a Convention right is the ambit of the remedy of 'just satisfaction' under Art 41 of the Convention. This remedy is expressly incorporated by ss 8(3) and 8(4) of HRA 1998. It is to be noted, however, that the question of what is necessary to afford justification under s 8(3) is subject to the 'circumstances of the case' including: (i) any other relief or remedy granted, or order made, in relation to the action in question (by that or any other court); and (ii) the consequences of any decision (of that or any other court) in respect of that or any other act. In respect of the requirement to have regard to other relief or remedies granted, the primary concern would appear to be to prevent 'double recovery'. As to the obligation to consider the consequences of the decision, this would seem to require consideration of the wider implications of the award of damages, whether in terms of opening the 'floodgates' for other claims or otherwise.

'Just satisfaction' can only take the form of compensation to the applicant. In particular, ECHR will not award non-compensatory types of damages, such as nominal damages or exemplary damages. 'Just satisfaction' in Convention terms covers three possible heads: pecuniary damage, non-pecuniary damage and costs. Only the award of damages is subject to Convention principles, so HRA 1998 leaves intact the domestic courts' jurisdiction to award costs.[9]

Unfortunately, the ECHR approach to the award of just satisfaction lacks any clear set of guiding principles. Beyond stating that an equitable approach is to be adopted, no detailed rules have been laid down. It is tempting to conclude that, far from proceeding according to consistent principle, the court is swayed primarily by the perceived merits of the application and of the applicant.

The basic distinction drawn is between pecuniary and non-pecuniary damage. Pecuniary damage is financial loss, including damage resulting from loss or damage to real or personal property. It appears that there is no limit on the amount that may be awarded under this head provided that a causal link is established. Non-pecuniary damage is damage to the person or to interests which do not have an obvious monetary value. The most common type of claim under this head is for damages for anxiety and distress. Although occasionally very high awards are

8 See s 8(2).
9 See s 8(4).

made by ECHR (particularly in cases involving the loss of property contrary to Art 1 of the First Protocol to the Convention), awards are generally modest. The court has applied two particular principles which tend to reduce the level of damages awarded.

Causation

The first of these restrictive principles is a strict requirement of causation. There must be a direct causal link between the violation of a Convention right and financial loss to the applicant. This requirement causes particular difficulties for applicants who have suffered breaches of their procedural rights, since the court is often reluctant to conclude that the outcome would have been any different if the correct procedures had been followed. A number of successful applicants claiming breach of the right to a fair trial contained in Art 6 of the Convention have failed to obtain any compensation for this reason.[10]

Unhelpfully, however, in another line of cases the court has adopted a more liberal approach, compensating the applicant for the loss of potential opportunity that would have resulted had a different lawful procedure been adopted. In *McMichael v United Kingdom,*[11] the applicants complained that they had been refused access to documents during care proceedings contrary to the Convention. The UK government argued that no compensation should be awarded even if the applicants' rights had been breached because it was impossible to maintain that the outcome of the proceedings would have been any different if the documents had been handed over. In contrast to its approach in *Saunders* and *Findlay*, the court held that it could not be said with certainty that no practical benefit could have accrued to the applicants if the procedural deficiencies had not existed. In considering non-pecuniary loss, the court further held that it was material that some of the distress suffered by the applicants flowed directly from their inability to see the documents in question, and this did not depend on the outcome of the proceedings. In the event, the court awarded compensation of £8,000.

No coherent rationale for the radically different approaches to causation adopted in these cases can be discerned from the court's judgments. This inconsistency of approach will thus provide no real assistance to domestic parties and courts in considering the effect of the obligation under s 8(4) of HRA 1998 to take into account the jurisprudence of ECHR in determining levels of damages. It is to be hoped that the domestic courts will develop a more coherent approach to the award of damages. Section 8(4) permits them to do this, provided that the jurisprudence of ECHR is taken into account. It is perhaps likely that principles analogous to those for determining when damages for 'loss of a chance' can be recovered in contract and tort for breach of private rights will be developed in the human rights context.

Necessity

The second principle limiting awards of damages by ECHR is that of necessity. Often the court has held that just satisfaction has been provided merely by virtue of the fact that it has found that the applicant's rights have been violated, and thus no award of damages is necessary. This limitation on the award of damages

10 See, for example, *Saunders v United Kingdom* A/702 (1996) 23 EHRR 313 and *Findlay v United Kingdom* A/734 (1997) 24 EHRR 221.
11 A/307-B (1995) 20 EHRR 205.

is expressly adopted by way of s 8(3) of HRA 1998. In substance, the principle of necessity has been used by the court to avoid awarding compensation to undeserving applicants, even in cases of serious violation of Convention rights. A stark example of the application of this principle is provided by *McCann v United Kingdom*,[12] in which the court found a breach of the right to life under Art 2 of the Convention arising from the killing by the SAS in Gibraltar of three suspected IRA terrorists. No compensation was awarded, in the light of the court's finding that the suspects had intended to plant a bomb.

Once it has been established that it is necessary to award compensation for loss caused by breach of a Convention right, the court seeks to value the loss and damage suffered under the two heads of pecuniary and non-pecuniary damage. Again, no clear guiding principles are to be found in ECHR case law, although the court's overall approach is relatively conservative. The main exception to this approach is provided by cases involving loss of property contrary to Art 1 of the First Protocol, in which very high compensation can be awarded.[13] The method of calculating the sum awarded, and the evidence relied on, are rarely stated in the court's judgments. As a rough guide, damages for non-pecuniary loss are generally of a similar order of magnitude to awards for injury to feelings under the domestic discrimination legislation, with typical awards lying in the range £1,000 to £15,000. There is a discretionary power to award interest on compensation for breach of a Convention right. The court has awarded interest only in a minority of cases, generally relating to the confiscation of property by the state. The court's recent approach, however, has been to provide for interest to be paid on any damages awarded from the date when payment is due, at the rate stipulated in the relevant national law. Thus in *Halford v United Kingdom*[14] the court ordered interest at 8% to be payable, but only from the expiry of the three-month period given to the UK for the payment of compensation. As regards retrospective interest, the domestic courts and tribunals may need to curb their usual approach of awarding interest on damages and compensation as a matter of course. By virtue of ss 8(3) and 8(4) of HRA 1998 they will be obliged to take into account the discretionary approach of the court, since interest is a component of damages.

Remedies other than damages

Section 8(1) of HRA 1998 expressly empowers courts and tribunals to grant such remedies within their powers as they consider just and appropriate. In addition, s 7(11)(a) empowers a minister to extend the range of remedies which can be awarded by a tribunal where he considers it necessary to ensure that the tribunal can provide an appropriate remedy.

In judicial review proceedings, the full range of remedies will be available where it is alleged that a local authority's act is unlawful on the ground that it breaches a Convention right: certiorari, mandamus, prohibition, declaration, injunction and damages (as to which see above). Similarly, the civil courts' injunctive jurisdiction will be available to plaintiffs who consider that their Convention rights have been, or are likely to be, breached. However, s 12 of HRA 1998 places a number of restrictions on the power of the courts to grant

12 A/324 (1995) 21 EHRR 97.
13 See for example, *Stran Greek Refineries v Greece* A/301-B (1994) 19 EHRR 293.
14 [1997] IRLR 471.

injunctions which might affect the exercise of the Convention right of freedom of expression. In particular, s 12 provides that:

- ex parte applications must be justified by compelling reasons;
- the plaintiff must establish that he is likely to succeed at trial;
- in considering whether or not to grant relief, the court must give particular weight to freedom of expression;
- in privacy cases, the court must consider various factors, including the public interest in publication, which are likely to weigh in favour of defendants.

The possibility of quia timet relief is expressly contemplated by the reference in s 8(1) to relief in respect of a 'proposed act'.

One area in which the order of mandamus and injunctive relief are likely to be sought is in child care cases brought by way of an application for judicial review. The courts will seek to ensure that local authorities comply with the rights of children and their parents, particularly under Art 8 of the Convention (the right to respect for private and family life). The remedy provided for any breach of such rights will be aimed to compel compliance with the relevant right Hence orders of mandamus and injunction are likely to be made where a Convention right has been breached.

DECLARATIONS OF INCOMPATIBILITY

A declaration of incompatibility is the only remedy available where a provision in an Act of Parliament is held to be incompatible with a Convention right.[15] It is also the only remedy available where the act of a local authority was required by, or calculated to give effect to, primary legislation of that kind.[16] Like all the remedies under HRA 1998, the declaration of incompatibility is a discretionary remedy. By s 4(6), such a declaration does not affect the validity of the provision or act in question, and is not binding on the parties to the proceedings in which it is made. The declaration of incompatibility thus provides no immediate practical remedy to the successful party at all. The absence of any remedy in damages for a violation of a Convention right caused by primary legislation is perhaps the major remedial gap in HRA 1998. Unless a system of ex gratia payments is established, this remedial gap is bound to invite proceedings in Strasbourg.

However, the making of a declaration pursuant to s 4 of HRA 1998 triggers the provisions of s 10, which permit (but do not require) the Government to take remedial action in the form of subordinate legislation to bring domestic law into line with the Convention. Schedule 2 to HRA 1998 contains detailed provisions as to the making of remedial orders. Paragraph 1(1)(b) of Sch 2 provides that a remedial order may be made so as to have effect from a date earlier than that on which it is made. The effect of such a retrospective order could, therefore, be to alter the law as it was at the time of the act which led to the proceedings in which a declaration of incompatibility was made. It is conceivable that a complainant might be able to go back to court to obtain a remedy in damages following the making of a remedial order, notwithstanding that such a remedy would not have been available previously.

15 See s 4.
16 See s 6(2).

Chapter 2

Implications for Employment Law

This chapter considers the significance of the Human Rights Act 1998 ('HRA 1998') for the following particular areas of employment law and practice: unfair dismissal (Wallington); internal disciplinary proceedings (Nicholls); and freedom of association and trade union rights (Morris). Reference should also be made to the chapter on discrimination under Art 14 which appears later in the book.

This chapter demonstrates the range of contexts in which Convention rights may be relevant to local authorities as employers. This introductory section provides a general overview of the implications of HRA 1998 for employment law. It is itself divided into three sections. The first considers the legal contexts in which issues relating to HRA 1998 may arise. The second examines specific articles of the Convention. The third summarises the measures which local authorities should take in order to minimise the risk of challenge to their employment practices.

THE LEGAL CONTEXTS IN WHICH THE ACT IS RELEVANT

Legislation

The obligation to read and give effect to legislation in a way which is compatible with Convention rights so far as possible (s 3) will be important in a number of areas including constructive dismissal (conduct which violates a Convention right may constitute a breach of the implied duty of trust and confidence), unfair dismissal and freedom of association. It should be noted that there is authority to support the view that employees can claim to have been constructively dismissed and so mount an unfair dismissal claim (provided that other qualifications to claim are met) without resigning from the employment on the basis that their existing employment contract has been breached.[1]

Common law

The duty on courts and tribunals to act compatibly with the Convention (ss 6(1)(a) and (3)(b)) is likely to have implications for the interpretation of contractual rights and obligations. Decisions relating to the scope of the managerial prerogative, and the corresponding duty on employees to obey lawful and reasonable orders,

1 *Hogg v Dover College* [1990] ICR 39 and *Alcan Extrusions v Yates* [1996] IRLR 327.

will need to take account of Convention rights. Express contractual powers which interfere with the exercise of a Convention right may also require justification by employers,[2] although the relationship between Convention rights and contract is a complex area which will require further exploration by the courts.[3]

Direct or collateral challenge

The acts of local authorities as employers are susceptible to challenge under s 7(1) even if they occur in contexts which are traditionally regarded as private for the purposes of judicial review.[4] The European Court of Human Rights ('ECHR') has held that dismissing or threatening to dismiss a worker for activities which the Convention guarantees will constitute an interference with the exercise of that right.[5] A lesser disciplinary penalty, such as suspension or a reprimand,[6] or the threat of disciplinary action,[7] may also be sufficient. However, to date it has rejected the argument that denial of employment, or the confirmation of employment, for exercising a Convention right is capable of giving rise to a violation of the Convention.[8] The distinction between prejudicial treatment during employment and denial of employment for exercising a Convention right does not appear in the Convention. The US Supreme Court has affirmed that public employment cannot be made conditional on the surrender of constitutional rights which cannot be abridged by direct governmental action. This is a principle which does not depend on the applicant being able to demonstrate a 'right' to the benefit which is being denied.[9] It remains to be seen whether UK courts will be persuaded to adopt the US view.[10]

ARTICLES OF PARTICULAR RELEVANCE TO EMPLOYMENT

The rights guaranteed by Arts 3, 6, 8-11 and 14 may all be relevant to the acts of local authorities as employers.[11] Article 3 may be violated by excessively long disciplinary proceedings and discrimination. Of the remainder, the application

2 Application 12242/86 *Rommelfanger v Germany* 62 DR 151 (1989); cf. Application 11308/84 *Vereniging Rechtswinkels Utrecht v Netherlands* 46 DR 200 (1986).

3 See further Gillian Morris, 'The European Convention on Human Rights and Employment: To Which Acts Does it Apply?' (1999) *European Human Rights Law Review* , Issue 5 (forthcoming).

4 See further Gillian Morris, 'The Human Rights Act and the Public/Private Divide in Employment Law' [1998] 27 *Industrial Law Journal*, 293.

5 *Vogt v Germany* judgment of 26 September 1995, [1996] 21 EHRR 205, para 44.

6 Application 10293/83 *B v United Kingdom* 45 DR 41 (1985); Application 11389/85 *Morissens v Belgium* 56 DR 127 (1988).

7 *Young, James and Webster v United Kingdom* judgment of 13 August 1981 (1981) 4 EHRR 38; see also *Dudgeon v United Kingdom* judgment of 22 October 1981 (1981) 4 EHRR 149, paras 40, 41.

8 *Glasenapp v Germany* judgment of 28 August 1986 (1986) 9 EHRR 25; *Kosiek v Germany* judgment of 28 August 1986 (1986) 9 EHRR 328.

9 *Keyishian v Board of Regents* 385 US 589 (1967), 605; *Perry v Sindermann* 408 US 593 (1972), 597.

10 See further Morris, note 3.

11 Article 4 is also potentially relevant to employment (for example it may be arguable that junior doctors' working hours, which are not protected by the Working Time Regulations, could constitute a violation), but it is unlikely that any local authority practices would constitute a breach.

of Art 6 is analysed in detail by Nicholls, Art 11 by Morris and Art 14 by Ivimy (in chapter 7). This section examines the implications of Arts 8, 9 and 10.

Article 8: The right to respect for private and family life, home and correspondence

Article 8(1) has been given an expansive interpretation in ECHR jurisprudence. 'Private life' covers actions in the workplace as well as the domestic sphere, and mail and telephone communications fall within 'private life' and 'correspondence' regardless of whether they concern personal or professional matters.[12] The following practices are among those capable of raising issues under Art 8(1):

(i) surveillance of employees by monitoring telephones, e-mail or other forms of communication. The leading case is *Halford v United Kingdom,*[13] where Ms Halford, the Assistant Chief Constable of Merseyside Police, complained that her employers had infringed Art 8(1) by intercepting calls made from her office relating to her sex discrimination claim against them. ECHR held that she had a reasonable expectation of privacy for such calls, particularly as her employers had given permission for her to use her office telephones for this purpose. If an employer expressly warns that telephone calls will be monitored, there will probably be no interference with the right, provided that adequate alternative provision is made, for example, payphones. However, surveillance of 'private' areas, such as toilets and staff canteens, is likely to constitute an interference, regardless of a warning;
(ii) psychological or personality testing which requires individuals to reveal information about their private lives;[14]
(iii) dress codes and hair styles;
(iv) penalties for sexual conduct, or misconduct outside the workplace.

Practices which interfere with the right to respect for the areas which Art 8(1) protects may be justified under Art 8(2). The Commission recently accepted the justification for rules requiring 'appropriate' dress at work designed to safeguard the employer's 'public image' and held that the male applicant's dismissal for wearing women's clothes at work was inadmissible.[15] However, it was stressed that the rules in question did not affect his freedom to dress as he chose at other times. Restrictions which intrude on conduct outside work will be more difficult to justify. Thus, rules on hair length which are based

12 *Klass v Germany* judgment of 6 September 1978 (1978) 2 EHRR 214; *Niemietz v Germany* judgment of 16 December 1992 (1992) 16 EHRR 97; *Halford v United Kingdom* judgment of 25 June 1997 (1997) 24 EHRR 523.
13 *Halford v United Kingdom* (1997) 24 EHRR 523. Following this judgment OFTEL has published guidance on the monitoring and recording of employees' personal telephone calls.
14 In the case of both (i) and (ii) the implications of the Data Protection Act 1998 will also need to be considered.
15 Application 36528/97 *Kara v United Kingdom* [1999] EHRLR 232. The applicant's complaint that his dismissal violated Art 14 in conjunction with Art 8 also failed: that the range of dress considered appropriate for a woman may be wider than that for a man did not mean that he had been subjected to a different rule on the basis that he was a man.

purely on 'conventional standards' are unlikely to withstand challenge.[16] In many contexts it will be more difficult to show a 'pressing social need' and to satisfy the proportionality test if not all authorities adopt the practice challenged.[17]

Article 9: Freedom of thought, conscience and religion

The most common issues for employers under Art 9 relate to time off work for religious services and holidays. To date, Convention jurisprudence has not been sympathetic to employees' claims that the requirements of religious observance should prevail over their contractual obligations. In *Ahmad v United Kingdom*[18] a Muslim teacher left his full-time job because his employers would not allow him 45 minutes time off every Friday to attend a mosque and instead sought to employ him on a 4½ day week at a reduced rate of pay. The majority of the Court of Appeal rejected his argument that he had been constructively dismissed,[19] and the Commission held that the employer's action did not constitute an interference with his Art 9(1) right. It noted that an individual may have to take account, in the exercise of his freedom to manifest his religion, of his professional and contractual position. Here, the applicant had 'of his own free will' accepted obligations which prevented his attendance at Friday prayers. Similarly in *Konttinen v Finland*[20] the dismissal of a clerical worker in the Finnish State Railways, who became a Seventh Day Adventist, for leaving work early on six Fridays in the period 1992-93 was found by the Commission to be motivated by his refusal to respect his working hours rather than his religious convictions.

In holding that existing contractual rights prevailed, the Commission decisions in *Ahmad* and *Konttinen* overlook the fact that Art 9(1) specifically guarantees the right to change religion, a point which may be taken in domestic courts. In *Stedman v United Kingdom*[21] the Commission went one step further in holding that there was no interference with the applicant's Art 9(1) right when she was dismissed for refusing, on religious grounds, to sign a new contract with her employer which included Sunday as a normal working day. She had been dismissed 'for failing to agree to work certain hours rather than for her religious beliefs as such'. In all these cases freedom to resign from the employment was regarded as the ultimate guarantee of the right to freedom of religion. UK courts may be persuaded to adopt a different view.

Although, as presently interpreted, Art 9(1) does not require employers to grant time off for religious purposes, if time off is given employers should not discriminate between religions.

Rules regulating dress or other aspects of appearance may also give rise to complaints under Art 9(1). ECHR has emphasised that Art 9 does not protect every act motivated or inspired by a religion or belief.[22] It remains to be seen

16 Cf. *Smith v Safeway plc* [1995] IRLR 132, where the dismissal of a male assistant on a delicatessan counter because he had a pony-tail, a style permitted to women, was found not to contravene the Sex Discrimination Act 1975.
17 See *Vogt v Germany* judgment of 26 September 1995 (1995) 21 EHRR 205 (relating to freedom of expression).
18 Application 8160/78 (1982) 4 EHRR 126.
19 *Ahmad v Inner London Education Authority* [1977] ICR 490.
20 Application 24949/94 87 DR 68.
21 Application 29107/95 (1997) 23 EHRR CD168.
22 See, for example, *Kalac v Turkey* judgment of 1 July 1997, (1997) 27 EHRR 552.

whether penalising non-conformity with rules which run contrary to religious practices will be regarded by domestic courts as 'interfering' with the exercise of the right, so requiring justification under Art 9(2).

Article 10: Freedom of expression

The Convention jurisprudence in relation to freedom of expression has centred on Art 10(2), with a wide interpretation being accorded to the concept of 'expression'. Dress codes may give rise to freedom of expression issues if they prevent an individual expressing a particular opinion or idea.[23]

Article 10(2) states that the exercise of freedom of expression is subject to 'duties and responsibilities'. This qualification has led the court to conclude that public servants accept certain restrictions (a 'duty of discretion') as being inherent in their duties, and that 'a certain margin of appreciation' is left to the national authorities in determining whether any given interference is proportionate to the aim which is being pursued. In *Ahmed v United Kingdom*[24] the court had regard to this in finding that the restrictions on the political activities of local government workers were not a disproportionate interference with their rights under Art 10(1). The 'duty of discretion' may also justify constraints on public sector workers criticising their employer or making use of information gained in their official capacity.[25] Although any such constraints will now be subject to the Public Interest Disclosure Act 1998 ('PIDA 1998'), disciplinary action for 'whistleblowing' disclosures which are not 'protected' by PIDA 1998 could probably be justified under Art 10(2).

As in the case of Art 8(1), restrictions on freedom of expression which are confined to the workplace will be easier to justify than those which extend to life outside work.

MEASURES WHICH LOCAL AUTHORITIES SHOULD TAKE

Local authorities should take immediate steps to review their contracts of employment, staff handbook and other documents relating to employment policies and practices to ensure that they are compatible with Convention rights. Ideally this should be done by authorities on a co-ordinated basis. This will mean that if a policy or practice is challenged and found to interfere with a Convention right, it will be easier for the respondent authority to justify it than if it is not universally applied to the category of workers in question.

23 Application 11674/85 *Stevens v United Kingdom* 46 DR 245 (1986). In *Kara v UK*, above note 15, the Commission held that in the applicant's case the restriction did not interfere with his freedom of expression.

24 Judgment of 2 September 1998 [1999] IRLR 188; see further Gillian Morris, 'The Political Activities of Local Government Workers and the European Convention on Human Rights' [1999] Public Law 211.

25 Application 10293/83 *B v United Kingdom* 45 DR 41 (1985); Application 18957/91 *Haseldine v United Kingdom* 73 DR 225.

Unfair Dismissal

INTRODUCTION

The right not to be unfairly dismissed is not one of the rights recognised by the European Convention. Consequences for the law of unfair dismissal following the incorporation of substantive parts of the Convention by the Human Rights Act 1998 ('HRA 1998') will therefore necessarily be indirect.

Local authorities are clearly public authorities within HRA 1998 and are therefore bound not to act in a way which is incompatible with an individual's human rights as protected by HRA 1998, unless (in effect) compelled to do so by some statutory provision.[1] A local authority is a public authority without the need to have recourse to the extended definition in s 6(3)(b) 'any person certain of whose functions are functions of a public nature'. It is a 'pure' public authority.[2] It is not excused from compliance with human rights standards if the nature of the act in issue is private, as would be the case for a s 6(3)(b) public authority by virtue of s 6(5). It is therefore irrelevant whether acts done by a local authority in the capacity of employer are 'private', and in particular whether the public/private divide which has proved problematical in judicial review applies to define the substantive obligations of local authorities under s 6.

Courts and tribunals are also public authorities under s 6(3)(a). This entails an obligation to apply legislation, such as the statutory test of fairness of a dismissal,[3] in such a way that the disposition of a particular claim is not incompatible with the human rights of the applicant, unless the tribunal is compelled by the wording of HRA 1998 (or some other material statutory provision) to determine the matter in an incompatible way (substantially or procedurally).

As public authorities, local authorities are liable to proceedings for damages under s 7 for violations of human rights which may be the same as, or closely interrelated with, the matters in issue in unfair dismissal proceedings. An example would be conduct relied on as the basis for a constructive dismissal claim which is also asserted as an impermissible interference with privacy under Art 8 of the Convention. It is not yet known whether employment tribunals will be designated as 'appropriate' for the purposes of s 7. If not (as seems more probable) there will nevertheless be an issue whether in awarding a remedy for a constructive unfair

1 HRA 1998 s 6(1), (2).
2 See Gillian Morris [1998] 27 ILJ 293 at 294-297.
3 Employment Rights Act 1996, s 98(4).

dismissal which is also an interference with privacy, the compensatory award can be increased to reflect this additional factor. This is discussed further below.

There is a statutory obligation on courts and tribunals to have regard to relevant jurisprudence of the European Court of Human Rights ('ECHR') and the (former) Commission, (which until the reformed procedures under the Convention came into effect on 1 November 1998 determined the admissibility of claims). There is relatively little case law on employment law issues and it is largely concerned with collective rights rather than individual protection from dismissal. Some relevant cases are referred to below. In the absence of a substantial body of case law, there will be more opportunity for tribunals (and the higher courts on appeal) to develop and apply concepts of protected human rights to issues in the employment context. In this process, they may well be assisted by reference to the jurisprudence of other jurisdictions.

The substantive rights secured by the Convention and incorporated by HRA 1998 must be secured without discrimination on any of an open-ended range of inappropriate grounds. Article 14 specifically refers to sex, race, religion and political or other opinion, but also 'other status', which may be held to extend to disability and/or sexual orientation. Article 14 is also incorporated by Sch 1 to HRA 1998. It does not follow that a dismissal involving discrimination on grounds within Art 14 will *necessarily* render the dismissal unfair, although this will no doubt be argued in tribunals. The EAT has held back from saying that a dismissal which is an act of unlawful sex discrimination is per se unfair,[4] and this must at least be equally so for discrimination (for example, on grounds of sexuality) which is not as such unlawful under domestic law. However, where a dismissal entails a breach of a substantive right such as freedom of religion or expression, or discrimination between employees in relation to substantive rights, the s 6 duty of the tribunal is likely to drive it to the conclusion that the dismissal is unfair. (This is without prejudice to any other remedy that may be pursued against the employing authority in any other judicial forum).

The jurisdictional limits to the right not to be unfairly dismissed

It is unlikely that a challenge could successfully be mounted under HRA 1998 to any of the jurisdictional limits to the right not to be unfairly dismissed. As stated above, the right is not in itself protected and therefore the kinds of challenge mounted under EU law in *R v Secretary of State for Employment, ex p Seymour-Smith*[5] and *Nash v Mash t/a Roe Group Ltd*[6] could not plausibly be argued on the basis of discriminatory effects of the jurisdictional restrictions impacting on individuals under Art 14. The Commission has rejected a challenge to the two-year qualifying period of employment.[7] The limit has, in any event, for dismissals since 1 June 1999, been reduced to one year.

It is also likely that challenges to the statutory time limits for presenting unfair dismissal claims[8] will be rejected. Article 6 of the Convention requires that anyone is entitled to a hearing before an independent and impartial tribunal of any claim in relation to his civil rights or obligations. However, the jurisprudence of the court clearly establishes that this does not preclude reasonable time limits for the

4 *Clarke v Eley (IMI) Kynoch Ltd* [1983] ICR 165.
5 [1997] IRLR 315.
6 [1998] IRLR 168.
7 *Stedman v United Kingdom* (1997) 23 EHRR CD168.
8 Employment Rights Act 1996, s 111.

bringing of proceedings.[9] The existence of the discretion to extend time where compliance with the primary three-month limit was 'not reasonably practicable' provides a safety net likely to satisfy any requirement of reasonableness. Nevertheless, the application in specific cases of the test of reasonable practicability is bound to come under fresh scrutiny if applicants argue that Art 6 requires the tribunal not to deny them a hearing where a late application was the result, for example, of incorrect advice or ignorance of rights. It remains to be seen how far these arguments will result in a more relaxed approach to late claims (and indeed to interlocutory decisions preventing a party from pursuing, or defending, a claim).

Constructive dismissal

There may be cases where the ambit of constructive dismissal is widened by HRA 1998. The duty of public authorities not to act incompatibly with individuals' human rights may be regarded as an implied term of any contract to employ an individual, in the same way that the courts have recognised the implied contractual duty not to expose the employee to the risk of injury by disregarding statutory health and safety duties. The same result may also (or alternatively) be achieved by further refinement of the implied duty not to undermine mutual trust and confidence.[10] If an implied term is recognised, acts or omissions of a public authority employer incompatible with the human rights of an individual employee would (unless the authority was bound by statute so to act) be grounds for the employee to treat himself as constructively dismissed. An example would be refusal to allow an employee to take a holiday on a day regarded as holy in his religion (arguably in breach of the freedom of religion safeguarded by Art 9, although the Commission has thus far taken a narrower view on this point).[11]

Procedural unfairness

It should be made clear that Art 6 does not necessarily require particular procedural standards in internal disciplinary proceedings. However, there may be ways in which procedures leading to dismissal infringe individuals' human rights in ways relevant to the fairness of the dismissal. The possible range of circumstances makes any attempt to identify likely examples random and speculative. However, some possible areas of difficulty can be anticipated:

(1) excessively long suspension (unfortunately not unknown in local authority practice). This may, in an extreme case, be argued to be inhuman or degrading treatment of the individual, in breach of Art 3 of the Convention;
(2) the imposition of restrictions on an individual during a period of suspension. A prohibition on contacting the press, for instance, could provide grounds for challenge under Art 10 as an improper restriction on freedom of speech;
(3) over-intrusive investigations during suspension pending the disciplinary hearing, such as questioning work colleagues about aspects

9 See, for example, *Stubbings v United Kingdom* (1996) 23 EHRR 213.
10 See *Mahmud v Bank of Credit and Commerce International SA* [1998] AC 20.
11 Cf *JH Walker Ltd v Hussain* [1996] IRLR 11, an indirect racial discrimination claim.

of the employee's private life or unnecessary surveillance, could involve breach of the rights to privacy in Art 8.[12]

Substantive unfairness

Clearly there is scope for tribunals to take into account the human rights of a dismissed employee as part of the circumstances to be considered in determining whether the employer acted reasonably in dismissing the employee, without needing to resort to HRA 1998. The Act will raise the question whether a tribunal is required to find a dismissal unfair where a violation of the employee's human rights is involved. It is likely to feel obliged to do so for one or more of the following reasons:

(1) a dismissal incompatible with the employee's human rights will generally be a breach of the local authority's duty under s 6 of HRA 1998;
(2) the tribunal as a public authority has a duty in determining the dispute arising from the dismissal to act in a way that is not in-compatible with the applicant's human rights (unless constrained to decide otherwise by statute). This would, at least, arguably necessitate finding such a dismissal unfair, since a finding that the authority had acted fairly (for example, reasonably) in violating the employee's human rights would be inconsistent with those rights, and is not required by the statutory test of fairness in s 98(4) Employment Rights Act 1996;
(3) if the employment tribunals are designated as appropriate under s 7 of HRA 1998, the issue to be determined would simply be whether the authority had acted in breach of its s 6 duty. It would be artificial not to answer that question in proceedings to which it was relevant in the event that the tribunals are not so designated.

Nevertheless, in practice relatively few situations will arise where a dismissal which violates the human rights of the dismissed employee would not be held to be unfair on ordinary principles. Some examples where the scope for a finding of unfair dismissal may arise are noted below:

(1) interference with private or family life, dismissal for reasons related to sexual orientation or sexuality,[13] or because of private conduct of the employee outside the employment context;
(2) dismissal in circumstances where the employee sought to practise his religious beliefs (as in the example given above of an individual being denied a holiday for a religious festival) or to manifest them in dress or appearance;
(3) dismissal for participating in political activity or expressing political opinions (but the circumstances where such a dismissal would be held to be incompatible with human rights are likely to be significantly restricted by the decision of ECHR in *Ahmed v United Kingdom)*;[14]

12 See the decision of ECHR in *Lustig-Prean v United Kingdom* 27 September 1999, unreported.
13 See, *Lightman and Bowers* [1998] EHRLR 560 at 576-8; and n 12 above.
14 [1999] IRLR 188: see Morris [1999] PL 211-218.

(4) dismissal for informing the proper authorities (or, more debatably, the media) of alleged wrongdoing by the employer (but it is likely that dismissals not rendered automatically unfair by the Public Interest Disclosure Act 1998 would also not be regarded as incompatible with human rights).

Other examples of reasons for dismissal that would be regarded as infringing human rights can, no doubt, easily be identified but most are likely to be clearly unfair under established criteria (for example, dismissal for supporting an unpopular religious group) or even automatically unfair (for example, dismissal for trade union membership). In addition it must be remembered that the rights safeguarded by the Convention are subject to extensive qualification under the terms of the Convention itself, often extensively interpreted in the jurisprudence of the court and Commission. It is unlikely that a dismissal which violates any of the core rights and for which no exemption arises under the Convention, would satisfy the criteria of reasonableness applied by Tribunals under s 98 Employment Rights Act 1996.

Remedies

Where an act, such as dismissal, is a violation by a public authority of the victim's human rights, an appropriate remedy is required. In principle, the appropriate route to obtaining a remedy would be to apply to a court or tribunal designated under s 7 and the effects of HRA 1998 on unfair dismissal remedies are likely to be indirect. However, the abolition of the limit on compensation for sex discrimination following the decision of the ECJ in *Marshall v Southampton and South West Hampshire Health Authority (No 2)*,[15] is perhaps a pointer to challenges to the maximum compensatory award for unfair dismissal (which is to be increased to £50,000 and index-linked under the Employment Relations Act 1999, but not, as had been proposed in the 1998 White Paper 'Fairness at Work', abolished). Nevertheless, it is unlikely that a Marshall-type challenge to the statutory limit would succeed. Neither an employment tribunal nor the EAT will have the power to make a declaration that the statutory provision is in breach of the Convention. The Court of Appeal would, no doubt, be influenced by the argument that the remedy in issue is for unfair dismissal not violation of human rights. A further consideration is that Art 13 of the Convention, which requires the provision of an effective remedy for any violations of Convention rights, has not been incorporated into Sch 1 to HRA 1998.

A potentially more fruitful challenge would be to the case law limiting the recoverable loss in unfair dismissal claims to strictly financial losses, excluding injury to feelings, distress or any form of compensation for the affront involved in being unfairly dismissed. Where the dismissal is, or involves, a violation of the individual's human rights a tribunal would arguably fail to comply with its s 6 duty if it failed to award appropriate compensation for that factor. There is no statutory restriction, within the overall maximum, except that the tribunal must 'have regard' to the employee's losses. The general injunction that compensation should be 'just and equitable',[16] gives scope for some creative jurisprudence even (possibly especially) at tribunal level. The amount of any additional compensation

15 [1993] ICR 893.
16 Employment Rights Act 1996, s 123(1).

a tribunal might award would be limited by the jurisprudence of ECHR on what constitutes 'just satisfaction' for a violation of rights: see s 8(3), (4) HRA 1998.

Conduct of tribunal proceedings

Complaints of unfair dismissal require the determination of civil rights and obligations and must therefore be decided in accordance with Art 6(1) of the Convention. Excessive delay in determining a tribunal claim has been held by ECHR to be a violation of the requirement to give a determination within a reasonable time,[17] and this will no doubt be a point made by parties suspicious of the reasons for applications for adjournments or other apparent delaying tactics by the opposing party.

Other procedural issues likely to arise are the practice of tribunals sitting in private at directions hearings (which not infrequently involve determinations of issues of considerable importance to the parties) or for pre-hearing reviews, and the determination of interlocutory matters without affording the parties the opportunity of a hearing. Following the enactment of HRA 1998 there has already been a change of practice of tribunals as to the status of directions hearings, which are now classed as public.

A related issue (applicable equally to other types of cases heard by employment tribunals) is the common and growing practice of the tribunal reading witness statements privately and taking the evidence as read. While this may make the proceedings speedier and more efficient, there is room for argument that they are not truly 'public', since members of the public (and the press) attending the hearing do not have a right of access to the evidence given in this way.

The majority of unfair dismissal claims are settled before any public hearing, and local authorities, like many other employers, commonly ask for confidentiality clauses as a condition of settlement. It is likely that any such clause would be unenforceable if tested in subsequent proceedings by reason of its interference with freedom of expression and information under Art 10. The permitted exception for the protection of information given in confidence could hardly apply to provisions in settlement agreements precluding disclosure of the circumstances leading to the claim, and it would be self-serving for a local authority to rely on an obligation of confidentiality introduced at its initiative rather than arising from the nature of the information itself.

Indeed, the act of insisting on confidentiality as a condition of settlement might arguably be open to challenge by media interests as an act incompatible with Art 10, on the basis that it denies the media access to information that may be a proper matter of public interest.

The arbitration scheme due to be introduced by regulations under the Employment Rights (Dispute Resolution) Act 1998 is not likely to be successfully challenged since it will be dependent on the consent of the parties to refer the dispute to arbitration. However, any future proposal to make the scheme obligatory would inevitably fall foul of Art 6, at least if arbitrations were to be held in private. Agreements having the effect of excluding the (ex-) employee from recourse to the tribunal are already subject to stringent restrictions on enforceability (for example, Employment Rights Act 1996, s 203) and the current judicial tendency to enforce the conditions of validity of compromise agreements strictly is likely to be reinforced by the incorporation of Art 6.

17 *Darnell v United Kingdom* (1993) 18 EHRR 205.

CONCLUSION

Whereas the impact of HRA 1998 in some areas of the law, including areas of employment law, is likely to be significant, unfair dismissal is one area where the impact can be expected to be both patchy and largely indirect. However, as in other areas the safest predictions are that HRA 1998 will be heavily relied on by litigants, often imaginatively so, and that the actual outcome of the expected flurry of litigation cannot be predicted.

Freedom of Association and Trade Union Rights

INTRODUCTION

There are two Articles of the European Convention on Human Rights which are relevant to freedom of association and trade union rights. Article 11(1) provides that:

> everyone has the right to ... freedom of association with others, including the right to form and to join trade unions for the protection of his interests.

In addition Art 10, which protects the right to freedom of expression, may apply to some aspects of trade union activity.

Both these rights may be restricted to protect specified interests. Article 11(2) states that restrictions may be imposed where these are:

> prescribed by law and are necessary in a democratic society in the interests of national security or public safety, for the prevention of disorder or crime, for the protection of health or morals or for the protection of the rights and freedoms of others.

The current jurisprudence of the European Court of Human Rights ('ECHR') and European Commission of Human Rights ('the Commission') leaves many issues yet to be determined in the areas of freedom of association and trade union rights.

FREEDOM OF ASSOCIATION IN ENGLISH LAW

There is no positive right to freedom of association in English law, although ss 137-167 of the Trade Union and Labour Relations (Consolidation) Act 1992 ('TULRCA 1992') accord limited protection to trade unionists who are discriminated against by employers. These protections may currently be claimed only by 'employees' or prospective employees, although the Employment Relations Act 1999 empowers the Secretary of State to extend their application.

Who may claim the right to freedom of association under the Convention?

Articles 10 and 11 apply to 'everyone'. There is, thus, a extensive body of potential 'victims' (including unions) who may bring proceedings against local authorities which act in ways which are incompatible with the rights they guarantee.

Article 11 does not prevent the imposition of 'lawful restrictions on the exercise' of the right to freedom of association by 'members of the armed forces, of the police or of the administration of the state'.

In Britain the police are forbidden to join trade unions but no other groups of workers are subject to statutory restrictions. Convention jurisprudence suggests that local government workers do not constitute 'members ... of the administration of the state'.[1] Thus, if any future Government were to impose restrictions on the freedom of association of local government workers, such restrictions would almost certainly have to be justified by reference to one of the alternative criteria set out in Art 11(2).

Does the Convention apply to participation in union activities?

In addition to being limited to employees, the protections established by TULRCA 1992 have further gaps. Protection against discriminatory hiring applies only on grounds of union membership, not activities.[2] Protection against dismissal and action short of dismissal extends to participation in the activities of an independent trade union, but showing that activities are those of the union can be difficult. How far does the Convention extend beyond these provisions?

In *X v Ireland* the Commission considered that threats of dismissal or other actions intended to make an employee relinquish the office of shop steward could, in certain circumstances, seriously restrict or impede the lawful exercise of freedom of association under Art 11.[3] This reasoning could be applied to discriminatory hiring if ECHR or domestic courts were to be persuaded (contrary to the current Strasbourg jurisprudence) that denial of employment could give rise to a violation of a Convention right. Article 10 may also be relevant in this context. In *Vogt v Germany,* ECHR held that the dismissal of a civil servant from her teaching post because she had engaged in various political activities for the German Communist Party (including holding Party office) violated both Arts 10 and 11. In doing so, it reiterated a point made on previous occasions that '[t]he expression of personal opinions is one of the objectives of freedom of association'.[4] In *Ahmed v United Kingdom*[5] standing for political office was again regarded by ECHR as involving the exercise of freedom of expression.

A right not to join a union?

Article 11 does not specify a right not to join a union and the *travaux preparatoires* indicate that it was not intended to be covered. Despite this, ECHR has concluded that Art 11 does incorporate a negative right, and closed shop agreements may be difficult to justify under Art 11(2).[6] In practice this is unlikely to present an

1 Application 11603/85 *Council of Civil Service Unions v United Kingdom* (1988) 10 EHRR 269 (workers at GCHQ within this concept because its purpose resembled that of the armed forces and the police in protecting national security); *Vogt v Germany,* judgment of 26 September 1995 (1995) 21 EHRR 205, para 67.

2 There is some doubt as to how far the concept of membership includes using union facilities and services: *Discount Tobacco and Confectionary Ltd v Armitage* [1990] IRLR 15; *Associated Newspapers Ltd v Wilson; Associated British Ports v Palmer* [1995] ICR 406; *Speciality Care plc v Pachela* [1996] IRLR 248.

3 [1971] Application 4125/69.

4 *Vogt v Germany*, above note 1, para 64.

5 Judgment of 2 September 1998 [1999] IRLR 188.

6 *Sigurour A Sigurjonsson v Iceland,* judgment of 30 June 1993 (1993) 16 EHRR 462, para 35.

issue for the UK courts in the foreseeable future. TULRCA 1992 provides that employers cannot dismiss or take action short of dismissal against employees who refuse to join a union.

Article 11 and employee representation

Article 11 states that an individual has the right to join a union 'for the protection of his interests'. ECHR has accepted that this safeguards the freedom to protect the occupational interests of trade union members by trade union action and that union members have a right 'that the trade union should be heard'.[7] However, this does not imply a right for unions to be recognised or consulted by employers, nor, *a fortiori*, is there a right that the state should conclude a collective agreement with them; rather, each state has:

> a free choice of the means to be used towards that end ... What the Convention requires is that under national law trade unions should be enabled, in conditions not at variance with Art 11, to strive for the protection of their members' interests.[8]

If there is no mechanism whatsoever by which a union can be 'heard' by a local authority employer, however, this may constitute a breach of Art 11.

The recognition procedure contained in the Employment Relations Act 1999 will not necessarily change this position. If an authority refuses recognition to a union which fails to meet the statutory criteria for mandatory recognition, that union or its members may nevertheless be able successfully to argue that there should be some conduit for hearing members' views. Moreover, if a union (or group of unions) is accorded exclusive recognition the same reasoning will probably apply. The employer should still provide a channel for the views of members of non-recognised unions to be heard.[9] Differences in treatment between unions are unlikely to violate Arts 11 and 14 together, provided that the employer can demonstrate a legitimate aim, such as the desire to avoid a large number of bargaining partners (see Ivamy, chapter 7).[10] However, if the employers' aim is to marginalise a 'militant' union which has a large membership among the workforce this may be more difficult to justify.

Article 11 and 'personal contracts'

In *Associated Newspapers Ltd v Wilson; Associated British Ports v Palmer*[11] the House of Lords held that making a pay rise for employees conditional on a transfer from collectively-agreed terms and conditions of employment to 'personal

7 *National Union of Belgian Police v Belgium,* judgment of 22 October 1975 (1975) 1 EHRR 578, para 39.
8 See also *Swedish Engine Drivers' Union v Sweden,* judgment of 6 February 1976 (1976) 1 EHRR 617; *Gustafsson v Sweden* judgment of 28 March 1996, (1996) 22 EHRR 409.
9 *Swedish Engine Drivers' Union v Sweden.* In this case although it was not incompatible with Art 11 for the Swedish National Collective Bargaining Office to restrict the number of organisations with which collective agreements were concluded, it was material that the applicant union was still able to make representations to the Government for the protection of its members' interests.
10 *Swedish Engine Drivers.*
11 [1995] ICR 406.

contracts' did not constitute action short of dismissal against those trade unionists who did not agree to transfer. A complaint that these acts of discrimination constitute a breach of the Convention has been declared admissible by the Commission.[12]

The Employment Relations Act 1999 provides powers for the Secretary of State to make regulations to protect workers from detriment and dismissal if they refuse to change from a contract which incorporates the terms of a collective agreement to one with different terms. However, paying higher wages or giving other monetary benefits to workers who do transfer will not constitute a detriment to those who refuse, provided that these additional benefits reasonably relate to services provided by those workers under their contracts of employment and there is no inhibition against union membership in the contract.[13] It is difficult to determine at this stage whether regulations made under this provision will be regarded as compatible with Art 11.

The right to strike

There is no mention of the right to strike in Art 11, and ECHR has refused to imply such a right, taking the view that while it is 'one of the most important' of the means by which the occupational interests of trade union members may be protected, 'there are others'.[14] It could be deduced from this that if a union had no other means of conveying its members' interests a right to strike could be implied, but this argument seems unlikely to succeed.

A CAUTIONARY NOTE

Article 11 has been narrowly interpreted by the Strasbourg organs in relation to some aspects of trade union rights. However, in this area in particular it is important to remember that UK courts are not bound to follow their decisions. Those adjudicating on other international instruments take a wider view. Thus, the supervisory bodies of the International Labour Organisation (ILO) have seen the right to strike as integral to freedom of association, although it is nowhere mentioned in ILO Conventions 87 and 98 relating to this area, and have developed an elaborate jurisprudence relating to its scope.[15] Moreover, the European Social Charter of 1961 (like the Convention, a treaty of the Council of Europe) specifically includes the rights to bargain collectively and to strike. This may be regarded as persuasive by the UK courts in deciding the scope of Convention rights.[16] Argument before the UK courts in the areas of freedom of association and trade union activity is unlikely to be confined to the jurisprudence of ECHR and the Commission.

12 *Wilson, Palmer and Doolan v United Kingdom*, Applications 30668/96, 30671/96, 30678/96.

13 See also TULRCA 1992, s 148(3).

14 *Schmidt and Dahlstrom v Sweden* (1976) A/21 1 EHRR 632, para 36.

15 International Labour Office, *Freedom of Association: Digest of decisions and principles of the Freedom of Association Committeee of the Governing Body of the ILO* (4th edn, 1996).

16 Note also that the ECJ, in adjudicating on an internal staffing matter, has also seen representational rights as integral to trade union activity: *Maurissen and European Public Service Union v Court of Auditors* Cases C-193, 194/87 [1990] ECR I-95.

Article 6 and the Right to a Fair Hearing

Article 6 of the Human Rights Act 1998 ('HRA 1998') contains the right to a fair hearing. So far as relevant, Art 6 provides as follows:

> '(1) In the determination of his civil rights and obligations … everyone is entitled to a fair and public hearing within a reasonable time by an independent and impartial tribunal established by law. Judgment shall be pronounced publicly but the press and public may be excluded from all or part of the trial in the interests or morals, public order or national security in a democratic society, where the interests of juveniles or the protection of the private life of the parties so require, or to the extent strictly necessary in the opinion of the court in special circumstances where publicity would prejudice the interests of justice'.

The Article also contains provisions about criminal proceedings which do not concern local authorities but which are relevant to the argument which will be developed below.

So far as local authorities are concerned the question which arises is whether, having regard to s 6 HRA 1998, it will be necessary to amend any internal disciplinary or other procedures in order to ensure that those procedures comply with Art 6. Some commentators have hinted that this a possibility on the grounds that Art 6 may apply to internal procedures as well as to court hearings.[1]

The basis for this view is that in some cases the court assesses the question whether a person has had a fair hearing by looking not only at the court hearing but also at earlier stages. This may occur where, as a condition precedent to the right to bring legal proceedings, a person must proceed through some other procedure or avail himself of some other remedy.

The author's opinion is that Art 6 does not impose any such obligation on local authorities conducting internal procedures involving their employees. Even if it did, the duties imposed would be no greater an obligation than that presently imposed by the duty to follow fair procedures prior to a dismissal.

First, the focus of Art 6 is the right to a fair trial in a court or tribunal. Its emphasis is on the right of an individual to secure a public remedy for a civil wrong rather than on any internal complaints mechanisms. Several features of the Article support this proposition. For example:

1 See *Lightman and Bowers* [1998] 5 EHRLR 560, 581.

– the stipulation that there be a public hearing;
– the requirement for a hearing before independent and impartial tribunals 'established by law';
– the inference that in usual circumstances the press and public should be admitted.

None of these provisions is consistent with the application of this Article to a local authority employer's internal decision making regarding employment issues. It may well be that an employee aggrieved by such a decision ought to have access to a court or tribunal in order to have his grievance resolved, but that is a different matter. It must, of course, be right that a court or tribunal adjudicating an employee's complaint about his employer's actions would have to comply with the requirements of Art 6. However, that is not the issue for present purposes. The issue is whether similar obligations are imposed on the local authority employer in coming to its decision.

Second, in a case where a person is aggrieved about his employment rights he will, subject to satisfying any qualifying criteria, have access to a court or tribunal. That forum will investigate the entire merits of the matter, and provide a hearing which accords with the requirements of Art 6. There is no obligation on a person first to pursue an internal remedy and it is therefore somewhat artificial to regard any internal process as a part of the 'hearing' for the purposes of Art 6. It is fair to say that there may be a difference between the UK and other European countries in this respect. For example, in France challenges to decisions of public sector employers are made by way of judicial review applications to administrative courts. By their nature, these courts tend to assess the legality of a decision rather than to review its merits. Therefore the only point at which the merits of the case would be assessed is when the employer takes the initial decision. In those circumstances it may be more readily understandable that the employer's decision should be regarded as part of the 'trial'. In the UK context, of course, employment tribunals and courts do investigate the merits of a decision. Thus, there is a good practical reason to regard only that hearing, and not the employer's decision, as being the trial for the purposes of Art 6.

There is an argument that s 13 of the Employment Rights Dispute Resolution Act 1998 may be said to mean that the employer's disciplinary hearing is a part of the whole process of the 'trial' because that provision may be said to impose an obligation on an employee first to exhaust internal remedies. If that argument were right, then there would be stronger grounds for ensuring that internal proceedings were part of the overall hearing. However, it is submitted that this is not the effect of s 13. Section 13 empowers a tribunal to make an adjustment to an award of compensation when an employee fails to pursue an internal appeals procedure. This provision does not make it a prerequisite of any claim that an employee has first exhausted internal mechanisms. Rather the provision merely empowers a tribunal, if it considers it just and equitable to do so, to reduce the remedy in the event that a person fails to pursue alternative remedies.

Third, there is a question whether decisions taken internally regarding employment issues fall within the purview of Art 6 at all. This is a difficult issue and involves consideration of somewhat opaque decisions of the court. Article 6 applies to the 'determination of [a person's] civil rights'. What is a 'civil right' has been a matter of some debate in the case law, often with unsatisfactory conclusions. There is a series of cases concerning employees of public bodies, which suggest that disputes between the employee and the public sector employer do not raise 'civil rights'. Two grounds may be discerned for this. One is that employment in the public service is a public law matter and not a matter of (private) civil rights. The other is that disciplinary proceedings do not concern civil rights.

As to the first, it has been held consistently that 'disputes relating to the recruitment, careers and termination of service of civil servants are as a general rule outside the scope of Art 6(1)'.[2] The basis for this is a distinction drawn between public authorities and private employees. The cases suggest that work in the public sector raises issues of public law and the discharge of public functions. Of course, many civil law systems do draw a distinction between public sector employment which is regarded as a matter of public law and private sector employment which is regarded as a matter of private law.[3] Hence it may be right to say that in, for example, the French system disputes concerning civil servants involve not private civil rights but administrative decision making. However, the position in English law is that disputes between workers and employers in the public sector are matters of private law not public law. Hence judicial review is usually not an appropriate remedy.[4] Therefore, to the English lawyer this ground for excluding Art 6 is somewhat unattractive.

As to the second ground, the court held in *Le Compte v Belgium*[5] that disciplinary proceedings do not ordinarily give rise to a dispute about civil rights. On this basis, one could argue that an internal disciplinary investigation conducted by a local authority was not within the ambit of Art 6. However, the same case indicated that in some circumstances disciplinary proceedings might affect civil rights so that Art 6 was applicable. Unhappily, the court failed to give any general guidance as to the circumstances in which there might be an exception to the general rule. In *Le Compte* it was held that the right to practise medicine was a civil right whose inhibition by disciplinary proceedings did fall within the ambit of Art 6. Clearly the extent to which disciplinary proceedings may be said to fall within Art 6 will have to await a case-by-case development. However in line with the general principle set out in *Le Compte,* it is submitted that local authorities' disciplinary actions should not be regarded as affecting civil rights within the meaning of that Article.

More recent case law has tended to suggest that civil rights are involved in any case which impacts on an economic right, such as the right to payment, in particular a payment after termination.[6] Thus, for example, a person who had been dismissed without notice and who claimed an entitlement to notice monies would plainly be relying on the infringement of a civil right. There may, however, be more difficult questions as to how close a connection there is between the conduct of which a person complains and the impact on his economic rights.

Fourth, it is submitted that until an authority has taken a decision, for example to dismiss, there is no dispute regarding civil rights which needs to be determined. This turns on an analysis of the point at which a complaint concerns the 'determination' of a civil right. It is only when a decision is directly decisive of a right that the decision involves the determination of the right.[7] There must be a dispute which is justiciable.[8] This provides a further reason why internal disciplinary and other proceedings do not require the protection of Art 6. Arguably

2 *Neigel v France,* 17 March 1997, *Huber v France,* 19 February 1998.
3 See *Neigel,* para 43.
4 See *McClaren v Home Office* [1990] ICR 824.
5 [1983] 5 EHRR 533.
6 *Huber v France, Cazenave de la Roche v France,* 9 June 1998.
7 *Le Compte v Belgium.*
8 *Van Marle v Netherlands.*

there is no dispute capable of judicial resolution until an authority has taken a decision (for example) to dismiss. Once the decision has been taken, there may be a dispute. But until an authority has acted in a manner which an employee disputes, there is no dispute which falls to be determined.

Finally, some support for the proposition that Art 6 does not apply to internal disciplinary proceedings is to be gleaned from the case of *De Compte v European Parliament*.[9] In that case, an employee of the Parliament was made the subject of disciplinary proceedings on the ground that he was suspected of financial misconduct. He challenged the decision to demote him, inter alia, on the ground that the decision was reached in breach of Art 6. The ECJ rejected the contention that Art 6 had any application, holding that it 'does not apply to what are strictly disciplinary matters within the public service' since those matters were not penal proceedings.[10]

If it is right to suggest that Art 6 concerns not internal proceedings but the right to complain to a court of breaches of civil rights, one class obviously excluded from such a right would be those employees with less than one year's service who are dismissed by their employer. Of course, for the present they may not complain of unfair dismissal. Does this exclusion from the legislation mean that these employees are deprived of the right to a fair hearing? The Commission rejected such an argument in *Stedman v UK*,[11] holding that the right of access to a court was not absolute but was subject to a state's 'margin of appreciation'. The UK government was entitled to limit unfair dismissal rights to those with (then) more than two years' service in order to prevent employers being burdened by claims brought by those who had not become established in employment. (The qualifying period has of course since been reduced to one year.)

If the analysis set out above is wrong and Art 6 would apply to internal disciplinary proceedings, the question arises whether authorities should be amending their procedures to comply with the substantive requirements of the Article. As previously indicated the requirements of Art 6, so far as they may sensibly be said to apply to internal proceedings, are that there be a fair hearing within a reasonable time. It is submitted that these requirements do not add to the requirements already developed by decisions of the employment tribunals and the appellate courts under the unfair dismissal legislation. Hence an authority whose procedure adheres to guidelines developed in cases such as *Clark v Civil Aviation Authority*[12] will, it is submitted, also discharge their obligations under Art 6.

9 [1991] ECR II-781.
10 at 813, para 94.
11 (1997) 23 EHRR CD 168.
12 [1991] IRLR 412

Chapter 3

Education

INTRODUCTION

Section 6(1) of the Human Rights Act 1998 ('HRA 1998') will make it unlawful for a public authority to act in a way which is incompatible with a Convention right. A public authority includes any person whose functions are of a public nature (although not where the nature of the particular act in question is private).[1] There is no doubt that local education authorities ('LEAs') are public authorities for all purposes.

Section 1(1) of HRA 1998 lists the Convention rights. Included among these rights is the right to education described in Art 2 of the First Protocol to the Convention. We consider this Convention right in detail below, along with the other Convention rights which we think are likely to be in play in the area of education law affecting local authorities.

Section 2(1) of HRA 1998 will require any court or tribunal determining a question arising under HRA 1998 in connection with a Convention right to have regard primarily to any judgment, decision, declaration or advisory opinion of the European Court of Human Rights ('ECHR'). Before considering what may be required of LEAs in the future in order that they may avoid acting incompatibly with Convention rights, our starting point is to have regard to this primary reference source with a view to describing the nature and content of the Convention rights which we think will be in play in this area of the law. Having painted the relevant legal backcloth (in Part 1), we next identify (in Part 2) the main subject-headings in education law affecting LEAs where we think questions could arise under HRA 1998. We indicate what those questions might be and how we think a court might answer them.

PART I

Article 2, First Protocol – right to education

> 'No person shall be denied the right to education. In the exercise of any functions which it assumes in relation to education and to teaching, the state shall respect the right of parents to ensure such education and teaching in conformity with their own religious and philosophical convictions.'

1 HRA 1998, ss 6(3)(b), 6(5).

The first and basic obligation: no person shall be denied the right to education

In spite of its negative formulation, the first sentence of Art 2 does enshrine a 'right'. (The text in its original form had provided 'every person has the right to education' but this was reworked to avoid what some states feared might prove to be an excessively burdensome positive obligation.)

What is guaranteed is a right of access to educational institutions existing at a given time and to recognition of any studies completed there:'"To make existing teaching available to all": this is the service which it is required of contracting states to perform'. There is no right to require the state to establish at its own expense, or to subsidise, education of any particular type or at any particular level. In the *Belgian Linguistic Case*[2] the court rejected the applicants' submission that Article 2 gave rise to 'obligations to take action'.

Whereas there is no obligation to establish new educational institutions, in regulating access to and providing education at such educational institutions as do exist, the state must act in accordance with the requirements of the Convention. 'The right to education guaranteed by the first sentence of Art 2 of the Protocol by its very nature calls for regulation by the state, regulation which may vary in time and place according to the needs and resources of the community and of individuals. It goes without saying that such regulation must never injure the substance of the right to education nor conflict with other rights enshrined in the Convention'.[3]

By way of illustration of the propositions set out above, whereas the state may allow private systems of education or permit children to be educated by their parents, if it does so, Art 2 does not require it to fund or subsidise these alternatives.[4] However, in the course of regulating private and public education, the state may not use its regulatory power to injure the substance of the Art 2 right, for example, by making it impossible to establish private schools.[5]

Education includes all forms of education provided or permitted by the state. The focus is on primary education.[6] 'Education' includes higher education. However, access to higher education may be restricted to those able to benefit

2 (1968) 1 EHRR 252, the leading case in this area, where public support and official recognition had been withdrawn from French-language schools because they were in areas designated as Dutch unilingual. See also, Application 10476/83 (1985) 9 EHRR 247 (complaint about failure of state to meet cost of textbooks and teaching aids for children attending Rudolf Steiner school in same way as for children in state schools and some independent schools held inadmissible: the state's obligations under Art 2 were met by permitting the Steiner school to be established). In *O'Connor v Chief Adjudication Officer* [1999] ELR 209, the Court of Appeal rejected the argument that the denial of income support to a student working towards examination resits was a breach of Art 2: a person's right to avail himself of existing means of instruction did not include a right to be subsidised by the state in the exercise of that right. In *R v Department for Education and Employment, ex p Begbie* [1999] 35 LS Gaz R 39, Maurice Kay J held that Art 2 does not provide or guarantee a right to an assisted places scheme, nor does it give rise to an obligation to keep one in being.

3 See pp 281-282.

4 *W and KL v Sweden* Application 10476/83 45 DR 143 (1985) at 148-149.

5 *Jordebo* [1987] 51 DR 125 at 128.

6 Application 5962/72 *X v United Kingdom* 2 DR 50 (1975); Application 7671/76 15 *Foreign Students v United Kingdom* 9 DR 185 (1977); Application 8844/80 *X v United Kingdom* 23 DR 228 (1980); Application 11655/85 *Glazewska v Sweden* 45 DR 300 (1985).

from the academic standards which it provides.[7] 'Education' does not extend to vocational training.[8]

Does 'education' within the first sentence of Art 2 imply education of any particular quality?

We think not. What is guaranteed is the right to avail oneself of such education as is available at any given point in time. Certain commentators, while accepting the propositions set out above, argue that there may be derived from the Belgian Linguistic Case the additional proposition that 'education' within the first sentence of Art 2 means an 'effective education'.[9] We read the judgment[10] as indeed requiring the right to education to be effective in the sense that that right should include the right to official recognition of any studies completed, but we do not read the judgment as requiring more than that. We therefore see no scope for the argument (although it is to run ahead) that a Convention right has been infringed if the standard of teaching received by a child at a LEA school is very poor. It may be another matter if no effective education is being received at all, for instance if a class is kept at home for want of a teacher to teach them or, for no good reason, a school fails to open its doors. However, and as the above-mentioned commentators note, where any challenge to the effectiveness of an education received depends on the resources or the organisation and pattern of the education system established by the state, the negative formulation of the Art 2 right will provide the state with a sufficient answer.

The second obligation: to respect parents' philosophical and religious convictions

This is a right belonging to parents. The right continues when the child is in care.[11] If the child is in the custody of one parent, it ceases for the other.[12] The right ceases for both parents if the child is adopted.[13]

The right applies to all the systems of education in the state, public and private, and to all the functions the state exercises in connection with education, whether academic or administrative.[14]

The second sentence of Art 2 does not solely imply the right for parents to have their children exempted from classes offering religious instruction of a denominational character. It enjoins the state to respect parents' convictions, be they religious or philosophical, throughout the entire state education programme.[15]

The second sentence of Art 2 is principally a protection against indoctrination by the state. However, it does not prevent states from importing through teaching or education information or knowledge of a directly or indirectly religious or philosophical kind (provided that it is conveyed in an objective, critical and pluralistic manner).[16]

7 Application 8844/80 *X v United Kingdom* 23 DR 228 (1980).
8 See for example, Harris, O'Boyle and Warbrick, *Law of the European Convention of Human Rights* [1995] at 542-43.
9 See especially at 281.
10 Application 10554/83 *Aminoff v Sweden* 43 DR 120 (1985) at 144.
11 Application 7911/77 *X v Sweden* 12 DR 192 (1977).
12 Application 7626/76 *X v UK* 11 DR 160 (1976).
13 *Campbell and Cosans v United Kingdom* (1982) 4 EHRR 293, paras 33-36.
14 *Kjeldsen, Busk Madsen and Pedersen v Denmark* (1976)] 1 EHRR 711, para 51.
15 *Kjeldsen*, para 53.
16 *Campbell and Cosans v United Kingdom.*

The expression 'philosophical convictions' denotes such convictions as are worthy of respect in a 'democratic society', which are not incompatible with human dignity, and which do not conflict with the fundamental right of the child to education (the whole of Art 2 being dominated by its first sentence).

A conviction that one's child should not be subjected to corporal punishment satisfied the above criteria in *Campbell and Cosans v United Kingdom* on the grounds that it had attained 'a certain level of cogency, seriousness, cohesion and importance'. Perhaps more important than these qualitative characteristics of the conviction was the fact that it related to a 'weighty and substantial' aspect of human life and behaviour, namely the integrity of the person.

The convictions which are to be taken into account are interpreted narrowly. In particular, parents' philosophical and religious convictions do not include their cultural and linguistic preferences. There is no right to receive education in accordance with one's cultural or linguistic preferences.[17]

There is no right for parents opposed to sex education classes for their children to have their children exempted from such classes (provided that the information and knowledge conveyed in such classes is conveyed in an objective, critical and pluralistic manner). Parents (in Denmark) who wish to dissociate their children from integrated sex education have the choice of sending their children to private schools where there is no integrated sex education or to educate them at home.[18]

The state is forbidden from pursuing an aim of indoctrination that might be considered as not respecting parents' religious and philosophical convictions. The competent authorities have a duty to take the utmost care that parents' religious and philosophical convictions are not disregarded by carelessness, lack of judgment or misplaced proselytism on the part of a given teacher.

Section 1(2) of HRA 1998 provides that the Convention rights (as defined in s 1(1)) are to have effect for the purposes of HRA 1998, subject to any designated derogation or reservation. At the time of signing the First Protocol, the United Kingdom made a reservation (the text of which is set out in Pt II of Sch 3 to HRA 1998) to the effect that the principle contained in the second sentence of Art 2 of the First Protocol was accepted by it 'only so far as it is compatible with the provision of efficient instruction and training, and the avoidance of unreasonable public expenditure'. The effect of this reservation was considered by the Commission in *Graeme v United Kingdom*,[19] in which parents complained that the placement of their child, who had learning difficulties, in a special school was contrary to their wishes in a number of respects. The Commission said, taking into account the UK reservation, that 'there must be a wide measure of discretion left to the appropriate authorities as to how to make the best possible use of the resources available to them in the interests of disabled children generally'.

The applicant who contends that the second sentence of Art 2 has been infringed must show the basis for, and content of, the belief which he claims has not been respected; that it is a belief which he holds; that holding it is the reason for his objection to what the state is doing; and that he has brought the reasons for his objection to the attention of the authorities.[20]

17 See the Belgian Linguistic case.
18 See the Kjeldsen case.
19 [64 DR 158 (1990).
20 *Campbell and Cosans v United Kingdom*; Application 9471/81 *Warwick v United Kingdom* 60 DR 5 (1986) at 18; Application 9303/81 *B and D v United Kingdom* 49 DR 44 (1986) at 50.

The duty 'to respect' parents' religious and philosophical convictions is subsidiary to the fundamental obligation of the first sentence of Art 2. However, that fundamental obligation, as we have noted, is interpreted narrowly. So, for example, a parent who objects to a system of corporal punishment operating in his child's state school, may remove his child from the school and seek to place him in a fee-paying school where the disciplinary regime does not offend his convictions. However, the state has no duty under Art 2 to subsidise that private education.[21]

Article 14 – Prohibition of Discrimination

'The enjoyment of the rights and freedoms set forth in this Convention shall be secured without discrimination on any ground such as sex, race, colour, language, religion, political or other opinion, national or social origin, association with a national minority, property, birth or other status.'

The obligation not to discriminate

The combination of Art 14 of the Convention and Art 2 of the First Protocol did not have the effect of guaranteeing to a child or to his parent the right to obtain education in the language of one's choice.[22] The object of these two Articles, read in conjunction, is more limited. It is to ensure that the right to education shall be secured by each Contracting Party to everyone within its jurisdiction without discrimination on the ground, for instance, of language.

The principle of equality of treatment is violated if a difference in treatment has no objective and reasonable justification. The existence of such a justification must be assessed in relation to the aim and effects of the measure under consideration, the relationship of proportionality between the means employed and the aim sought to be realised, and the legal and factual features which characterise the life of the society in question.

These principles were established in the Belgian Linguistic case, in which the parents of French-speaking children alleged that several of the schooling arrangements differentiated between their children and Dutch-speaking children. The court found that Art 14 had been infringed in one respect only. French-speaking children in a particular area could not attend the French-speaking schools in a particular bilingual district outside the area, whereas the Dutch-speaking schools in that district accepted all Dutch-speaking children, even those from outside the district. The court held that this differential treatment could not be justified under Art 14: 'The enjoyment of the right to education as the court conceives it, and more precisely that of the right of access to existing schools, is not therefore on the point under consideration secured to everyone without discrimination on the ground, in particular, of language'.

As we have seen, the state has no duty to establish or subsidise private schools in order that parents' religious or philosophical convictions may be respected. However, the question arises whether a state which subsidises some denominational schools will infringe Art 14 if the subsidies favour some

21 See also Application 9461/81 *v United Kingdom* (1982) 5 EHRR 480 (complaint about LEA's failure to contribute to applicant's costs of sending children to Rudolf Steiner school held inadmissible; there was no obligation on the state to set up or support any educational establishment serving particular religious or philosophical beliefs or convictions).

22 See the Belgian Linguistic case.

denominational groups over others. There is a powerful argument that, in order to avoid incompatibility with Art 14, the state must avoid such discrimination. However, it must be equally arguable that the state should be able to rely on the adequacy (or any surplus) of school places within the district in which the school may be located as constituting an 'objective and reasonable justification' for a decision not to subsidise.

Article 9 – Right to freedom of thought, conscience and religion

'1. Everyone has the right to freedom of thought, conscience and religion …
2. Freedom to manifest one's religion or beliefs shall be subject only to such limitations as are prescribed by law and are necessary in a democratic society …'

Right to freedom of thought, conscience and religion

The right to hold religious beliefs is absolute. The right to manifest those beliefs is qualified. ECHR case law with respect to Art 9 illustrates a restrictive approach to the application of this Article. For example, the Commission held that the decision of ILEA not to release a Muslim school teacher to attend mosque on Friday afternoons was not a breach of Art 9.[23]

Article 8 – Right to respect for private and family life

'1. Everyone has the right to respect for his private and family life, his home and his correspondence. …'

Right to respect for private and family life

Article 8(1) does not guarantee either a right to education or a personal right of parents relating to the education of their children. Its object is essentially that of protecting the individual against arbitrary interference by public authorities in his private and family life. In particular, Art 8 does not guarantee the right to be educated in the language of one's parents by the public authorities or with their aid. Measures taken in the field of education may affect the right to respect for private of family life, for example if their aim or result were to disturb private or family life in an unjustifiable manner, say, by separating children from their parents in an arbitrary way. Thus, in the Belgian Linguistic case the court agreed that French-speaking parents in Dutch-speaking areas who, rather than enrol their children in Flemish schools, boarded their children in French schools outside the relevant area, suffered an interference in their private and family life. However, the court's judgment was that this hardship resulted from the 'choice of the parents who place their children in schools situated outside the Dutch unilingual region with the sole purpose of avoiding their being taught in Dutch, that is to say, in one of Belgium's national languages'.

Article 3 – Prohibition of torture

No one shall be subjected to torture or to inhuman or degrading treatment or punishment,'

23 See, for example, *Ahmad v United Kingdom* (1981) 4 EHRR 126.

Freedom from torture, cruel and inhuman treatment and punishment

The obligation on the High Contracting Parties under Art 1 of the Convention to secure to everyone within their jurisdiction the rights and freedoms defined in the Convention, taken together with Art 3, requires states to take measures designed to ensure that individuals within their jurisdiction are not subjected to torture or inhuman or degrading treatment, including such ill-treatment administered by private individuals. Children and other vulnerable individuals are in particular entitled to state protection in the form of effective deterrence, against serious breaches of personal integrity.[24] In *A v United Kingdom,* the applicant's stepfather, who had caned him several times, was found not guilty of assault occasioning actual bodily harm on the ground that the chastisement was 'moderate and reasonable', a defence under English law. ECHR held that the applicant's treatment reached the level of severity prohibited by Art 3. The law of England and Wales not having provided adequate protection to the applicant, there was a breach of Art 3.

Article 6 – Right to a fair trial

> '1.In the determination of his civil rights and obligations ... everyone is entitled to a fair and public hearing within a reasonable time by an independent and impartial tribunal established by law. Judgment shall be pronounced publicly but the press and public may be excluded from all or part of the trial in the interests of morals, public order or national security in a democratic society, where the interests of juveniles or the protection of the private life of the parties so require, or to the extent strictly necessary in the opinion of the court in special circumstances where publicity would prejudice the interests of justice.'

Right to a fair hearing

Our view is that the better argument is that Art 6 concerns the right to complain to a court or statutory tribunal of breaches of civil rights. There is no scope, therefore, as we see it for schools' governing bodies or local authorities being required to amend their decision-making procedures in order to comply with Art 6.

In order for Art 6 to apply, there must first be a 'determination' of an individual's 'civil rights and obligations'. There is extensive Strasbourg jurisprudence devoted to the meaning of 'civil rights and obligations' as used within Art 6 and in particular to the distinction drawn in the earlier jurisprudence between rights and obligations in private law (which fell within the scope of this Article) and rights and obligations in public law (which did not). Although the requirement remains that the rights and obligations in question (in order to fall within Art 6) should be of a private law character, more recent jurisprudence has led to a position in which Art 6 regulates many kinds of disputes between the individual and the state which would not obviously fall to be classified as private law disputes (for example, rights to social security).[25] One might have thought it very arguable that decisions to refuse admission to, or to exclude from, schools concerned 'civil rights' in that such decisions affected the Art 2 right to education and that right should surely qualify as a 'civil right'. The argument might be thought all the stronger in the case of exclusions, where the relevant decision deprives the child

24 *A v United Kingdom* Decision of 23 September 1998. [1988] 3 FCR 597.
25 *Feldbrugge v Netherlands* A 99 (1986) 8 EHRR 425.

of an advantage already possessed by him (as opposed to a decision not to admit, where the child has the mere prospect of and is not the present holder of a school place). If it is the case (as is well-established) that Art 6 applies to a suspension of a doctor from medical practice,[26] the position of a child excluded from school would seem at the least analogous. One would also have thought that the parental rights under the Education Act 1996 to express a preference as to the school at which a child should be educated and to have that preference complied with (subject to qualifications) were perfectly capable of qualifying as civil rights within the meaning of Art 6. The decision in *Simpson v United Kingdom*[27] would seem to suggest, however, that the right not to be denied education is not a 'civil right or obligation' with Art 6(1). The case concerned a dyslexic child who complained about the failure of a LEA to educate him at a special school. An attempt to apply Art 6 to the decision of an old-style appeal committee adjudicating upon the child's statement of special needs failed. The Commission decided that the right not to be denied elementary education was a right squarely within the field of public law and was not a civil right within Art 6. The decision in *Simpson* would seem to cover cases of refusal to admit to, or exclusion from, state schools and decisions regarding the provision to an individual of state education generally.

Moreover, what Art 6 requires, is that there should be a 'determination of' a person's 'civil rights', not merely a decision regarding those rights. It is only when a decision is directly decisive of a right that that decision involves the determination of the right.[28] There must be a dispute which is justiciable.[29] The better argument, in our view, is that there is no dispute capable of judicial resolution until an authority, or governing body, has taken the decision which prompts the dispute. So, internal disciplinary proceedings culminating in the dismissal of a teacher may not need to comply with Art 6 (since until the dismissal occurs there will be no justiciable dispute).

PART 2

Parental choice

The second sentence of Art 2 of Protocol 1 declares the right of parents to have their philosophical and religious convictions respected in so far as concerns the education of their children. We have noted above the narrow interpretation given by ECHR to the expression 'religious and philosophical convictions'. Further (and also as noted in Part 1 above) the UK has entered a reservation with respect to Art 2 of Protocol 1 in the following terms:

Reservation

> '... in view of certain provisions of the Education Acts in the United Kingdom, the principle affirmed in the second sentence of Art 2 is accepted by the United Kingdom only so far as it is compatible with the provision of efficient instruction and training, and the avoidance of unreasonable public expenditure'.[31]

26 For which, see *Le Compte, van Leuven and de Meyere v Belgium* (1981) 4 EHRR 1.
27 Application 14688/89 64 DR 188 (1989).
28 *Le Compte v Belgium.*
29 *Van Marle v Netherlands* (1986) EHRR 483.
31 Following a review of the UK's reservations and derogations from human rights treaties, the Government has concluded that this particular reservation should be kept in place: White Paper, *Rights Brought Home: The Human Rights Bill*, Cm 3782 para 4.7.

The incorporation of the Art 2 right by HRA 1998 is limited by this reservation.[32]

The present law, in so far as it is reflected in s 9 of the Education Act 1996 ('EA 1996'), is on the face of it wider than Art 2 in that it enshrines 'the general principle that pupils are to be educated in accordance with the wishes of their parents' (emphasis added), a concept vaguer and more general than the religious and philosophical convictions of parents, as that concept has been interpreted by the court. However, just as the basic principle contained in the second sentence of Art 2 is subject to the express reservation set out above, so too the duty of LEAs and the funding authorities to have regard to the general principle in s 9 is expressly made subject to the need to ensure 'the provision of efficient instruction and training and the avoidance of unreasonable public expenditure'. Thus, the principle of parental choice is limited by considerations of efficiency and avoidance of significant[33] additional public expenditure.[34]

EA 1996 s 9 enshrines a general principle to which LEAs and the funding authorities are required to have regard 'in exercising or performing all their respective powers and duties under the Education Acts'.[35] This is consistent with the approach of the court in *Campbell and Cozens* where the court held that the principle contained in the second sentence of Art 2 applied to the organisation and financing of public education and the supervision of the educational system in general.[36]

Admission and removal

LEAs are under a general obligation to secure sufficient schools for providing primary and secondary education within their areas.[37] As we have seen in Part 1, such a duty would not be regarded as a necessary consequence of the 'right' to education under Art 2. However, once the state does provide education, Art 2 will control the manner of that provision. The first stage of the provision of education is admission.

Before the Education Act 1980 ('EA 1980'), parents wishing to exercise choice could only rely on what is now s 9 of EA 1996 (referred to above). Section 9 has now largely been superseded by the introduction of the concept of parental preference by EA 1980 (as consolidated by EA 1996).

Section 86 of the School Standards and Framework Act 1998 ('SSFA')[38] allows parents to express a preference for the county or voluntary school which they wish their child to attend. The general rule is that when such a preference is expressed the pupil (whether or not he lives in the area of the LEA concerned) must be admitted to the school concerned. Just as in the case of s 9, the general rule as expressed in s 86 has potentially broader scope than the principle enshrined

32 HRA 1998 s 1(2) and s 15.

33 In *Surrey County Council v P* [1997] ELR 516 the court held that for attendance to be incompatible with the efficient use of resources it has to result in *significant* additional expenditure.

34 See also *R v Dyfed County Council, ex p S* [1994] ELR 320 balancing considerations of parental preference, Welsh language policy and school transport policy.

35 The principle is also reflected in specific instances: see, for example, EA 1996 s 411 (school admissions).

36 *Campbell and Cozens v United Kingdom* (1982) 4 EHRR 293, para 35.

37 EA 1996 s 14.

38 The School Standards and Framework Act 1998 (c 31) ('SSFA 98') s 86 formerly EA 1996 s 411.

in the second sentence of Art 2 (in the sense that LEAs are required to respect parents' preferences, whether or not those preferences arise from religious or philosophical convictions). However, the general rule expressed in s 86 is subject to a number of exceptions.

The first of these is where compliance with the preference 'would prejudice the provision of efficient education or the efficient use of resources'.[39] This language is very similar to the language of the qualification contained in s 9 and the language of the UK reservation to Art 2.

The second exception is where compliance with the parental preference would be incompatible with 'any arrangements between the governing body and the [LEA] made under s 91'.[40] Section 91 concerns admission arrangements to preserve the character of an aided or special agreement school. Usually the characteristic of the school sought to be preserved is religious. Will admission arrangements aimed at preserving the religious character of a school survive a challenge under Art 14? Such arrangements are obviously discriminatory, so that the question which will arise is whether their discriminatory effect has an objective and reasonable justification.

In most, if not all, cases the preservation of the religious character of a school will itself provide an objective and reasonable justification for the consequent religious discrimination. However, the language of the Article allows some scope for creative argument. So, for example, whereas there may be good reasons in favour of preserving the religious character of a school, if the operation of admission arrangements aimed at preserving that religious character in fact produces the result that the pupils are almost all from a certain social class (for example, middle-class or professional class), it must at the least be arguable that the admission arrangements are discriminatory on grounds of social origin (contrary to Art 14) and that discrimination on that ground is not capable of objective justification, so that the arrangements concerned should be amended to avoid producing that result.

The third exception to the general rule in s 86 is effectively that parental preference may not override admission arrangements providing for admission only of pupils with high ability or aptitude.[41]

The fourth exception is that there is no obligation to follow parental preference where the child has been excluded from two or more schools.[42] In such cases, a policy not to admit potentially disruptive pupils may be lawful. However, at least as a matter of English law, there should be a fair hearing in each case before the policy is applied.[43]

In every case (other than a s 87(2) case) where an LEA or a governing body of an LEA-maintained county or controlled school refuses admission to a child, the parent has a right of appeal. In a s 87(2) case (where the child has been permanently excluded from two or more schools) and admission is refused, there is no right of appeal by the parent from the admissions decision, although there is a right for the governing body to appeal against a decision to admit a s 87(2) child.[44] Although

39 SSFA 1998 s 86(3)(a)
40 SSFA 1998 s 86 (3)(b).
41 SSFA 1998 s 86 (3)(c),
42 SSFA 1998 s 87.
43 Cf the obligation to consult before the closure of a school in *R v Secretary of State for Education, ex p Morris* [1996] ELR 162 (the Hackney Downs case).
44 SSFA 1998 s 95; cf s 94 containing the right of appeal in other cases.

it appears that this absence of any right of appeal for the parent of a s 87(2) child is contrary to Art 6 (in that it offends against the basic principle of equality of arms which is an acknowledged important element of the fair hearing requirement), as pointed out above[45] it seems that decisions regarding the provision to an individual of state education will fall outside Art 6(1). So far as the appeal procedure provided for in every other s 86 case is concerned, although there is no requirement for that procedure to satisfy Art 6, it would seem to us that it does satisfy that Article. If the child contends that the admission criteria themselves are unlawful (for example, because they offend against Art 14) then the child will have his remedy in judicial review proceedings or otherwise under HRA 1998.[46]

A related issue concerns the extent, if any, to which Art 6 will apply to decisions under the new schools adjudication system. The School Adjudicators will take decisions on School Organisation Plans, individual proposals for change to school organisation or issues relating to schools admission arrangements where it has not been possible to resolve the matter at a local level. In the case of most referrals, the complainant will be the LEA, the school organisation committee or an admission authority. These bodies exercising public functions will not qualify as victims under HRA 1998. However, parents (who as individuals would qualify as 'victims') are entitled to refer to the Adjudicator complaints against the continuation of existing partially selective admission arrangements. It must remain highly uncertain, however, (for the reasons discussed earlier) whether the decision to continue such arrangements would qualify as a determination of 'civil rights' as required by Art 6.

The removal of a child from a school is essentially a matter for the head teacher and the governing body.[47] The right of the state to regulate education includes the right to take disciplinary measures, including suspension and expulsion.[48] The rules of natural justice apply with respect to the decision to exclude.[49] Questions of proportionality are likely to arise in this context, as they have done already to some extent in domestic law.[50] Exclusions which might breach Art 2 are permanent or lengthy exclusions where no satisfactory alternative provision was made for the child's education and/or where the child was at a stage of his education where disruption was likely to prove particularly damaging. Non-compliance with dress requirements is clearly an insufficient basis for any sanction where it arises from legitimate cultural or religious reasons.[51] There may be an argument that the legal result should be the same if such non-compliance is a direct result of poverty or other problematical family circumstances which might constitute discrimination on grounds of social origin within Art 14. Further, given that the right conferred by the first sentence of Art 2 is a right which belongs to the child, it might be necessary to take particular care before excluding a child on account of parental conduct.

We have mentioned earlier the provision for appeals from admission decisions. With respect both to admission and exclusion there are specific provisions for appeals.[52] As noted above, it seems that, on current ECHR case law, these appeal

45 See text to footnote 27 above.
46 See SSFA 1998 s 67.
47 SSFA 98 ss 64 ff.
48 Application 24515/94 *Sulak v Turkey* 84–A DR 98 (1996).
49 *R v Governors of the London Oratory School, ex p Regis* [1989] Fam Law 67.
50 See *R v London Borough of Newham, ex p X* [1995] ELR 303 per Brooke J.
51 See DFE Circular 10/94 para 26.
52 SSFA 1998 Sch 18 and 24.

hearings need not comply with Art 6. We do draw attention, however, to commentary in Part 1 with respect to that provision and to the scope for respectable argument that both admission and exclusion decisions do amount to determinations of 'civil rights'. We make the point above that the argument (that Art 6 should apply) seems to be even stronger with respect to exclusions. However, even if Art 6 does apply to exclusion decisions, it is unlikely that a properly conducted appeal would infringe Art 6(1).

If the scope for challenges against admission and exclusion decisions under the Act is likely to be limited, the wider, but related, question of the provision of schooling generally within a particular area may prove more fertile ground for challenges. In our commentary relating to Art 14 in Part 1, we discussed the question whether, in order to avoid infringing Art 14, where the state subsidised some denominational schools, it was required not to discriminate between denominational groups by subsidising schools for some groups but not others. We think that there is a strong argument that the state's preferential treatment of one denominational school over another would be incompatible with Art 14 in the absence of sufficient justification for such preferential treatment. In our view, in many cases it should be possible to rely on the adequacy (or any surplus) of school places within the district in which the school might be located as constituting an 'objective and reasonable justification' for a decision not to subsidise.

Curriculum

UK schools operate within the confines of the National Curriculum.[53] The court considers that such matters fall within the state's margin of appreciation and so is unlikely to intervene on the substance of the curriculum.[54] There are, however, three areas of particular sensitivity: religious education, sex education and partisan politics.

Religious education

All registered pupils at every maintained school must have religious education provided for them and they must take part in an act of collective worship.[55] They may not be taught by way of catechism or formulary.[56]

So far as compliance with the second sentence of Art 2 (and the related Art 9) is concerned, the vital protection is provided by EA 1996 s 389 which provides that if a parent requests that his child be wholly or partly excluded from religious education and/or collective worship that request must be respected. Whereas it is most unlikely (for the reasons set out in Part 1) that a pupil who is withdrawn can claim to be entitled to funding for alternative religious education, the pupil must not be put at a disadvantage with respect to any other part of his education.

Sex education

Compulsory sex education does not violate Art 2, even if parents do not wish their children to be exposed to such teaching, provided that 'carelessness, lack of judgment or misplaced proselytism' by any given teacher does not in fact exceed the public interest pursued by such education. The court in *Kjeldsen* emphasised that the legislation before it 'in no way amounts to an attempt at indoctrination

53 See EA 1996 Part V.
54 *Kjeldsen*, para 53.
55 SSFA 1998 s 70 and Sch 20.
56 EA 1996 s 376(2).

aimed at advocating a specific kind of sexual behaviour. It does not make a point of exalting sex or inciting pupils to indulge precociously in practices that are dangerous for their stability, health or future or that parents may consider reprehensible'.[57] For completeness, we mention that EA 1996 s 405 provides that if a parent requests that his child be wholly or partly excused from receiving sex education at the school (other than sex education comprised in the National Curriculum), that request must be complied with. Since the biological dimensions and reproductive processes are taught within the National Curriculum, pupils cannot be withdrawn from this part of sex education on parental request. As with withdrawal from religious education or collective worship, schools must ensure that pupils' general education does not suffer as a result of withdrawal.

Contraceptive advice

We think that a parent's belief that his child should not be given individual advice on contraception by a teacher without the parent's consent is capable of amounting to a philosophical conviction within the meaning of Art 2 of Protocol 1. Teachers' caution about giving such individual advice, in the light of *Gillick*,[58] will in our view remain well-placed.

Secton 28?

This prohibits the intentional promotion of homosexuality and the promotion of the acceptability of homosexuality as 'a pretended family relationship'.[59] Section 28 does not prohibit teaching about homosexuality with the purpose of treating or preventing the spread of disease. The banning of homosexual acts may itself be in breach of Art 8 (the right to respect for private life).[60] What of the parent who maintains that the failure of a school (albeit in compliance with s 28) to promote homosexual relationships as familial relationships on a par with equivalent heterosexual relationships is contrary to his philosophical convictions and that the school (in failing to respect his philosophical convictions) is therefore acting contrary to Art 2 of the First Protocol? We think that a conviction that a monogamous homosexual relationship should be given the same respect (as a familial relationship) as a monogamous heterosexual relationship ought to be capable of qualifying as a philosophical conviction within the meaning of Art 2. This will especially be the case if the parent in question is party to a monogamous homosexual relationship himself (so that the child's perception of his family's and his own acceptability by the school is under challenge) and if the failure to respect the parent's convictions relied on consists, not merely of non-promotion of the monogamous homosexual relationship as a familial relationship, but active repudiation of such a relationship as a familial relationship. Unsurprisingly, the Government has recently confirmed its commitment to repeal s 28.

Treatment of political issues

EA 1996 s 406 forbids the promotion of partisan political views in the teaching of any subject in school. Section 407 requires the LEA, governing body and head

57 Kjeldsen, para 54.
58 *Gillick v West Norfolk and Wisbech Area Health Authority* [1986] AC 112.
59 Local Government Act 1988 s 28, inserting s 2A into the Local Government Act 1986.
60 *Dudgeon v United Kingdom* (1981) 4 EHRR 149; *Lustig-Prean v United Kingdom* (27 September 1999).

teacher to take 'reasonably practicable' steps to ensure that, when political issues are raised either at the school or out of school in extra-curricular activities, pupils are offered a balanced presentation of opposing views.

Sanctions

Following the court's ruling in *Campbell and Cosans* that the use of corporal punishment could infringe a parent's 'philosophical convictions', corporal punishment has been abolished in this country.[61] It is unclear the extent to which parents' unwillingness to have their children subjected to sanctions, short of corporal punishment, might similarly qualify as philosophical convictions within Art 2 which schools would be required to respect. The difference may be one of degree. Whereas we think it is doubtful whether a 'name and shame' disciplinary system which involved little more than writing on the blackboard the name of an errant pupil could seriously be objected to, the greater the humiliation or embarrassment involved with a consequential greater risk of damage to the child's self-esteem (for example, parading the errant pupil before the whole school assembly) the more likely that a parent's objection to such a system would qualify as a philosophical conviction within Art 2. Similarly, whereas a punishment requiring a child to hop on the spot a dozen times might be unobjectionable, the position might be very different if a young child was forced to run around a football pitch several times on a cold winter's day.

Detention as a means of discipline is now regulated by EA 1996 s 550B. It has been held that a punitive detention does not involve any 'deprivation of liberty' falling within Art 5 where no more onerous restrictions are entailed than are a normal incident of bringing up children.[62]

Overall responsibility for the maintenance of discipline in grant-maintained schools rests with the governing body and the head teacher.[63] In county, controlled and maintained special schools, overall responsibility rests with the governing body. However, the LEA has a reserve power, in order to prevent a breakdown of discipline, to take 'such steps ... as they consider are required'.[64]

The sanction for non-attendance lies on the parent, who (unless he is able to avail himself of one of the very limited statutory defences) commits an offence if he fails to secure the regular attendance of his child.[65] The absolute nature of this offence has been upheld by the Divisional Court.[66] Is a parent charged with commission of this offence 'charged with a criminal offence' within the meaning of Art 6?[67] We think he clearly is, in which case not only is the parent entitled to 'a fair and public hearing within a reasonable time by an independent and impartial

61 Education (No 2) Act 1986 ss 47-48; EA 1996 ss 548-550; and now SSFA 1998 s 131 (not yet in force).

62 *Family TV v Austria* 64 DR 176 (1989).

63 SSFA 1998 s 61.

64 EA 1996 s 155.

65 EA 1996 s 444. See also s 443(1): offence for a parent to fail to comply with a school attendance order. It is clearly arguable that Art 6 considerations will apply with respect to the making of such an order (under s 437), as well as with respect to a prosecution for failing to comply with the order.

66 *Jarman v Mid-Glamorgan Education Authority* [1985] LS Gaz R 1249; *Bath and North East Somerset District Council v Warman* [1999] ELR 81.

67 'Criminal charge' within Art 6(1) is an autonomous concept, it is for determination by the court which is not bound by the categorisation in domestic law: see *AP v Switzerland* [1998] EHRLR 88. Note also the very narrow defences to this charge.

tribunal established by law', but the parent is also entitled to certain 'minimum rights' under Art 6, namely, (1) to be informed promptly of the nature and cause of the accusation against him; (2) to have adequate time and facilities for the preparation of his defence; (3) to defend himself in person or through legal assistance of his own choosing or, if he lacks means, to be given legal assistance free when the interests of justice so require; (4) to examine or have examined witnesses against him and to obtain the attendance and examination of witnesses on his behalf under the same conditions as witnesses against him; and (5) to have the free assistance of an interpreter if he cannot understand or speak the language used in court.

An important question which arises is whether the legislation itself, in so far as it imposes a requirement on the parent to secure a result which it may be impossible for him to achieve (for example, in the case of an absconding and independent-minded 15-year old) might itself be held to be contrary to HRA 1998. We think that this is a real possibility.

Special Educational Needs ('SENs')

Section 316 of EA1996 imposes on the LEA a duty to ensure that a child with SENs is educated in a mainstream school unless 'incompatible with the wishes of his parent' and so long as integration in a mainstream school is consistent with, (1) his receiving the special educational provision his needs call for; (2) the pupils with whom he will be educated receiving efficient education; and (3) the efficient use of resources. In similar vein, the LEA must comply with parental preference unless the school is unsuitable or the placement would be incompatible with the efficient education of other children or with the efficient use of resources.[68]

We have noted above the wide measure of discretion granted by the court so far as the provision of education to disabled children is concerned. In *Simpson v United Kingdom*[69] the applicant was dyslexic. The LEA insisted that he be educated at the local comprehensive school. The applicant argued that the LEA should pay the fees for a place at a special private school on the basis that, in effect, the LEA was denying him the right to education, that is an education which was suitable to his needs. The Commission considered that this was an area in which the state has a wide margin of appreciation. On the facts, there was no breach. The applicant was at a school which had special teaching facilities for disabled children, albeit that it was a mainstream school.[70]

Similarly (and as noted above) the Commission has stated that Art 2 requires a balance to be drawn between the child's right to have as effective an education as possible and the wishes expressed by the parents. 'There must be a wide measure of discretion left to the appropriate authorities as to how to make the best use possible of the resources available to them in the interests of disabled children generally'.[71]

68 EA 1996 Sch 27 para 3(3).
69 Application 14688/89, 64 DR 188 (1989).
70 Compare Application 28374/95 (1989) *Ford v United Kingdom* EHRR 534 where the applicant objected to being placed in a special school, claiming that the refusal to allow him to attend a mainstream school infringed his right to education – application dismissed.
71 Application 13887/88 *Graeme v United Kingdom* 5 February, 64 DR 158 (1990). Note the emphasis on the importance of the LEA's assessment in *R v East Sussex County Council, ex p Tandy* [1997] 3 WLR 884.

We have referred to *Simpson v United Kingdom* above[72] on the question whether Art 6 is likely to require changes to be made to the procedures for decision making in the education field. It seems, on current Strasbourg case law, that decisions about access to state education may not qualify as determinations of civil rights within the meaning of Art 6. The decision in *Simpson* at least would suggest that a determination by a SENT is unlikely to qualify as a 'determination of civil rights and obligations' within Art 6. Even were Art 6 to be held to apply to SENT hearings, apart from the restrictive provisions on the admissibility of late evidence (which in some cases might prejudice the fairness of the hearing) we think that few difficulties under the Article would arise in practice.

An interesting question which arises is whether, if the LEA has acknowledged its obligation to provide education to meet the special educational needs of a child but fails to deliver on that obligation, the consequential impact on the quality of life enjoyed by that child may form the basis of a successful challenge under Art 8 (on the grounds that the LEA failed to take sufficient or appropriate steps to protect the physical and psychological integrity of the child and/or other members of the family) with the prospect of an award of damages against the LEA under s 8 of HRA 1998. We think it is plainly arguable that a breach of Art 8 or Art 2 might be found in a case in which a LEA had accepted (or the SENT had imposed) a duty to make a particular form of provision, but that duty had simply not been carried out over a long period.

Access to education – miscellaneous points

Failing schools

The UK reservation (providing for compliance with the principle contained in the second sentence of Art 2 only so far as is compatible with the provision of efficient instructions and training and the avoidance of unreasonable public expenditure) does not apply generally. However, in our view it is likely that in the same way that the 'right' to education arises only once the state has decided to establish a school, the same right cannot require the state to keep open a school which is failing.[73]

Bullying

If a child ceases to attend school in response to a bullying campaign which the school has failed to take appropriate action to end, could it be said that there has been a breach of the primary obligation under Art 2 to provide access to education? We think that this may well be arguable and that it ought not to be a sufficient answer to point to a neighbouring school to which the child might be transferred. The point may be capable of being made even more strongly if the child is in the course of preparing for public examinations at the original school and the likelihood is that transfer to another school would disrupt his course of studies, jeopardising his examination prospects.

72 See footnote 27 above.

73 This leaves open the question of when a school can be said to be 'failing'. What of a school which adopts a certain broad, liberal approach to education but which attains such low results that it is closed? It is at least arguable that this would breach the second sentence of Art 2, the parents preferring the 'broad' approach to education rather than the 'narrow', results-based approach.

Provision of education for children with SENs
Similarly, we think that there must be a good argument that the LEA will be in breach of Art 2 where it fails to diagnose correctly the nature of a child's SENs with the result that it fails to make a proper assessment or statement of special needs, so that the LEA fails to provide the child with any appropriate schooling.

Damages
If a court holds that there has been a breach of Art 2 in either of the respects set out above, it will be open to the court under s 8 of HRA 1998 to award damages.[74]

Discrimination
Provision is made in English law against sex and race discrimination in the education context.[75] Clearly, Art 14 has much broader application, covering discrimination 'on any ground' and we have noted above certain issues which may fall for consideration under Art 14.

Intervention
From 1 October 1998, broader powers of intervention have been introduced.[76] Two principal questions arise. To what extent, if any, will LEAs and the governing bodies of schools be able to challenge the exercise of intervention powers by, respectively, the Secretary of State or LEAs? To what extent, if any, will Art 6 apply to the interventionist measures taken? For example, if the LEA exercises its intervention powers to remove or replace governors, will that constitute a 'determination' of 'civil rights' such that the requirements of Art 6 will need to be satisfied? So far as concerns the first question, in order to have standing to bring proceedings under HRA 1998 s 7 requires that the person mounting the challenge 'is (or would be) a victim of the unlawful act.' To be a victim, the challenger must be a 'person, non-governmental organisation or group of individuals.' Governmental organisations such as local authorities are excluded and so too are any authorities which exercise public functions.[77] We think that a LEA complaining about the exercise of intervention powers by the Secretary of State would not be able to rely on HRA 1998, and nor (probably) would a governing body be able to complain about the exercise of such powers by a LEA. An individual governor would, of course, qualify as a victim so that if he had grounds under HRA 1998 for challenging a decision to remove him, he would have standing to mount such a challenge. Such challenges, however, are likely to be rare. So far as the second

74 Note also the recent judgment of ECHR in *Osman v United Kingdom* [1999] 1 FLR 193 in which it was held that the effective immunity of the police from a negligence suit was in breach of Art 6. Cf the effective immunity of social workers following *X v Bedfordshire County Council* [1995] 2 AC 633 and of educational psychologists following the decision of the Court of Appeal in *Phelps v Hillingdon London Borough Council* [1998] ELR 587. See also *Barrett v Enfield* London Borough Council [1999] 3 All ER 193 in which the House of Lords allowed an appeal against the striking-out of a negligence claim relating to the treatment afforded to a child whilst in care. The Commission has declared admissible an application by the unsuccessful plaintiff in *Bedfordshire.* The case has not yet been heard by the Court at the time of writing. As to damages on the closure of a school see *Meade v Haringey London Borough Council* [1979] 1.

75 Sex Discrimination Act 1975 ss 22–28; Race Relations Act 1976 ss 17 to 19. Note in particular the exception in the former for single sex schools – SDA s 26.

76 SSFA 1998 ss 14-19.

77 Application 15090/89 *Ayuntamiento de M v Spain* 68 DR 209 (1991).

question is concerned, we think that Art 6 should not apply to the exercise of intervention powers. We do not think that the entitlement to membership of a school's governing body stands to be treated as a 'civil right' within the meaning of Art 6.

CONCLUSION

Generally (and largely as a result of the controversy in the negotiation of the right) education is an area which the Convention has left broadly to the state. Moreover, the UK's reservation to Art 2 of Protocol 1, preserved by HRA 1998, considerably limits the potential scope of the second sentence of that Article. The result is that, in contrast to certain other areas of the law affecting local authorities, HRA 1998 is likely to have relatively limited impact for local authorities in the area of education.

That is not to say, however, that potential claimants will shy away from employing creative and imaginative argument with a view to mounting challenges based on alleged breaches of Art 2 and indeed the related Articles discussed in Part 1 above. In particular, we would expect to see, at least in the early days following introduction of HRA 1998, and notwithstanding the UK reservation, a number of challenges under HRA 1998 put on the basis that parents' philosophical convictions have not been respected. The beliefs which may be advanced as constituting such philosophical convictions may be various but the present ECHR jurisprudence establishes a narrow gateway to be passed through. We anticipate that Art 6 will also generate litigation, given the uncertainty as to the extent to which administrative tribunals (such as appeal panels and SENTs) need comply with its requirements. Article 14 may well also prove a fertile source of litigation, given the range of matters on which discrimination is prohibited, a range which goes far beyond the scope of any current UK anti-discrimination legislation. Finally, the general principle enshrined in the first sentence of Art 2 itself may prove to be the sleeping dog which barks when disturbed. We anticipate one or more test cases aimed at discovering whether action (or inaction) by LEAs, short of negligence, which disrupts a child's schooling or results in his obtaining inappropriate schooling should be regarded as conduct incompatible with Art 2 and therefore unlawful under HRA 1998.

Chapter 4

Social Services

The sections in this chapter illustrate the importance of the Human Rights Act 1998 ('HRA 1998') on social services law and practice. The responsibilities of local authorities and the ways in which they exercise their functions in the areas of community care, child care, mental health and asylum seekers and the relief of destitution are all likely to be affected.

Articles in the Convention of particular relevance in this context are Art 5 (the right to liberty and security of the person), Art 6 (the right to a fair trial) and most importantly Art 8 (the right to respect for private and family life). To a lesser extent Art 2 (the right to life) and Art 3 (freedom for torture or inhuman or degrading treatment) require consideration.

In *Botta v Italy*,[1] the European Court of Human Rights ('ECHR') considered the scope of the concept of 'respect' for 'private life' set forth in Art 8. In the court's view:

> 'Private life ... includes a person's physical and psychological integrity; the guarantee afforded by Art 8 of the Convention is primarily intended to ensure the development, without outside interference, of the personality of each individual in his relations with other human beings' (para 32).

The court continued:

> While the essential object of Art 8 is to protect the individual against arbitrary interference by the public authorities, it does not merely compel the state to abstain from such interference: in addition to this negative undertaking, there may be positive obligations inherent in effective respect for private or family life. These obligations may involve the adoption of measures designed to secure respect for private life even in the sphere of the relations of individuals between themselves. However, the concept of respect is not precisely defined. In order to determine whether such obligations exist, regard must be had to the fair balance that has to be struck between the general interest and the interests of the individual, while the state has, in any event, a margin of appreciation' (para 33).

1 (1998) 26 EHRR 241.

The recent decision in *R v North and East Devon Health Authority, ex p Coughlan*[2] demonstrates, as Clive Sheldon suggests, how English courts may be prepared to accept arguments based on HRA 1998 when reviewing decisions of local authorities to close homes maintained by them under Part III of the National Assistance Act 1948 ('NAA 1948'). Where the local authority had decided to close down a purpose-built facility for the disabled, even though the applicant had been given a 'promise' that this facility would be her 'home for life', the court held that there had been a breach of Art 8 of the Convention. Further, it held that the local authority had not made out a case that the exception in Art 8(2) applied. Indeed, the determinative issue in most cases is whether the local authority can bring itself within Art 8(2).

In the area of child care, there does not appear to be any fundamental conflict between the emphasis on family life in Art 8 and the paramount importance in English law of the welfare of the child. Paul Nicholls suggests, therefore, that it is necessary to focus on the procedures which have been adopted in reaching the decision under challenge, since ECHR has repeatedly held that the procedures followed by a public authority in applying for orders such as care orders are relevant to the Art 8(2) exemption. The court has placed considerable emphasis on the provision of procedural safeguards against arbitrary treatment. An example of child custody procedures in breach of Art 8 is *McMichael v United Kingdom*[3] where the applicants were refused access to important documents submitted by the local authority in care proceedings.

The only Article which specifically focuses on the area of mental health is Art 5 which guarantees the liberty and security of the person. This general principle is subject to the right to detain 'persons of unsound mind'.[4] However, as ECHR declared in *Winterwerp v The Netherlands*:[5]

> '... sub-paragraph (e) of Art 5(1) obviously cannot be taken as permitting the detention of a person simply because his views or behaviour deviate from the norms prevailing in a particular society. To hold otherwise would not be reconcilable with the text of Art 5(1), which sets out an exhaustive list of exceptions calling for a narrow interpretation. Neither would it be in conformity with the object and purpose of Art 5(1), namely, to ensure that no one should be dispossessed of his liberty in an arbitrary fashion. Moreover, it would disregard the importance of the right to liberty in a democratic society (at pp 401-402).

In this area also, it is the procedures adopted by local authorities that are likely to be subjected to challenge. The court in *Winterwerp v Netherlands* said that:

> '... for its part [it] considers that the words 'in accordance with a procedure prescribed by law' essentially refer back to domestic law; they state the need for compliance with the relevant procedure under that law.
>
> However, the domestic law must itself be in conformity with the Convention, including the general principles expressed or implied therein. The notion underlying the term in question is one of fair and

2 [1999] 2 CCL Rep 27.
3 A/307-B (1995) 20 EHRR 205.
4 Article 5(1)(e).
5 (1979) 2 EHRR 387.

> proper procedure, namely, that any measure depriving a person of his liberty should issue from and be executed by an appropriate authority and should be not be arbitrary' (para 45).

Clive Sheldon makes the point that if the English courts accept that the right to respect for family life is being threatened by the local authority's decision, then it will scrutinise its decision, not just on traditional grounds of *'Wednesbury'* unreasonableness, but will test it against principles of 'proportionality' (para 12). There may, therefore, be a closer scrutiny of the decision on its facts than a traditional *Wednesbury* test would suggest. This could lead, in the context of community care, for example, to an examination by the court of the cost consequences of two competing service provisions and a consideration of whether the difference in the cost of rival care provision is so great that it is necessary to interfere with the right to respect for family life. For similar reasons, my section with Nigel Giffin on asylum seekers suggests that had HRA 1998 been in force there might well have been a different outcome in the cases of *R v Newham London Borough Council, ex p Plastin*[6] and *R v Croydon London Borough Council, ex p Gou.*[7]

Challenges under Art 8 are often linked to arguments made under Arts 2 and 3. For example, challenges to closures of residential homes based on Art 8 may also raise issues under Art 2. In particular, where a social services department takes on the responsibility for the well-being of a person, it should also consider its obligations under Art 2 with regard to the protection of the life. Following *Olsson v United Kingdom*[8] it is clear that Art 2 can be breached not only where an authority takes a positive decision, but also where it fails to take appropriate steps to protect life. Therefore, where a local authority has accommodated persons in particular Part III accommodation, and plans are being made to alter the position, it may be necessary for the authority to have in mind its obligations under Art 2 before implementing those plans. Similarly, in the context of mental health, Arts 2 and 3 come into play. Andrew Hillier suggests that in *St George's Healthcare NHS Trust v S* Art 2 might have provided powerful support for the argument that the interests of the foetus had to be considered and might, in appropriate cases, override the rights of the mother. My section with Nigel Giffin also considers that on the evidence of the attitude already taken in *R v Hammersmith and Fulham London Borough Council, ex p M*[9] and *R v Brent London Borough Council, ex p D*,[10] English courts may be well disposed to an argument that Art 2 does not permit the state simply to leave a person to starve. The same should go for Art 3. In addition there may be a breach of Art 2 or Art 3 in some cases where no 'safety net' provision is made, either under NAA 1948 or under the Immigration & Asylum Bill 1999.

Difficulties may arise in this area in relation to the application of Art 6. For example, it is uncertain whether a local social services authority deciding whether a person falls within s 21 of NAA 1948 is exercising a function to which Art 6 applies. Certainly, the applicability of the Article cannot be ruled out. On the other hand, action which is directly decisive for the right to respect for family

6 [1997] 1 CCL Rep 305.
7 CO/2142/98, Ognall J, 21 August 1998.
8 A/1017, decision of 28 October 1998.
9 [1997] 1 CCL Rep 85.
10 [1998] 1 CCL Rep 234.

life, such as decisions placing children in care[11] or concerning parental access to children[12] or adoption[13] have been held to be regulated by Art 6. Indeed in *W v UK*, ECHR held that the availability of judicial review was insufficient in a case in which parents wish to challenge, on the merits, a local authority decision restricting access to a child in care. The court stated that in such a case, Art 6 required that the tribunal have 'jurisdiction to examine the merits' (para 82).

By contrast, as Clive Sheldon points out, Art 6 protection will probably not apply to the majority of social service benefits for which local authorities are responsible, as these are largely discretionary, but where there is an entitlement to a particular social service benefit the position may be different. Article 6 may, therefore, apply where the circumstances of the applicant are so severe that some level of service must be provided, for example, under the Chronically Sick and Disabled Persons Act 1970.[14] However, decision-making procedures of local authorities at present are unlikely to satisfy the requirements of a fair hearing under Art 6. The issue will be whether the availability of judicial review in a particular case is sufficient to comply with Art 6.

In summary, it is clear that HRA 1998 will in certain important respects have an impact on local authorities performing their functions in the social services area. In particular, local authorities will need to review their procedures to ensure that they best protect themselves from challenge.

11 *Olsson v Sweden* A/130 (1988) 11 EHRR 259.
12 *W v United Kingdom* A/121 (1987) 10 EHRR 29.
13 *Keegan v Ireland* A/290 (1994) 18 EHRR 342 para. 57.
14 See *R v Gloucestershire County Council, ex p Barry* [1997] AC 584.

Community Care

The Human Rights Act 1998 ('HRA 1998') will provide applicants' lawyers with an invaluable tool to pursue arguments against local authorities which would previously have had little prospect of success, to bolster arguments which were already persuasive, and to advance entirely new arguments as well. It is not clear to what extent arguments based on HRA 1998 will prevail, but local authorities in the exercise of their social services function must be alert to the potential for challenge.

In this chapter, some of the areas where potential challenges may be made on the basis of HRA 1998 are highlighted. There will undoubtedly be others.

Closure of residential homes – right to respect for private life/and the right to life

It is well accepted that local authorities are entitled to close homes maintained by them under Part III of the National Assistance Act 1948 ('the 1948 Act'). Before making the decision to close any homes, local authorities are under a duty to act fairly and to consult with interested parties.[1]

The recent decision in *R v North and East Devon Health Authority, ex p Coughlan*,[2] demonstrates how English courts may be prepared to accept arguments based on HRA 1998 in this context. In *Coughlan*, it was held by Hidden J that there had been a breach of Art 8 of the European Convention of Human Rights ('the Convention'), where the local authority had decided to close down a purpose-built facility for the disabled even though the applicant had been given a 'promise' that the facility would be her 'home for life'.

Article 8 of the Convention provides that:

> '1. Everyone has the right to respect for his private and family life, his home and his correspondence.
> 2. There shall be no interference by a public authority with the exercise of this right except such as in accordance with the law and is necessary in a democratic society in the interests of national security, public safety or the economic well-being of the country, for the prevention of disorder or crime, for the protection of health or morals, or for the protection of the rights and freedoms of others.'

1 See *R v Devon County Council, ex p Baker* (1992) 91 LGR 479.
2 [1999] 2 CCL Rep 27 (upheld on this point by the Court of Appeal: see Times Law Reports, 20 July1999).

In *Coughlan*, the local authority was held by Hidden J and the Court of Appeal to have violated the applicant's right to respect for 'private life', by resiling from its 'promise' to her. This was on the basis that closing the institution interfered with the applicant's occupation of her home, as that is where she lived permanently. The local authority had also not made out a case that the exception in Art 8(2) applied. The savings to the local authority in terms of economic and logistical efficiency by closing the residential home did not outweigh the loss of the applicant's home.

In *Coughlan*, the argument based on Art 8 merely bolstered the applicant's general arguments on unfairness and irrationality. With the advent of HRA 1998, courts will be able to consider Art 8 as not merely 'persuasive authority as to the content of the common law', but as part of English law.

In addition to challenges to closures based on Art 8, it is possible that arguments may be made using Art 2 of the Convention. Article 2 provides that:

> 'Everyone's right to life shall be protected by law. No one shall be deprived of his life intentionally save in the execution of a sentence of a court following his conviction of a crime for which this penalty is provided by law.'

In one case, the European Commission of Human Rights ('the Commission') has stated that the positive obligation to protect life 'enjoins the state not only to refrain from taking life intentionally but, further, to take appropriate steps to safeguard life'.[3]

It is arguable, therefore, that where a public authority (such as a social services department) takes on the responsibility for the well-being of a person, then it is under an obligation to take responsibility for protecting the life of that person and not putting them in danger. Where, therefore, a local authority has accommodated persons in particular Part III accommodation, and plans are being made to alter the provision, it may be necessary for the authority to have in mind its obligations under Art 2, before implementing those plans. One can easily imagine arguments to the effect that closure of a residential home and transfer to alternative accommodation may endanger the life of residents (particularly the elderly).

Nature of facilities afforded in residential homes - 'inhuman and degrading treatment'

Article 3 of the Convention provides that:

> 'No one shall be subjected to torture or to inhuman or degrading treatment or punishment.'

It is arguable that this Article will provide a recipient of social services with a minimum standard of care. The minimum standard may not be that high, however, as 'inhuman and degrading' treatment suggests extremely poor treatment. It is unlikely, therefore, that merely placing residents in insanitary accommodation would contravene this Article.[4]

3 Application 7154/75 *X v United Kingdom* 14 DR 31 (1978) at 32 (public vaccination scheme).

4 See for example, detention cases: *Guzzardi v Italy* (1980) 3 EHRR 333, *B v United Kingdom* (1984) 6 EHRR 204.

Residential placement versus domiciliary care – right to respect for family life

Imaginative lawyers may seek to invoke Art 8 of the Convention to challenge decisions of local authorities as to how social services needs are met. In *R v Lancashire County Council, ex p Royal Association for Disability and Rehabilitation*,[5] the court held that the local authority was entitled to decide that a disabled person's need for 24-hour care could be met by residential placement in a nursing home, rather than 24-hour domiciliary care which was preferred by the applicant, and that the cost resources effect of the two alternatives could be considered by the authority.

With the advent of HRA 1998, it could be argued that the domiciliary care option must be followed unless there are overwhelming arguments to the contrary, as this option respects the applicant's 'family life' under Art 8. The argument would be that Art 8 requires the local authority to pay proper regard to the right of the individual concerned to maintain his or her family life, as well as the right of the remaining members of the family to respect to their life together. This right embraces the right of families to live together, so that members of the family may enjoy each other's company. It is accepted that the right to family life embraces not only the relationship between husband and wife, and parent and child, but also between siblings and grandparents and grandchildren.

If the courts accept that the right to respect for family life is being threatened by the local authority's decision, then it will scrutinise its decision not just on traditional grounds of 'Wednesbury' reasonableness, but will test it against principles of 'proportionality'. This invites a greater degree of scrutiny of the local authority's decision making, and will give the courts greater opportunity to interfere with the local authority's conclusion. There will be an examination of the cost consequences of the two competing service provisions, and the court will then ask whether the difference in the cost of rival care provision was so great that it was necessary to interfere with the right to respect for family life.

Article 6 – decision-making process

There will surely be arguments under HRA 1998 that local authority decisions as to whether, and what, social services provision should be made available to an individual does trigger the right to a fair hearing pursuant to Art 6 of the Convention. Article 6 provides that:

> 'In the determination of his civil rights and obligations . . . , everyone is entitled to a fair and public hearing within a reasonable time by an independent and impartial tribunal established by law.'

The case law of the Convention indicates that, in determining what is a 'civil right' for the purposes of Art 6, a distinction is drawn between (i) social benefits which are entitlements deriving from statute and affect an applicant's means of subsistence[6] where Art 6 is held to apply, and (ii) those benefits which are in the discretionary gift of the state,[7] where Art 6 is held not to apply.

5 [1996] 4 All ER 421, 439d-440b.
6 See *Salesi v Italy* (1993) 26 EHRR 187.
7 See *Lombardo v Italy* A/249-B (1992) 21 EHRR 188; *Machatova v Slovak Republic* (1997) 24 EHRR CD44.

Accordingly, if the Convention jurisprudence is followed, it is unlikely that Art 6 protection would apply to most social service benefits which fall within local authority responsibility, as these are largely discretionary. Where, however, there is an entitlement to a particular social service benefit, then Art 6 may well be invoked. It could therefore apply to the provision of the benefits under the Chronically Sick and Disabled Persons Act 1970, where the circumstances of the applicant are so severe that some level of service must be provided.[8]

If Art 6 is found to apply, then this would entitle potential service recipients to receive a fair hearing as to the level and nature of their welfare provision. The right to a fair hearing requires that (i) proceedings should be completed within a reasonable period (in *FM v Italy* (1992) 18 EHRR 570, the Commission was of the view that 'disputes over welfare provisions generally call for a speedy resolution'); (ii) the proceedings should be impartial; (iii) legal aid may need to be available when essential for effective access to the tribunal; (iv) the hearing should be in public, subject to exceptions for the private life of the parties, or in the interests of juveniles; and (v) procedural rules must not be such as to impede effective access.

It is clear that local authority decision-making procedures would not satisfy the requirements of a fair hearing under Art 6. That need not matter where there is available a further right of review by a judicial body which does satisfy the Art 6 guarantees. Presently, however, challenges to decisions made by local authorities in this area are made by way of judicial review and the case law of the Convention suggests that judicial review supervision may not be sufficient. It is understood that there should be full appellate jurisdiction over the decisions.[9]

If it is held, therefore, that Art 6 does apply to local authority decision making, then this should encourage local authorities to take steps to secure that their decision making is even more comprehensive, and defensible, than at present, so as to withstand a full hearing before the courts.

Registration and closure of residential homes – Article 6

It is most likely that Art 6, and the right to a fair hearing, would apply to decisions to register or close residential care homes. This may be characterised as the deprivation of property (akin to the withdrawal of a licence) triggering Art 6. It is likely, however, that the statutory procedures set out in the Registered Homes Act 1984 and the Registered Homes Tribunal Rules 1984, with the right of appeal to the Registered Homes Tribunal, will be adequate to comply with Art 6.

The imposition of charges for social services – Article 6

It is probable that charging decisions for social services (for example, under s 22 of the 1948 Act, or s 17 of the Health and Social Services and Social Security Adjudications Act 1983) will not attract the requirements of Art 6. The case law on the assessment of taxes (which is somewhat analogous) suggests that Art 6 protection would not apply, but there is room for doubt given the decision in *Schouten v Netherlands*[10] (social security contributions).

8 See *R v Gloucestershire County Council, ex p Barry* [1997] AC 584.

9 Compare *W v United Kingdom* A/121 (1987) 10 EHRR 29 holding that a court should have jurisdiction to consider the merits of a local authority decision restricting access to a child in care, with *Bryan v United Kingdom* (1995) 21 EHRR 342.

10 (1994) 19 EHRR 432.

There is, however, certainly scope for arguing that Art 6 should apply to cases under s 21 of the 1983 Act where assets have been transferred with a view to avoid charges for residential accommodation, and local authorities hold the transferees liable for the costs of the accommodation.

CONCLUSION

At this stage it is unclear the extent to which HRA 1998 will, in reality, affect social services departments. It is clear, however, that challenges will be made to traditional practices, and new arguments pursued on the basis of HRA 1998. Social services departments must be alert to the potential for challenge.

The Impact on Mental Health Law

This section examines the likely impact of the Human Rights Act 1998 ('HRA 1998') on mental health law, particularly in the context of the responsibilities of local social service authorities (SSA) and social workers employed by them.

The governing statute which sets out the rights and obligations of health authorities, trusts and local authorities is the Mental Health Act 1983 ('MHA 1983') as amended by the Mental Health (Patients in the Community) Act 1995. As recently announced, there are likely to be some major changes in connection with the care of the mentally ill.[1] Already there are suggestions that some of them may be incompatible with the Convention

The only Article which specifically focuses on the area of mental health is Art 5, which guarantees the liberty and security of the person. This general principle is subject to the right to detain 'persons of unsound mind'.[2] However, such detention must be effected in accordance with a procedure prescribed by law and any person so detained 'shall be entitled to take proceedings by which the lawfulness of his detention shall be decided speedily by a court and his release ordered if the detention is not lawful'.[3] Other Articles which come into play are Art 3 (which guarantees freedom from inhuman or degrading treatment), Art 8 (which guarantees respect for private and family life, home and correspondence) and to a lesser extent Arts 9, 10 and 12. It is convenient to examine the various powers and duties against these Articles. The context is not only in terms of the potential liability of an SSA, but also in terms of the social worker's responsibility to his or her client whose Convention rights are arguably being violated.

THE POWER TO DETAIN

MHA 1983 sets out the power of hospital authorities to detain, assess and treat those suffering from 'mental disorder' and the rights of such patients to appeal against such orders. The social worker plays a key role in the process as being one of the two categories of persons entitled to make an application for detention. In the recent *St George's Hospital* case,[4] the Court of Appeal stressed the importance

1 Modernising Mental Health Services. Department of Health, 1998.
2 Article 5(1)(e).
3 Article 5(4).
4 [1998] 2 WLR 936.

of the social worker exercising an independent judgment when performing this function. In terms of the duty of care, the validity of that judgment will continue to be measured by reference to the accepted standards of that profession.

Article 5 permits what it terms 'lawful' detention of those of unsound mind. The leading judgment of the European Court of Human Rights as to what constitutes lawful detention is to be found in *Winterwerp v Netherlands* decided in 1979.[5] It was held that three conditions have to be satisfied. First, the decision to detain must be supported by 'objective medical expertise', for example, medical evidence. Second, the evidence must show that the patient's disorder is of a kind warranting compulsory confinement. Third, the detention should only continue so long as the disorder warrants it. The first two of these principles are subject to the qualification that, in an emergency, detention may be justified even though the necessary medical evidence has not been obtained.

How does the statutory power to detain fare against these principles? Medical evidence is a prerequisite to detention in all cases except two. First, the police have a power to detain under s 136 (place of safety orders) for a period of 72 hours. A social worker may be asked to attempt to find suitable accommodation or may decide to begin the process of sectioning. Since the purpose is to enable the individual to be examined, the detention would be treated as justified by the urgency of the case and as not violating the Convention. Second, and more problematic, there is the power of recall exercisable by the Home Secretary under s 42(3) of MHA 1983, in the case of a restricted patient who has been conditionally discharged. The patient will frequently be subject to the supervision of a local authority social worker whose responsibility is to assist him to settle into the community and monitor his progress and, if there are signs of his condition deteriorating, to take steps to see that he is recalled to hospital. When exercising this power of recall, the Home Secretary does not need the support of any medical evidence.[6] It is arguable that, in this respect, the procedure does violate the Convention. Although the SSA is unlikely to be liable in such a situation, it would be advisable in the future for the social worker to try to arrange a medical examination of the patient. This will obviously be subject to the urgency of the situation.

As to the justification for detention, the treatability of the patient's condition will be an essential requirement. This has important implications in the context of psychopaths, the treatability of whose condition is currently the subject of much professional debate.[7]

The third requirement set out in the *Winterwerp* decision, that detention should cease immediately the grounds for such detention cease, is not expressly set out in MHA 1983. Social workers should be alert to two aspects of the discharge procedure which may arguably be incompatible with the Convention. First, while in the case of non-restricted patients, discharge from formal detention generally follows as soon as the Registered Medical Officer ('RMO') considers it is no longer warranted, discharge of restricted patients requires the approval of the Home Secretary or of a tribunal. This will not necessarily follow on the recommendation of the patient's RMO. There is scope here for challenge although

5 (1979) 2 EHRR 387.

6 *R v Secretary of State for the Home Department, ex p K* [1991] QB 270 where the Court of Appeal said that it was for the Home Secretary to balance the patient's interests against those of public safety.

7 *Reid v Secretary of State for Scotland* [1999] 1 All ER 481.

it might well be held that it is permissible to await formal determination of the matter before the obligation to discharge the patient crystallises.

Second, there may be a violation where a tribunal decides that although a person is no longer suffering from mental disorder, the discharge is not to take effect immediately but at some future date to enable hostel accommodation to be found. In the case of *Johnson v United Kingdom*[8] the applicant had first become a restricted patient in 1984 when he was detained at Rampton. In 1989, a tribunal held he was no longer suffering from mental disorder but his discharge was made conditional on a suitable hostel place being found. None could be found as a result of the reluctance of any hostel to admit him. It was not until 1993 that the tribunal gave him an absolute discharge so that he could finally leave hospital. The court upheld the applicant's complaint that his continued detention in these circumstances violated Art 5. It accepted that the tribunal was entitled to proceed with caution and to decide that, even in the case of a person no longer suffering from mental disorder, a phased discharge might be appropriate to protect the community since the medical assessment is not an exact science. However, the extent of the delay in this case had been unacceptable. The onus was on the authorities to secure a hostel willing to admit the applicant. This decision therefore could have important repercussions for an SSA where a tribunal's order for discharge is dependent on suitable accommodation being found. The authority might be liable if it failed to provide suitable accommodation in such circumstances within a reasonable time.[9] However, where the delay relates only to the transfer from one secure institution to a more liberal institution, there will be no infringement of Art 5.[10]

There are two further areas where social workers should be alert to the possible illegality of a client's 'detention'. The first concerns the case of 'informal patients'. In *R v Bournewood Community and Mental Health Trust, ex p L*,[11] the House of Lords upheld the right of a hospital to provide care and treatment for a compliant adult who lacked the mental capacity to give a valid consent. Although the decision was unanimous, the House was divided on the question whether the patient should be regarded as being detained against his will. Two of their lordships held that he should. Lord Steyn, describing the suggestion that the patient was as free to go as a 'fairy tale', expressed considerable reservations about the consequences of the decision. It meant that such patients were effectively detained but were without any of the safeguards provided by HRA 1983. If it is right that the patient is detained, it is strongly arguable that such detention violates Art 5(4) which guarantees the right to take proceedings to challenge the lawfulness of such detention. The other category to be considered consists of those who are in prison but who are mentally ill, of whom there are large numbers. It is certainly arguable that where a mentally ill prisoner requires, but is not receiving, adequate treatment for his mental disorder, his detention may violate Art 3 (inhuman or degrading treatment) or Art 5.[12]

8 (1997) 27 EHRR 296.
9 As to this duty, see *R v Mental Health Review Tribunal, ex p Hall* [1999] 3 All ER 132.
10 *Ashingdane v United Kingdom* (1985) 7 EHRR 528.
11 [1999] 1 AC 458.
12 In *Aerts v Belgium*, No 61/1997/845/1051, the court held that there must be some relationship between the ground of permitted deprivation of liberty and the place and conditions of detention.

THE PATIENT'S NEAREST RELATIVE

The concept of a patient's 'nearest relative' is important in connection with the power to detain and the power to discharge. A social worker applying for an order for detention of a patient under s 3 must consult with, and obtain the approval of, the nearest relative and under s 2 (assessment) must inform the nearest relative after the event. MHA 1983 provides a hierarchy of kinships for the purposes of defining the nearest relative. On occasions, the relative may be someone with no knowledge of the patient or whom the patient seriously distrusts. The powers given to the nearest relative are intended to safeguard the patient's interests. Yet, in such situations, they may provide no safeguard at all. Conversely, someone to whom the patient is very close would have no rights. While MHA 1983 provides for the displacement of the nearest relative in certain circumstances, it may be argued that these powers are too limited.[13] Article 8 (which guarantees family rights and privacy) may support an argument that the designation of an inappropriate person as the nearest relative would constitute a violation of these principles. It is arguable that in the context of MHA 1983, the social worker should be alert to see that the patient's nearest relative is not someone to whom the patient clearly objects, where there is a more suitable alternative. [14]

COMPULSORY TREATMENT

The provisions of MHA 1983, governing the right to administer compulsory treatment to detained patients, set out extensive safeguards for such patients. While the provisions do not involve the social worker once the patient has been admitted, social workers are not infrequently faced with the dilemma about how to deal with a client who is refusing to undergo essential medical treatment. Compulsory treatment can only be given for the patient's mental illness. The courts in the UK have given a wide meaning to the term 'treatment' in this context. For example, it has been held that in the case of a patient suffering from mental illness which includes symptoms of anorexia nervosa, it is permissible to feed the patient forcibly as part of her treatment programme.[15] So, a social worker would be entitled to apply for the detention of a person in that situation to enable treatment to be given. This approach is unlikely to violate the Convention.

The court has rejected the argument that compulsory treatment can be considered in the context of Art 5. Provided that the detention is in a hospital, clinic or other institution that is able to provide appropriate treatment, the Article is not concerned with the suitability of the conditions or treatment.[16] However, in exceptional cases it might be possible to invoke Art 3. It was successfully relied on against the UK by a patient challenging the seclusion procedures at Broadmoor.[17]

Article 3 was also considered in *Herczegfalvy v Austria*.[18] The court, somewhat surprisingly, found that there had been no breach of Art 3 where a mentally ill

13 See ss 26 and 29.
14 This issue is currently being considered by the Commission in Application 26494/95 *JT v United Kingdom*.
15 *B v Croydon Health Authority* [1995] 1 All ER 683.
16 See *Ashingdane v United Kingdom* (1985) 7 EHRR 528.
17 Application 6840/74. Report of the Commission 16 July 1980.
18 (1992) 15 EHRR 437.

patient had been handcuffed and attached to a security bed. While such a decision would be unlikely today, the judgment is instructive for the test which the court applied. It said that the relevant criteria were whether the conditions and approach conformed to the 'psychiatric principles generally accepted at the time'. It therefore effectively applied a *Bolam* test to the question.[19]

In this context, Art 3 is linked with Art 8 (which guarantees a person's right to respect for private and family life, his home and his correspondence). UK law already jealously protects the right of a person of sound mind to refuse treatment however drastic the consequences of the refusal. Perhaps the high water-mark of this approach is the decision of the Court of Appeal in *St George's Healthcare NHS Trust v S*.[20] In that case an expectant mother, able to make an informed decision, was adamant that she did not want to have a Caesarean even though the consequences would be fatal for her and the unborn child. An approved social worker applied under s 2 of MHA 1983 for the compulsory admission of the mother to hospital on the grounds that she was evidencing signs of depression. Soon after her admission to a mental hospital, she was transferred to a general hospital. The hospital authorities applied for a declaration that a compulsory Caesarean could lawfully be performed without the patient's consent. The High Court granted the declaration and the mother was safely but forcibly delivered of her baby by Caesarean in the sense that she did not consent to the anaesthetic. On appeal, the Court of Appeal delivered a swingeing criticism of both the decision and the procedure that led to it. They held, clearly rightly, that there were no grounds for detention under MHA 1983 and that, even if there were, there was no right under MHA 1983 to administer compulsory treatment which was unrelated to the mental illness itself. They held that the mother was fully aware of what she was doing and of the consequences and was able to give an informed consent. In the circumstances, there were no valid grounds for dispensing with her consent.

The decision has serious implications for hospital authorities and for SSA. If the declaration had been refused, the various professionals involved would have been required to override what they rightly believed to be their professional obligations to the mother and the expected child.

Might the Convention have influenced the outcome? It would not provide any support for permitting the compulsory treatment in normal circumstances. Here Arts 3, 5 and Art 8 would reinforce the principle of the individual's autonomy. However, Art 2 (which guarantees the right to life) might have provided powerful support for the argument that the interests of the foetus had to be considered and might in appropriate cases override the rights of the mother. The Court of Appeal rejected the argument that in English law the foetus had any rights. Cases under the Convention have touched on whether the unborn child has any rights under Art 2 but have yet to rule definitively on the issue. The Commission has ruled that, if there is such a right, it is not absolute and that abortion is therefore justified.[21] On the other hand, this suggests that in other circumstances the foetus may be considered to have rights. It might well be that an English court, faced with prospect of the death of both the mother and the child, and struggling for a legitimate basis to overcome the mother's refusal, would find the interests of the

19 *Bolam v Friern Hospital Management Committee* [1957] 1 WLR 582.
20 [1999] Fam 26.
21 Application 8416/78 *X v United Kingdom* (1980) 19 DR 244.

unborn child under Art 2 sufficient to legitimise the operation. It would be open to the SSA to bring the matter before the court on this basis.

The Court of Appeal concluded its judgment in the case by giving guidelines as to how such applications are to be dealt with in future. It emphasised the heavy responsibility weighing on the social worker in such cases. All local authority legal departments should ensure that they have those guidelines well in mind.

CARE IN THE COMMUNITY

At present there are only very limited powers to control the mentally disordered within the community. Control is imposed principally by way of guardianship orders with the corresponding power of the social services authority to impose a residence requirement, leave of absence from hospital with the corresponding right to recall and conditional discharge of restricted patients. Finally, there are the powers introduced by the Mental Health (Patients in the Community) Act 1995. None of these controls are likely to give rise to complaints under MHA 1983.

Most importantly, there are currently no powers to treat patients compulsorily in the community. However, the proposed changes referred to in the Government's consultation paper are likely to introduce more extensive controls and in particular to result in the introduction of a form of compulsory community treatment order. In the past, such a power has been strongly resisted by many mental health pressure groups and there can be little doubt the Convention will be relied on to challenge any such power. In this context, it is worth noting that the Commission has rejected a complaint that making treatment a condition of discharge amounted to a deprivation of liberty. It held that the compulsory treatment was permissible as it was necessary for the health of the patient.[22]

The duty to provide after-care, set out in s 117, is unlikely to be affected by the Convention except where a failure to do so leads to the continued detention of a patient who is otherwise well enough to leave hospital.

CONCLUSION

The Convention will profoundly influence the climate in which decisions relating to the detention and treatment of the mentally disordered are determined. In the main, the current legislation and jurisprudence of the UK courts is consistent with the principles of the Convention. However, there may well be challenges in a number of areas as outlined above. The proposed changes relating to compulsory treatment in the community may also be subject to challenge .

22 Application 12778/87 DR 59.

Child Care

Decisions which local authorities have to take concerning children and their care can be among the most difficult and emotive decisions which an authority is called on to take. The issues raised are capable of affecting the most fundamental of human interests, namely the relationship between parents and their children. This chapter addresses the question to what extent the Human Rights Act 1998 ("HRA 1998') will impact on the dealings of local authorities with parents and children.

There is no doubt that many and inventive attempts will be made to invoke the Convention for the Protection of Human Rights and Fundamental Freedoms ('the Convention') and HRA 1998 in seeking to challenge local authority actions concerning child care. However, it will be argued that many of the requirements of the Convention related to decisions about child care are already present in domestic law and practice. One prediction is that the effects of HRA 1998 may be substantially less dramatic than might have been expected. Further, it may be difficult as a matter of practice to challenge the substance of particular decisions. Both the domestic courts and the European Court of Human Rights ('ECHR') decline to engage in fact-finding. Numerous ECHR cases (see those cited below) also make it plain that the judgment of the court does not concern the merits of individual decisions. A more promising line of challenge may be the procedures and structures put in place by local authorities.

THE RELEVANT PROVISIONS OF THE CONVENTION

There are three provisions of the Convention which might be said to be relevant: Art 6 on the right to a fair trial; Art 8 on the right to respect for private and family life; and Art 13 on the right to an effective remedy. HRA 1998 has not given effect to Art 13 as a 'Convention Right',[1] and no more will be said about that Article.

Article 8 provides:

> '1. Everyone has the right to respect for his private and family life, his home and his correspondence.
> 2. There shall be no interference by a public authority with the exercise of this right except such as is in accordance with the law and is necessary in a democratic society … for the protection of health or morals, or for the protection of the rights and freedoms of others'.

1 See s 1 of HRA 1998.

THE APPLICATION OF THE CONVENTION

The relevance of the provisions of the Convention is that it is unlawful for a public authority to act in a way which is incompatible with a 'Convention right'.[2] By s 7, a 'victim' of an act, committed by a public authority, which is alleged to be incompatible with a Convention right may bring proceedings against the authority on that ground. Further an aggrieved victim would be likely to rely on an alleged breach of Convention rights in addition to other grounds of challenge.

DECISIONS OF LOCAL AUTHORITIES WHICH ARE LIKELY TO RAISE CONVENTION RIGHTS

In the context of decisions about child care, there will no doubt be many occasions when aggrieved parties invoke the Convention. Without being able to provide a comprehensive review of every case in which Convention rights may play a part, four specific areas in which it seems likely that a party may seek to rely on a Convention right are as follows:

(1) applications by authorities for care orders;
(2) applications by authorities for child assessment orders;
(3) applications by authorities for emergency protection orders; and
(4) decisions to put a child's name on a child abuse or child protection register.

The requirements of the relevant Convention rights are in the context of these four areas.

Care orders

In cases where an authority decides to make an application to take a child into care, with the consequence that the parents will no longer be in sole control of the child or have sole parental responsibility for the child, there is a plain basis for contending that there is an interference with family life. The consequence of the care order will be the intervention of the state with the family relationship. The child will remain with the authority rather than with its parents. The authority will have parental responsibility for the child.[3] The effect of the order will be to interfere with the mutual enjoyment by parent and child of one another's company, a matter which the court has consistently held to be a fundamental element of the right to respect for the family.[4]

Therefore there is prima facie a breach of Art 8(1). The issue is whether the decision of the authority falls within the exception created by Art 8(2). Hence, one must ask whether the interference is in accordance with the law and necessary in a democratic society. In addressing that question, the court has held that it is necessary to consider several issues. Are the aims, which are being pursued as those identified in Art 8(2), legitimate? Is there a pressing social need which necessitates action? Are the steps which are taken proportionate to the aim? In respect of the last two mentioned matters, national governments enjoy a wide

2 See HRA 1998, s 6.
3 Children Act 1989 ('CA 1989'), s 33(3)(a).
4 See, for example, *W v United Kingdom* (1987) 10 EHRR 29, *Olsson v Sweden* (1988) 11 EHRR 259, *R v United Kingdom* [1988] 2 FLR 445, *Eriksson v Sweden* (1989) 12 EHRR 183.

'margin of appreciation'. This means that ECHR will not seek to define what are pressing social needs and what steps are to be regarded as proportionate. Rather it is recognised that a given situation may lead to a range of responses, each of which is justifiable. Only if the acts of the national government fall outside that permissible range will the court hold that the government has failed to make Art 8(2) exemption. In addition to these matters, the court has repeatedly held that the procedures followed by a public authority in applying for orders such as care orders are relevant to the Art 8(2) exemption. Hence, to take an extreme example, the Art 8(2) exemption did not apply when a government body which put a man's child up for adoption without his knowledge or consent.[5]

Numerous judgments of ECHR follow the structure outlined above in assessing whether a public body, which has taken a child into care, has acted in breach of Art 8. Thus the determinative issue in the cases has usually been whether the state can bring itself within Art 8(2).[6]

Before considering Art 8(2) in the context of applications for care orders in the UK, it is relevant to consider a fundamental attack which was made on the English approach to applications involving children. In English law, the welfare of the child is always paramount in decisions affecting the child.[7] In *Re KD*,[8] a case about wardship, it was argued by counsel for the parent that there was a fundamental inconsistency between the right to respect for family life created by the Convention and the English law rule that the interests of the child are paramount. The House of Lords dismissed this contention, holding that there was no inconsistency between English law and the Convention right. Lord Oliver stated that if there was a difference between the position in English law and the judgment of ECHR in *R v United Kingdom*, any such difference was purely semantic.

Indeed the passage of the Children Act 1989 ('CA 1989') since *Re KD* has made it even more difficult to contend that English law is not consistent with the Convention. CA 1989 is based on the philosophy that children are best brought up in families.[9] That philosophy leads to a desire to curtail the frequency with which agencies of the state become involved in the up-bringing of children. Hence a care order will only be granted where the court is satisfied that the child is suffering or will suffer significant harm,[10] the granting of the order would be in the interests of the welfare of the child,[11] and the granting of the order 'would be better for the child than making no order at all'.[12] In other words, there is a presumption against the granting of the order. It is submitted that all these aspects of CA 1989 place more significance on the rights or interests of the family and confine the circumstances in which it is legitimate for the state to intervene.

In these circumstances, it is submitted that English law, as set out in CA 1989 complies with the requirements necessary to make out the Art 8(2) exemption. A local authority may only apply for a care order when the significant harm criterion

5 *Keegan v Ireland* (1994) 18 EHRR 342.
6 See the judgments cited above.
7 See now CA 1989 s 1(1); also Guardianship of Infants Act 1925; Guardianship of Minors Act 1921, *J v C* [1920] AC 668.
8 [1988] AC 806.
9 Cretney, *Principles of Family Law*, p 775.
10 CA 1989, s 31.
11 See s 1(1).
12 See s 1(5).

is satisfied. Hence the application is made for a legitimate reason, 'to protect the health or morals of the child', and there is a pressing social need to make the application. The court may only make the order where it is in the interests of the welfare of the child and where the presumption against making the order is defeated. Hence, the grant of the order will generally be proportionate to the aim which the authority seeks to secure.

On the question of procedure, there are several important safeguards. It is usual for issues relating to children to be discussed at case conferences which the parents may attend, albeit there is no statutory right for a parent to attend. Hence, they are able to know what the authority is planning and to have input into the decision-making process. Before a child is taken into care, this step should be discussed with the parents.[13] If proceedings are to be taken, the parents must be notified in advance so they may present their case.[14] That was a case of alleged sexual abuse but the language of the judgment suggests that the principle is of general application.

It is submitted that these are important elements already present in English law and practice which will assist authorities to resist complaints of breach of Art 8. However, it is obvious that in some difficult situations action may be taken without adequate steps to involve or notify parents. Unless the authority can provide a sound reason why the parent was not involved in such circumstances, it may be at risk of being held to be in breach of Art 8.

Once a decision has been taken to take a child into care, difficult issues may arise as to parental contact. Under s 33(3)(b) of CA 1989, an authority has power to determine the extent of parental responsibility. Under s 34(4), the authority has the power to apply for an order authorising it to refuse parental contact. In many cases there is a tension between a parent's right of access to a child and adherence to an authority's plan for the care of the child. On the one hand there is a presumption that a parent is to be allowed reasonable contact with a child in care.[15] On the other, it may well be the authority's judgment that contact will hamper the child's progress and be inconsistent with the authority's long-term plan for the child. It is likely that Art 8 will be relevant to determining how the balance between the rights of contact and the authority's plans should be resolved if the two conflict. However, it is submitted that the invocation of Art 8 is unlikely to change the present approach of the courts. This approach is to require the authority to justify refusal of contact and to seek to balance parental rights and the authority's plan, having regard always to the principle that the rights of the child are paramount.[16] It is submitted that the balancing act described in *Re B* is a good example of a government body acting within its 'margin of appreciation'.

Article 6 and the right to a fair trial can be dealt with more briefly. First, there is a preliminary question whether disputes about care orders and other orders affecting children fall within the ambit of Art 6. That Article applies in cases involving the 'determination of … civil rights and obligations'. It has been held that parental concern about the rights of access to a child do fall within the realm of 'civil rights' and therefore within Art 6.[17] Article 6 presents no problems in the case of care orders because a hearing will have to be held before such an order is

13 Children Act Guidance and Regulations, vol 1, para 368.
14 *R v Hampshire County Council, ex p K* [1990] 2 QB 71.
15 See s 34(1).
16 See *Re B* [1993] Fam 301.
17 *W v United Kingdom* (1988) 10 EHRR 29.

made.[18] There is more difficulty concerning disputes which arise in the course of care. For example, under s 33(3)(b) an authority has the power in certain circumstances to 'determine the extent to which a parent or guardian of the child may meet his parental responsibility for him'. However, there is no mechanism for a hearing or an appeal about any such decision. It may be possible to seek a judicial review of such a decision but judicial review hearings do not, by their nature, consider the factual merits of the decision. They have, therefore, in the context of child care been held not to be adequate hearings for the purpose of Art 6.[19] Hence this omission may well be contrary to Art 6.[20]

As indicated above, any attempt by an authority to restrict the rights of parental access must be the subject of a court order for which a hearing will be required.[21]

Child assessment orders

Many of the same points of principle, developed above, apply to the child assessment order. In particular, the different uses of the child assessment order and the emergency protection order demonstrate the presence within CA 1989 of a principle of proportionality. By providing for remedies of differing degrees of severity depending on the circumstances, Parliament has provided means by which local authorities can ensure that the steps which they take are appropriate for the problems which they face. The existence of these different remedies does give rise, however, to a trap for the unwary. If an authority were to apply for, and obtain, an emergency protection order (in particular if combined with an exclusion order) in circumstances which did not warrant such a draconian sanction, there would plainly be a strong basis for the argument that the authority had acted disproportionately and so in breach of Art 8.

Emergency protection orders

In addition to the points made about the risk that this order might be regarded as disproportionate, particular issues arise in connection with the emergency protection order. No appeal lies against the grant of an emergency protection order. An application may be made to discharge an order (since such orders may be sought without notice). In these circumstances, it is at least arguable that the grant of such orders involves the breach of Art 6.

Child abuse or child protection registers

It is questionable whether a decision to enter a child's name on such a register could be said to involve an interference with the right to respect for family life at all. Even if it could, plainly a decision to take this protective step in the interests of the child would satisfy the requirements of Art 8(2).

What is of more interest is the question whether Art 6 would apply. Two issues arise. First, whether such a step would involve the 'determination of … civil rights'. It is submitted that there would be no such determination of rights. The step taken does not involve any determination. It is an interim protective measure.

18 See s 31.
19 *W v United Kingdom* (1987) 10 EHRR 29.
20 Eekelaar [1989] New LJ 760.
21 See s 34(4).

Of course the act of entering a child's name on a register may lead to a further step, such as a application for a care order, which would involve the determination of civil rights. But that does not mean that the decision to place a child's name on the register involves such a determination. Second, however, if Art 6 does apply there may be grounds for saying that present law and practice would need adjustment to conform with that Article. Decisions about placing a child's name on a register are usually taken as a result of a case conference. In *R v East Sussex County Council, ex p R*[22] the authority maintained a practice of refusing to allow parents to attend the case conference at which such decisions were taken. Instead, the parents could make written representations. The High Court refused to hold that this approach was unlawful. The same case further decided that applications for judicial review against such decisions should be made only in exceptional circumstances. Thus the right of a hearing to review the original decision is curtailed. There may well therefore be an argument that one or both elements of the approach adopted by the court in that case will need to be revisited in the light of Art 6.

22 [1991] 2 FLR 358.

Asylum Seekers and the Relief of Destitution

THE IMMIGRATION AND ASYLUM BILL 1999

At the time of writing, the Immigration and Asylum Bill 1999 ('IAB 1999') has completed its Commons stages and the Committee stage in the House of Lords. Part VI of IAB 1999 should be read with the draft process manual and 'information document' published by the Home Office in the early part of 1999. IAB 1999 is designed to give effect to the proposals in the White Paper 'Fairer, Faster and Firmer – A Modern Approach to Immigration and Asylum' (CM 4018), ch 8 of which dealt with asylum seeker support. IAB 1999 has both a negative effect (excluding asylum seekers from the National Assistance Act 1948 ('NAA 1948') and the Children Act 1989 ('CA 1989'), as well as from the benefits and homelessness legislation) and a positive effect (creating an alternative support system). It is expected that IAB 1999 will receive royal assent in November 1999, and that the new asylum seeker support system will come into effect from 1 April 2000, with transitional provisions operating meanwhile.

As to the negative aspect, clause 111 of IAB 1999 excludes persons subject to immigration control[1] (not just asylum seekers) from entitlement to various statutory benefits, including income support, housing benefit and child benefit. Clause 114 maintains the general exclusion of such persons from the allocation of local authority housing accommodation and other housing assistance.[2] Clause 112 will insert a new s 21(1A) into NAA 1948, providing that a person subject to immigration control may not be provided with residential accommodation if his need for care and attention has arisen solely because he is destitute or because of the physical effects, actual or anticipated, of his being destitute. A person is destitute if, in the judgment of the local authority, he does not have adequate accommodation or any means of obtaining it, or if he cannot meet his other essential living needs.[3] What is contemplated, therefore, is that a person subject

1 A person is subject to immigration control if he requires leave to enter or remain in the UK but does not have it; if his leave is subject to a condition that he does not have recourse to public funds; if it has been given as a result of another person's written undertaking to be responsible for his maintenance and accommodation; or if he has leave to enter or remain only as a result of a statutory extension pending an appeal against a decision varying or refusing to vary his leave to remain.

2 Although clause 114 in effect permits the Secretary of State to exempt classes of person from the exclusion, and allows also for tenancies or licences of council housing stock to be granted pursuant to the asylum seeker support arrangements.

3 These concepts are more fully defined by clause 90 and regulations to be made under it.

to immigration control may still qualify for assistance under Pt III of NAA 1948 if, for instance, he needs care and attention because of some underlying medical condition or because of old age.

The positive aspect of IAB 1999 is the creation of a new asylum seeker support system. In particular, clause 90 empowers the Secretary of State to provide, or arrange for the provision of, support for asylum seekers or their dependants where they appear to the Secretary of State to be destitute, or likely to become destitute within a prescribed period.[4] A decision that a person does not qualify for support under clause 90, or that the provision of support should cease (but not decisions as to the nature of the support given) may be appealed to an Asylum Support Adjudicator.[5]

Clause 91 provides that the support may consist of adequate accommodation for the supported person and any dependants, provision for their essential living needs, the meeting of non-legal expenses incurred in connection with the asylum claim, or other forms of support in exceptional cases. Subject to the Secretary of State's power to provide otherwise by order, support may not be provided by the making of payments to the persons being supported. The Secretary of State will be obliged to have regard to prescribed matters, but IAB 1999 itself points him in the direction of arranging temporary accommodation in an area where there is a ready supply of accommodation and positively forbids him from having regard to any preference as to locality expressed by the supported person.[6]

In relation to children, clause 118 provides that where an 'eligible person' (that is, one who appears to the Secretary of State to be eligible for support under clause 90) applies for support, and has in his household a dependant under 18, the Secretary of State must exercise his clause 90 powers by offering (and arranging, if the offer is accepted) adequate accommodation and essential living needs for the child as part of the eligible person's household.

THE ROLE OF LOCAL AUTHORITIES UNDER THE BILL

Although the power to support asylum seekers and dependants is conferred on the Secretary of State, local authorities will have an important role in the implementation of the scheme. Clause 95 empowers an authority to provide support in accordance with arrangements made by the Secretary of State under clause 90 and clause 96 imposes a duty to give the Secretary of State, on request, such assistance as is reasonable in the circumstances. Clause 97 empowers the Secretary of State to direct an authority to make accommodation available for the purposes of support arrangements if the accommodation is otherwise unoccupied and likely to remain so for the foreseeable future and if the authority is within an area designated by the Secretary of State as a 'reception zone'.

IMPACT OF THE HUMAN RIGHTS ACT 1998 ON THE NEW ARRANGEMENTS

The Convention rights which are most obviously material in a substantive way are those conferred by Art 2 (the right to life), Art 3 (the right not to be subjected

4 Clause 94 provides for the possibility of temporary support in cases of possible destitution whilst the applicability of clause 90 is investigated.

5 See clauses 98, and 99 and Sch 9.

6 See clause 92. Further details of the support scheme may be prescribed pursuant to clause 93.

to, in particular, degrading treatment) and Art 8 (the right to respect for private and family life and home). These rights might, at first, appear of limited relevance because they are expressed in terms which suggest a merely negative prohibition on the taking of steps by the state which would infringe the rights in question. However, the jurisprudence of the European Court of Human Rights strongly suggests that there may, in certain circumstances, be a positive obligation on the state to take positive steps so as to avoid the consequences set out in Arts 2, 3 and 8.

This is most clearly established in relation to Art 8. It was held in *Botta v Italy*[7] that the right to private life was intended to ensure the development, without outside interference, of the personality of each individual in his relations with other human beings, that this extended to the individual's 'physical and psychological integrity' and that the existence of positive obligations might be inherent in effective respect for that right. It was further held that, in determining whether the failure to take positive steps amounted to an infringement of Art 8, a fair balance had to be struck between the general interest and the interests of the individual.[8]

So far as Art 2 is concerned, in *X v United Kingdom*,[9] the Commission indicated that the state's obligation under Art 2 extended to taking 'appropriate steps to safeguard life' (as opposed to merely refraining from intentional killing) but this arose in the context of a vaccination programme and may have meant no more than that there was an obligation not to vaccinate without taking care to ensure that the vaccines were safe. However, in *Scialacqua v Italy*,[10] the Commission did express the view that Art 2 imposed an obligation to take adequate measures to protect life and was prepared to assume that this might extend to meeting the costs of medical treatment which was essential to save life. The jurisprudence under Art 2 is likely to develop in a manner similar to the cases under Art 8 and, on the evidence of the attitude already taken in *R v Hammersmith and Fulham London Borough Council, ex p M*[11] and *R v Brent London Borough Council, ex p D*[12], English courts may be well disposed to an argument that Art 2 does not permit the state simply to leave a person to starve.

The same should go for Art 3. Even if an applicant could not show that his life was endangered by the lack of support, the suffering which it caused might be sufficient to rank as inhuman or degrading treatment within the meaning of Art 3.[13] Another way of reaching the same result would be for the applicant to argue that the absence of any support in the United Kingdom amounted to a form of forced deportation, which may involve a breach of Art 3 where there is no country willing to accept the deportee.[14] However, it is important to note that in *Machatova v Slovak Republic* (a case about an unsuccessful application for welfare benefits)[15] it was held that the ECHR does not confer any right to be relieved from hardship as such.

7 26 EHRR 241.
8 See also *Myszk v Poland* (1998) 26 EHRR CD76, and *Passannante v Italy* (1998) 26 EHRR CD153.
9 Application 7154/75 *X v United Kingdom* 14 DR 31 (1978).
10 (1998) 26 EHRR CD164.
11 (1997) 1 CCL Rep 85.
12 (1998) 1 CCL Rep 234.
13 Cf Application 9330/81 *Bulus v Sweden* 35 DR 57 (1984).
14 See Application 10798/84 *Harabi v Netherlands* 46 DR 112 (1986); Application 7612/76 *Giama v Belgium* 21 DR 73 (1980); and *D v United Kingdom* (1997) 24 EHRR 423.
15 (1997) 24 EHRR CD44.

Challenges under the Human Rights Act 1998 ('HRA 1998') might be expected to fall into two basic categories. First, there will be those persons for whom no form of provision is made. Second, there will be cases in which the adequacy of the provision is in issue.

Failure to make provision

The most obvious category of persons for whom there may be a failure to make provision consists of those subject to immigration control, whose need for care and attention results solely from destitution or its consequences and who are therefore outside the amended s 21 of NAA 1948, but are not within the support scheme under IAB 1999 because they are not asylum seekers. This may include illegal entrants or over-stayers, persons who obtained leave to enter or remain on the basis of a maintenance undertaking or a 'no recourse to public funds' condition and persons appealing against a refusal to vary their leave to enter or remain. Asylum seekers may also fall outside if, for instance, their claims for asylum are rejected or if they are evicted from their accommodation for breaching conditions or occupation.

There may be a breach of Art 2 or Art 3 in some such cases where no 'safety-net' provision is made, either under NAA 1948 or under IAB 1999. There is unlikely to be such a breach in a case where the individual concerned could reasonably be expected to solve his own predicament by leaving the country for a destination where he would have the ability to support himself. But in some cases that may not be a viable option: for instance, because there is no other country which will admit the individual, because he would be equally destitute anywhere else, because he lacks the means to travel, or simply for a limited period before he can make travel arrangements. The argument that the ECHR requires the safety-net in such circumstances is supported by the decisions of Moses J in *R v Brent London Borough Council, ex p D* and of Kay J in *R v Lambeth London Borough Council, ex p Sarhangi.*[16] In those cases it was held that illegal over-stayers, although in principle not entitled to rely on their own unlawful presence in the country so as to bring themselves within s 21 of NAA 1948, could nonetheless qualify for assistance because they were, respectively, too ill to travel and unable to gain admission to a safe third country.

It is unlikely that the courts will find a breach of a Convention right in cases where the applicant has caused his own eviction by serious or repeated misconduct for which he can properly be held responsible. It would be another matter if the misconduct was relatively trivial, if a proper and fair procedure had not been followed in finding the applicant guilty of that misconduct, or if the applicant could not fairly be held responsible for it (for example, if he suffered from learning difficulties). Hence, this category of case is likely to exemplify the situation in which the legislative scheme is in principle compatible with HRA 1998, but there may well be closer scrutiny of a decision on its facts than a traditional *Wednesbury* test would suggest. The same is likely to be true of a decision that a person is not destitute because he has some means of support open to him. So had HRA 1998 been in force, there might well have been a different outcome in the cases of *R v Newham London Borough Council ex p Plastin,*[17] *R v Croydon London Borough Council*

16 (1999) 2 CCLR 145.
17 (1997) 1 CCLR 304.

ex p Gou[18] and *R v Royal Borough of Kensington and Chelsea, ex p Kujtim.*[19] It is also doubtful that it is consistent with the ECHR to withdraw support from a person whose asylum application has failed, but who has obtained permission to apply for judicial review of that decision.

Adequacy of provision

In principle, it is unlikely that challenges to the adequacy of accommodation or provision for essential needs will succeed on HRA 1998 grounds. While it is clear that the level of provision is intended to be relatively basic, it would have to be deplorable indeed before it was likely to amount to 'degrading treatment' within the meaning of Art 3. Also, while having to live in shared hostel accommodation with very basic facilities might possibly represent a prima facie breach of Art 8, it would almost certainly be held that there was in fact no breach once the public interest, as perceived by the government, was balanced against the private interests of the individual asylum seekers. It is possible, however, that there may be some scope for a HRA 1998 challenge if accommodation has been provided on the express assumption that it need only be such as is adequate for a stay of a few months, but in practice the process continues to take much longer than that.

THE CONTINUING IMPORTANCE OF NAA 1948

Clearly there will still be cases in which s 21 of NAA 1948 (and s 17 of CA 1989) will be of relevance to the relief of destitution. The nature of the amendment made by the Bill is to entrench rather than to reverse the interpretation given to s 21 in *R v Hammersmith & Fulham LBC, ex p M*, albeit to create an important exception in the shape of s 21(1A). Such cases will include any situation in which the person seeking assistance is not a person subject to immigration control, yet for some reason has no entitlement to state benefits. There will also be cases where a person subject to immigration control has some personal characteristic (such as old age or physical handicap) which keeps them within the ambit of s 21. In dealing with such cases, ECHR considerations which are set out above in relation to the new scheme of asylum seeker support will again be relevant.

It is most unlikely that the arrangements made by local authorities under s 21, certainly once they are relieved of the burden of dealing with the great mass of unsupported asylum seekers under NAA 1948, will be of such low quality as to breach HRA 1998. A slightly more difficult question is whether a local social services authority deciding whether a person falls within s 21 is exercising a function to which Art 6 applies. The answer to this question is not clear, but the applicability of Art 6 cannot be ruled out. If Art 6 does apply, the initial decision by the local authority is unlikely in itself to offer the kind of hearing and tribunal that Art 6 requires. So the critical issue is whether the possibility of an application for judicial review will represent sufficient compliance, bearing in mind the limitations imposed by *Wednesbury* principles. Some cases suggest that it is consistent with Art 6 for a measure of respect to be accorded by the reviewing court to decisions of administrative

18 [1998] CO/2142/98, Ognall J, 21 August.
19 *The Times*, 5 August 1999.

authorities.[20] Nevertheless, there is a strong possibility that, particularly where the procedure leading to the initial decision is likely to fall well short of the standards that Art 6 would normally require, a more rigorous test than *Wednesbury* will be required if the possibility of judicial review is to fill the gap.

Further, s 21 may remain important in cases where the absence of any support would otherwise breach HRA 1998 (see above). Persons subject to immigration control are excluded from s 21 only if their need for care and attention arises *solely* from destitution or the physical effects of destitution. The word 'solely' leaves considerable scope for judicial interpretation and application to ensure that s 21 remains available as a safety net where a person subject to immigration control falls outside the asylum seeker support system in circumstances such that HRA 1998 requires that he should be supported. Indeed, such an approach is foreshadowed by the judgment of the Court of Appeal in *ex p M*, where it was held that entitlement under s 21 did not arise merely from the lack of money and accommodation, and reference was made to other factors such as language difficulties and the stress of travelling to the UK. In a case where the absence of any right to support would breach HRA 1998, it is very likely that a court will be able to find that some additional factor is present, with the result that the exclusion in s 21(1A) does not apply, and a local authority which has refused to provide accommodation under s 21 will be subject to judicial review.

20 See, in particular, *Vilvarajah v United Kingdom* (1991) 14 EHRR 248 and *Bryan v United Kingdom* (1995) 21 EHRR 342. But contrast the recent decision in *Smith and Grady v United Kingdom* (case no 33985/96).

Chapter 5

Property Rights and Respect for the Home

INTRODUCTION

This chapter is in four parts. They are:

(1) the provisions of the Convention which bear on the subject of this chapter;
(2) a brief look at some of the jurisprudence on the Convention in this field;
(3) a survey (by no means complete) of the some of those parts of the housing legislation which are likely to be affected by the Human Rights Act 1998 ('HRA 1998'), or which, it may be argued by enterprising applicants for judicial review, are so affected;
(4) a conclusion.

THE PROVISIONS OF THE CONVENTION

Two provisions of the Convention will be considered in detail as being particularly relevant to local authorities' activities in the sphere of property rights.[1] They are Arts 8 and 1 of the First Protocol. However, local housing authorities must also be conscious of the impact of Art 3 (the right not to be subjected to torture or to inhuman or degrading treatment or punishment),[2] Art 5 (the right to liberty and

1 Schedule 2 to HRA 1998.

2 It may seem odd to mention this Article in this context, but the court has shown a willingness to deploy this right in what, to an English lawyer, is a surprising context. In *D v United Kingdom* (1997) 24 EHRR 423, the court held that there was an infringement of the rights under this Article of a drug trafficker in the following circumstances. He was arrived in England and sought leave to enter as a visitor. This was refused, and he convicted of possession of a substantial amount of cocaine, and sentenced to six years' imprisonment. While in prison he developed AIDS. He was given appropriate medical treatment, and counselling. When he was released on licence, he was placed in immigration detention pending removal to St Kitts, his country of origin. Because the treatment for AIDS which he had received in the UK was not available in St Kitts, so that his short life expectancy would be reduced, and because he had built up relationships with his counsellors, his proposed deportation was a breach of his rights under Art 3. The court said that 'It [the court] is not ... prevented from scrutinising the applicant's claim under Art 3 where the source of the risk of proscribed treatment ... stems from factors which cannot engage directly or indirectly the responsibility of the public authorities of that country, or which, taken alone, do not in themselves infringe the standards of that Article. To limit the

security), Art 6 (the right to a fair hearing)[3] and Art 14 (Convention rights are to be enjoyed without discrimination on grounds such as sex, race, colour, language, religion and so on).[4] Articles 8 and 1 of the First Protocol are as follows:

Article 8

Right to respect for private and family life
(1) Everyone has the right to respect for his private and family life, his home and his correspondence.
(2) There shall be no interference by a public authority with the exercise of this right except as in accordance with the law and is necessary in a democratic society in the interests of national security, public safety, or the economic well-being of the country, for the prevention of disorder or crime, for the protection of health or morals, or for the protection of the rights and freedoms of others.

The First Protocol

Article I

Protection of property
Every natural or legal person is entitled to the peaceful enjoyment of his possessions. No one shall be deprived of his possessions except in the public interest and subject to the conditions provided by law and by the general principles of international law.

The preceding provisions shall not, however, in any way impair the right of a State to enforce such laws as it deems necessary to control the use of property in accordance with the general interest or to secure the payment of taxes or other contributions and penalties.

THE INTERPRETATION OF THE CONVENTION

Article 8

'In accordance with the law' means in accordance with some specific legal rule or regime which authorises the act in question.[5] If the law concerned confers a wholly

application of Art 3 in this manner would be to undermine the absolute character of its protection.' The court appeals to 'the standards of Art 3' without explaining how they are violated on these facts.

3 The relevant part of Art 6.1 provides: 'In the determination of his civil rights and obligations ... everyone is entitled to a fair and *public* hearing within a reasonable time by an independent and impartial tribunal established by law. Judgment shall be pronounced publicly but the press and public may be excluded from all or part of the trial in the interests of morals public order or national security in a democratic society where the interests of juveniles or the protection of the private life of the parties so require or to the extent strictly necessary in the opinion of the court in special circumstances where publicity would prejudice the interests of justice.' It is doubtful whether the practice in the Queen's Bench Division of hearing all interlocutory injunctions in Chambers squares with this.

4 The concept of discrimination is much wider than that against which English legislation protects.

5 *Silver v United Kingdom* A/61 para 86 (1983) 5 EHRR 347. The rule may be one of international law or EU law: *Groppera Radio AG v Switzerland* A/173 para 68 (1990) 12 EHRR 321..

unfettered discretion on a decision-maker, his decision will not be 'in accordance with the law' for these purposes.[6] 'Necessary in a democratic society' connotes an element of proportionality. The court must be satisfied that the interference corresponds 'to a pressing social need and, in particular, that it is proportionate to the legitimate aim pursued.[7] This involves the concept of the margin of appreciation which is accorded by the court to the state in order to assess whether the interference is justified.[8] One factor which may be significant is whether there is a European consensus on the question.[9] An analogous doctrine is likely to apply in the domestic courts, such that public authorities will have an appropriate margin of discretion when interfering with Art 8 rights.

According to Harris, O'Boyle and Warbrick[10] in cases on Arts 8-11, the European Court of Human Rights has adopted a five-stage approach:

(1) to identify the right, including its positive aspects;
(2) to identify the interference with it;
(3) to consider whether that interference is prescribed by law (both as understood domestically and by the court);
(4) to determine what aims the interference seeks to protect;
(5) to decide whether that interference is 'necessary in a democratic society' (that is whether the state asserts, and supports with evidence, relevant and sufficient reasons for the interference and those are proportionate to the limitation of the applicant's enjoyment of his right). Here the margin of appreciation is important.

Because the decisions of the court are made against an evolving social background, and because different states may adopt different approaches to similar problems, the value of those decisions as precedents is somewhat limited.

The combination of the drafting of Art 8 and the court's interpretation of it makes prediction in this area difficult. It is clear that decisions concerning civil rights must be taken in a way that conforms with Art 6.[11] 'Private life' has been given a wide meaning by the court, so as to encompass not only protection for personal information and privacy but also the right to establish relationships, physical integrity and sexual preference.[12] The salient point for local housing authorities, however, is that Art 8 does not confer a right to be provided with housing, and does not therefore impose any duty on authorities to provide housing. The source of all such duties continues to be domestic housing legislation.

In *Lopez Ostra v Spain*[13] the court held that a failure by the state to protect the applicant from pollution produced by a waste disposal plant was a failure to

6 *Kruslin v France* A/176-A (1990) 12 EHRR 528; *Huvig v France* A/176-B (1990) 12 EHRR 528, which concerned telephone tapping.
7 *Olsson v Sweden* A/130 para 67 (1988) 11EHRR 254.
8 See, for example, *Handyside v United Kingdom* A/24 paras 48-49 (1976) 1 EHRR 737.
9 *Marckx v Belgium* A/31 para 41 (1979) 2 EHRR 330, which concerned inheritance rights for illegitimate children.
10 *The Law of the European Convention on Human Rights* (1996) Butterworths at 301.
11 'In the determination of his civil rights and obligations .... everyone is entitled to fair and public hearing within a reasonable time by an independent and impartial tribunal established by law. Judgment shall be pronounced publicly ...': see, for example, *Olsson v Sweden (No1)* [1988] A 130.
12 As the recent decision of the Court of Human Rights in *Lustig-Prean v UK* graphically illustrates.
13 [1994] A 303-C.

respect her home and family life. 'Family life' has an extended meaning. It covers not only the conventional family but less formal relationships and those not traditionally regarded as legitimate. It is 'essentially a question of fact and degree, depending on the real existence in practice of close personal ties'.[14] 'Home' can include business premises.[15] The rights over a home which are protected are rights of access and occupation.

There can be an overlap between rights protected by Art 8 and by Art 1 of the First Protocol, as in *Howard v United Kingdom*[16] which concerned a compulsory purchase order. The obligation to respect these rights may connote not merely abstention from positive interference by the state itself, but also positive obligations,[17] even extending to obligations to minimise interference by others.

Article 1 of the first Protocol

'Possessions', consistently with the French text ('biens'), signifies a wide range of interests (all types of personal property and real property). There can be interference with this right, falling short of seizure and control.[18] This Article consists of three rules:

(1) the principle of peaceful enjoyment of property;
(2) deprivation of possessions is made subject to conditions;
(3) a recognition that states are entitled to control the use of property in accordance with the general interest.[19]

These rules are not distinct. Rules (2) and (3) 'are to be construed in the light of the general principle enunciated in the first rule'. In deciding whether rule (1) has been met, the court applies a 'fair balance' test.[20] Generally the court has accorded a wide margin of appreciation to states in applying Art 1.

HOW WILL THE ACT AFFECT LOCAL AUTHORITIES' HOUSING FUNCTIONS?

Introductory tenancies

Local authorities may operate an introductory tenancy regime under s 124 of the Housing Act 1996 ('HA 1996'). The main difference between an introductory tenancy and a secure tenancy is that apart from procedural safeguards contained in ss 128 and 129 of HA 1996, the authority has an apparently unfettered right to seek possession of a dwelling let under such a tenancy, as the Court of Appeal recently emphasised in *Manchester City Council v Cochrane*.[21] Of course, such a discretion is subject to the principles of administrative law. Further, any apparently unfettered discretion which may bear on Convention rights must now, in the light of s 3 of HA 1996, be read as subject to those rights. Thus HA 1996 imposes duties on local authorities to consider carefully the impact of a decision to seek

14 Application 11468/85 *K v United Kingdom* 50 DR 199 (1986) at 207.
15 *Niemietz v Germany* A/251-B para 30 (1992) 16 EHRR 97.
16 Application 10825/84 52 DR 198 (1985).
17 *X and Y v Netherlands*] A/91 para 23 (1985) 8 EHRR 235.
18 *Sporrong and Lònroth v Sweden* A/52 para 60 (1982) 5 EHRR 35.
19 *Sporrong and Lònroth v Sweden* A/52 para 61 (1982) 5 EHRR 35.
20 *Sporrong and Lònroth v Sweden* A/52 para 69 (1982) 5 EHRR 35.
21 [1999] 1 WLR 809.

possession on the private and family life and home of the tenant. It will usually be the case that the local authority will be able to justify a decision to seek possession under Art 8(2), but such justifications should be carefully considered and articulated both in the reasons provided under s 128(3) of HA 1996 and in any review decision made under s 129. Reasons and review decisions may also be affected by Art 1 of the First Protocol. Similar points will obviously apply when local housing authorities seek possession of accommodation held under a secure tenancy.

Injunctions against anti-social behaviour

Depending on the scope of such injunctions, there may be arguments that the local authority in applying for, and obtaining, such an order may infringe Convention rights of the anti-social actor against whom such an order is sought (for example under Art 8 or under Art 10).[22] Again, the message is that any decision to apply for such an injunction must be carefully considered and articulated, so that the local authority may be seen to have taken into account the anti-social behaviour concerned, and weighed it and its effects on the other occupiers of the accommodation to which s 152(2) of HA 1996 applies, against any Convention right which may arguably be interfered with by any such injunction. This is particularly important in view of the fact that powers of arrest may attach to such injunctions under s 153 of HA 1996. Further, under s 12 of HRA 1998, the power of any court to grant relief which may interfere with freedom of expression is expressly subject to procedural safeguards and a duty to have particular regard to the importance of the Convention right to freedom of expression. Local authorities must also bear in mind that they may interfere with the Convention rights of their well-behaved tenants if they do not take action under s 152 against anti-social behaviour. Provided that the local authority follows the legal process correctly and has patently and demonstrably weighed the competing considerations in coming to any decision, it should weather any challenge successfully.

Allocation of housing

Local housing authorities are bound to allocate housing in accordance with s 159 of HA 1996. Similar considerations will apply to the allocation of housing. So in making their decisions about qualifying persons under s 161, and their allocation scheme under s 167, authorities should bear in mind the possible impact of Arts 8[23] and 14. The question whether s 161(2) of HA 1996 (which provides that a person subject to immigration control is not qualified to be allocated housing) may infringe Convention rights is an interesting one. Since Art 8 does not guarantee a right to be provided with housing, it may be thought that it does not. In any event, local authorities are bound to implement it and are protected by s 6(1) of HRA 1998 when they do so. The Secretary of State who makes regulations for procedures for scrutinising allocation decisions by review under section 165(1) of HA 1996 will need to look at Art 6(1) of the Convention.

22 Which protects freedom of expression, subject to such 'formalities, conditions restrictions or penalties as are prescribed by law and are necessary in a democratic society' for various purposes.

23 For example, they should take into account the impact of a particular allocation decision on the applicant's right to his family life.

Homelessness

Similar points apply to the powers and duties of local housing authorities in relation to homelessness. While, as has already been pointed out, there is no Convention right to be provided with a home, the impact of any decisions on the applicant's right to respect for his private and family life should be considered. The impact of Art 6(1) on the review process provided for by s 202 should be borne in mind, though as under s165(1) of HA 1996 it is the Secretary of State who is responsible for devising the relevant procedures. The question whether ss 185 and 186 (which render persons from abroad, persons who are subject to immigration control and asylum seekers in temporary accommodation ineligible for assistance) infringe Convention rights is not for the local housing authority to decide. Their duty is to apply the statute as it stands (see s 6(2) of the Act).

Succession

Readers may well be aware of two relatively recent decisions on succession. One, *Kingston upon Thames Royal London Borough v Prince,*[24] that a minor can succeed to a secure tenancy,[25] was a result of statutory construction and owes nothing to the Convention. The other, *Fitzpatrick v Sterling Housing Association*[26] concerns rights of homosexual partners to succeed to a statutory or protected tenancy. By a majority, the court held that such a partner had no statutory right of succession. The court was bound by *Harrogate Borough Council v Simpson*[27] which decides that a homosexual partner cannot succeed to a secure tenancy, because they do not live together 'as man and wife' and do not otherwise fall within the definition of 'family' in s 113 of the 1985 Act. Ward LJ, dissenting, referred[28] to the fact that while the Commission appears to have recognised the rights of a transsexual in the context of Art 8,[29] it has not yet recognised the rights of a homosexual partner in that context. It remains to be seen whether it will do so.

Repairs and slum clearance

Local housing authorities' powers under Part VI of the 1985 Act may raise questions under Art 1 of the First Protocol. Prima facie the exercise of these powers could involve an interference with the right of a property owner peacefully to enjoy his possessions. This is not to say that such interventions are not capable of justification under Art 1, but local authorities should be alert to the need to justify such actions in accordance with that Article. Similar considerations apply to the powers conferred on local authorities by Part IX of the 1985 Act in respect of slum clearance. Questions under Art 6 may arise in relation to appeals in this context, and questions under Art 8 in relation to the exercise of powers of entry.

24 [1999] 1 FLR 593, CA 1989.
25 Defined in s 79 of HA 1985; rights of succession are dealt with in ss 87 and 113(1) of HA 1985.
26 [1998] Ch 304, CA 1989.
27 (1986) 17 HLR 205.
28 At pp 251 H-252 F.
29 *X, Y and Z v United Kingdom* (1995) 20 EHRR CD6.

Unauthorised campers

In *R v Wolverhampton Metropolitan Borough Council, ex p Dunne and Rafferty*[30] the local authority gave a direction under s 77 of the Criminal Justice and Public Order Act 1994 to unauthorised campers to leave occupied land. The court was of the view that, given the nature of the power under s 77, it was all the more important for authorities to bear in mind the guidance offered in Circular 18/94 before exercising it. But in *R v Brighton and Hove Council, ex p Marmont*[31] the authority proceeded by RSC O113 (summary possession), Tucker J holding that the Circular had no application in these circumstances. Article 8 will probably be invoked in such cases in the future.

Enjoyment of the home

Peaceful enjoyment of the home is part of the concept of the right to respect for the home.[32] Local authorities as landlords will doubtless find Art 8 cited against them when tenants are subjected to disturbing behaviour either from other tenants or from others. But the common law of nuisance, and contractual rights arising out of the tenancy, may provide as much protection as Convention rights do: see further *Baxter v Camden London Borough Council*; *Southwark London Borough Council v Mills*.[33]

Fair hearing

Under Art 6(1) a person has a right to a fair hearing in the determination of his 'civil rights'. Though Strasbourg has generally restricted the applicability of Art 6 to matters of private law, certain social security entitlements are covered by the principles in Art 6(1).[34] It is likely that authorities will soon face arguments that, for example, reviews of housing benefit and other circumstances in which a dispute has arisen (the existence of a dispute is a pre-requisite for Art 6(1)'s applicability) attract the protection of Art 6.1 with all that it entails. The answer to such a claim may be that where a court has jurisdiction over the decision-making process which the local authority undertakes, the law does not require the full rigours of Art 6 to be applied to the determination of the dispute before it reaches court.

CONCLUSION

This has necessarily been a speculative look at only some of the provisions of the Housing Acts which may be affected by HRA 1998. Although HRA 1998 does have potentially far-reaching consequences, the basic message is that undue panic would be premature. In the vast majority of cases where local authorities are accustomed to making thoroughly considered and well-documented decisions in the exercise of their existing discretions, the impact of HRA 1998 should simply be to make for more careful procedures and explicit consideration of the implications of decisions for the Convention rights of those affected by them.

30 (1996) 29 HLR 745.
31 (1998) 30 HLR 1046.
32 *Powell and Rayner v United Kingdom* (1990) 12 EHRR 355.
33 (1997) 30 HLR 501; [1999] 1 WLR 409, both appealed to the House of Lords; judgment awaited.
34 See *Massa v Italy* (1993) 18 EHRR 266.

Chapter 6

Environment, Planning and Licensing

INTRODUCTION

As will be seen from this chapter, there are many ways in which the responsibilities of local authorities for environmental, planning and licensing matters may be affected by the Human Rights Act 1998 ('HRA 1998'). Some of those ways may be less immediately obvious than in fields such as employment and discrimination law. However, they are no less far-reaching.

They may pull in either direction. As the sections on Gypsies and Travellers and on Local Authority Licensing indicate, HRA 1998 may affect the ways in which local authorities exercise their functions, for example in relation to licensing and in relation to enforcement. In particular, such decisions may impact on property rights, or in some cases on the right to family life. At the general level, they will also often involve issues of a 'fair hearing'.

These aspects of HRA 1998 may be seen by authorities as potentially making it more difficult for them to protect properly the local environment, by slowing up, or even precluding entirely, the range of actions which would otherwise be available. Certainly, internal procedures will need to be reviewed to ensure that the relevant Convention rights have been considered. Authorities will also need to address the proportionality of the actions proposed, in terms of the desired outcome and the effect on the Convention rights in question.

Much of this may already be part of good administrative practice however, whether provided by existing government guidance or by the rules of natural justice. Also HRA 1998 and the Convention will not apply in an absolute way in this respect. The case law of the European Court of Human Rights ('ECHR') already recognises that a balance needs to be struck between Convention rights and objectives such as the protection of public health and amenities, and the preservation of public order. Both local authorities and the courts will need to develop the ability to strike that balance.

In England, a great deal will depend on how interventionist the courts prove to be in coming to the conclusion that the balance may have been wrongly drawn. While HRA 1998 will almost certainly require more stringent scrutiny than would be necessary under traditional principles of administrative law, there is still room for the court to draw the conclusion that the local authority is the person best placed to strike that balance. Such an approach can be seen in *Tandbridge District Council v Delaney and Connors*[1] where the local authority was seeking interlocutory

1 (29 January 1999, unreported).

injunctions to enforce against breaches of planning control involving caravans and related structures. There had been a long history of planning and enforcement procedures relating to that issue on the site. The agent for one of the defendants argued that Art 8 of the Convention (the right to respect for private and family life) had been infringed:

> 'My client has a right to his home; he has a right to his family life and to the education of his children at a school of his choice. The action authorised by the Sub-Committee and particularly compliance with the time-scale required in your letter would deny him those rights.'

The Deputy Judge, Nigel McLeod QC, put the counter-argument in this way:

> '... it is submitted by the Plaintiff that the Defendants' needs have been considered and weighed against the public interests and preservation of the Green Belt on numerous occasions, two of which have been the subject of unsuccessful appeals to the Planning Inspectorate. It is contended that it is primarily for those bodies to decide where the balance of interest lies subject to the right of appeal to the High Court under the Town and Country Planning Act 1990 and that that procedure affords sufficient safeguards of the Defendants' rights under Art 8, and it is contended that accordingly there is no breach of Art 8. I agree with that submission.'

The case illustrates therefore what may become both a common argument and a common response.

The other side of the coin is the case where Convention rights are deployed to aid the cause of environmental protection. These are the cases where local residents or national interest groups argue that not enough has been done or that wrong decisions have been reached. It is here that Convention rights may have their most radical impact.

While the courts have generally liberalised the tests of standing for third parties in judicial review proceedings in recent years, the fact remains that it is difficult to challenge many decisions of local authorities for failure to do enough.

Unless there is a clear statutory duty to act (as in statutory nuisance), more often than not, the third party will be challenging the exercise of a statutory discretion on restrictive administrative law grounds. In the field of planning law, for example, there is no right of appeal by third parties on the merits against a decision to grant planning permission. Where such decisions affect the property or civil rights of third parties, the lack of such a right of appeal may not be enough so far as the Convention is concerned.

The other important aspect to remember is that local authorities may potentially fall foul of HRA 1998 by not doing enough to protect the Convention rights of others. Failure to take appropriate action may result in local people being subject to harm to their personal health, to their property or to the reasonable enjoyment of their home. As the cases described in the section on Environmental Pollution and Nuisance make clear, although the jurisprudence of ECHR on this issue may be at an early stage, it offers definite possibilities for arguments that local authorities are in breach by having permitted such harm or, equally importantly, the risk of such harm.

One difficulty in this area is that breach of a Convention right involves a 'victim'. Whereas in many areas it will be transparently obvious who the victim is, this may not always be the case in relation to environmental matters. Deficient action by the local authority in such matters may affect a wide range of people to varying degrees. Not all such people will necessarily be 'victims' entitled to vindicate Convention rights. Indeed, in some cases there may be no 'victim' at all, in the sense that it is the general environment which suffers rather than any individual or group of individuals. Again, these are issues with which ECHR will have to grapple as the case law develops.

Finally, there is the question of how Convention rights may impact on the substantive law relevant to this area. For example, Art 14 states that rights and freedoms under the Convention are to be secured without discrimination on any ground such as sex, race, colour, language, religion, political or other opinion, national or social origin, property, birth or other status.

It might, in future, be argued that Art 14 is infringed where differential standards are applied in the protection of health or home life. If more lenient standards are applied in relation, for example, to noise or air quality in areas which already have high ambient noise levels or poor air, and which may well be surrounded by disadvantaged or deprived communities, is that a possible breach of Art 14? As a matter of common law, will it be lawful any longer to say that what is a nuisance in Belgravia is not necessarily so in Bermondsey?[2]

Another example of potential difficulties in this area is the ruling of the House of Lords in *Hunter v Canary Wharf*[3] that someone without a proprietary interest could not take action in respect of private nuisance by noise and dust affecting their home. This would appear on the face of it to discriminate between individuals on the basis of 'property', contrary to Art 14.

As *Osman v United Kingdom*[4] makes clear, watertight exclusionary rules, which provide a defence to claims at common law without any consideration of competing policy issues or of the merits of the individual case, may amount to an unjustifiable restriction on the right to a proper hearing contrary to Art 6. The *Osman* case has potentially far-reaching repercussions which may impact on environmental law. The message is that local authorities should not assume that they will be safeguarded from liability for their acts or omissions by existing principles of law, however well-established.

As will be appreciated, the areas of environmental protection, planning and licensing may prove to be fertile ground for the application of human rights principles derived from HRA 1998 and the Convention. The sections in this chapter provide a starting point for consideration of those potentially far-reaching implications.

2 See *Sturges v Bridgman* [1879] 11 ChD 852.
3 [1997] AC 655.
4 [1999] 1FLR 193.

Pollution and Nuisance

From 1 April 1996, with the establishment of the Environment Agency,[1] there has been a reduction in the responsibilities of local authorities for pollution control. There are, however, important remaining responsibilities. These are notably in the fields of air pollution from industrial processes,[2] waste collection and disposal,[3] contaminated land,[4] nuisances,[5] clean air,[6] litter[7] and noise.[8] There are also environmental responsibilities as local planning authorities both in the context of considering applications for planning permission and in the enforcement of planning control.[9]

Moreover, all these responsibilities are enhanced by two external factors. The first is the fact that EU Directives may be capable of being directly enforceable against local authorities as emanations of the UK state.[10] The second factor is that, with the coming into effect of the Human Rights Act 1998 ('HRA 1998'), local authorities will be bound by the European Convention on Human Rights ('the Convention').

One result of HRA 1998 is that the positive actions of local authorities under environmental legislation will have to be compatible with Convention rights.[11] Notable amongst these is the right under Art 6 to a 'fair hearing'.[12]

LIABILITY FOR POLLUTION

Local authorities may also be liable for inaction, or insufficiently speedy and robust action, against polluters and the perpetrators of nuisance, or for the

1 EA1995, Pt I
2 EPA 1990 Pt I
3 EPA 1990 Pt II
4 EPA 1990 Pt IIA, to be brought into force on a date to be appointed
5 The Environmental Protection Act 1990 Pt III; Public nuisance may also be relevant
6 The Clean Air Act 1993
7 EPA 1990 Pt IV
8 EPA 1990 Pt III and the Noise and Statutory Nuisance Act 1993
9 See the section on Planning and Enforcement.
10 This will depend on considering the relevant provision of the Directive in question against the accepted test of whether the provision is sufficiently clear, precise and unconditional. Provisions in Directives which are intended to protect the public may well stand a good chance of meeting those criteria.
11 See s 6.
12 See Chap 2.

environmental consequences of development which they promote under economic development powers, or which they permit as landowners or as planning or licensing authority.

The possibilities of such liability are illustrated by a 1994 decision under the Convention.

Lopez Ostra v Spain[13] concerned the leather industry in Lorca. Several tanneries had a plant for the treatment of liquid and solid waste. The plant was built on local authority land with a public subsidy. It was close to Mrs Lopez Ostra's home. There were numerous complaints. The local authority took some action, but allowed certain activities to continue. It also rehoused residents.

Mrs Lopez Ostra brought proceedings on account of the local authority's inactivity in respect of the nuisances and risk caused by the waste-treatment plant. She relied on Article 8 of the Convention. The European Court of Human Rights ('ECHR') held unanimously that there had been a breach.

Under Art 8(1) everyone has the right to respect for his private and family life and his home. Under Art 8(2) there must be no unjustified interference by a public authority with this right. The court held[14] that:

(1) 'severe environmental pollution' may infringe the Art 8(1) right;
(2) this is so, irrespective of whether health is seriously endangered;
(3) whether the question is analysed in terms of a positive duty, to take reasonable and appropriate measures to secure the applicant's rights under Art 8(1), or in terms of an interference by a public authority, to be justified in accordance with Art 8(2), the applicable principles are broadly similar;
(4) in both contexts, regard must be had to the fair balance that has to be struck between the competing interests of the individual and of the community as a whole;
(5) in striking the balance, economic well-being and the rights and freedoms of others are relevant.

The court concluded[15] that a fair balance had *not* been struck between the interest of the town's economic well-being, that of having a waste treatment plant where there was a heavy concentration of tanneries and, on the other hand, Mrs Lopez Ostra's effective enjoyment of her right to respect for her home and her private and family life. There had accordingly been a violation of Art 8.

There are two relevant messages from the case:

(1) an authority may be held liable for inaction or insufficient action;
(2) it may be held to be liable for pollution for which it is indirectly responsible, because it provided land and/or subsidy for the process which produced the pollution.

Moreover, ECHR awarded damages. This was in respect of both pecuniary and non-pecuniary loss.

Nor is *Lopez Ostra* the only case at issue. In the more recent case of *Guerra v Italy*,[16] the 40 applicants lived in a town approximately a kilometre away from a

13 (1994) 20 EHRR 277.
14 *Lopez Ostra* para 51 at p 295.
15 *Lopez Ostra* para 58 at p 297.
16 (1998) 26 EHRR 357

chemical factory. They complained that the authorities had not taken appropriate action to reduce the risk of pollution by the factory. The ECHR held unanimously that Art 8 of the Convention had been infringed.

The court said[17] that although the object of Art 8 is essentially that of protecting the individual against arbitrary interference by public authorities, it does not merely compel abstinence from such interference: 'in addition to this primarily negative undertaking, there may be *positive obligations* inherent in effective respect for private or family life' (emphasis supplied).

The court reiterated[18] that 'severe environmental pollution may affect individuals' well being and prevent them from enjoying their homes in such a way as to affect their private and family life adversely'. The court found that there was a failure to secure the applicants' right to respect for their private and family life and that Art 8 was breached because the applicants had been deprived of 'essential information' that would have enabled them to assess the risks they and their families might run if they continued to live in the town.

PLANNING DECISIONS

Third parties who object to the grant of planning permission in the past had few rights in the UK. They have no statutory right of appeal to the Secretary of State. At the initial decision stage by the local planning authority, their private interests and personal circumstances are capable of being regarded as relevant only in exceptional circumstances.

This position contrasts with the Convention's emphasis on individual rights. These include property rights.[19]

In future, not only the wider public interest, but also affected private interests, may have to be taken into account, and seen to be taken into account, and indeed given due weight. This will apply both in the determination of individual planning applications and in the development plan process. A change of emphasis will be called for in the exercise of discretion in making planning decisions, including the enforcement of planning control.

17 *Guerra* para 58 at p 383.
18 *Guerra* para 60 at p 383.
19 See Chap 5.

Planning and Enforcement

OFFENCES AND ENFORCEMENT

Local authorities will have to assess how the Human Rights Act 1998 ('HRA 1998') bears on their enforcement role in relation to areas such as planning, public nuisance, air pollution, highways, trading standards and food safety.

Those functions may involve a variety of activities, such as inspections, the investigation of offences, prosecutions, the use of statutory enforcement powers, and in some cases, proceedings for injunctions to restrain breaches of the law.

The relevant Articles of the Convention are:

Article 6: right to a fair trial and 'minimum rights' of those charged with offences.
Article 7: no punishment without law, for example, criminal legislation cannot have retrospective effect.
Article 8: respect for private and family life.
Article 10: freedom of expression.
Article 11: freedom of assembly and association.
First Protocol, Article 1: entitlement to peaceful enjoyment of possessions.

Use of these Articles by companies

It is clear that commercial interests fall within the protection of the Convention. In *Niemietz v Germany*[1] it was found that the search of a commercial office by police could breach Art 8. Article 6 has been applied to commercial activities such as selling alcohol,[2] operating taxis[3] and storing liquefied petroleum gas.[4] However, rights may not extend to shareholders in the company affected.[5] A parent company with a controlling interest may however claim to be a 'victim'.[6]

Local authorities may therefore find that enforcement action which they take, or the legislation under which they take it, are challenged as unlawful or incompatible with Convention rights. This may take the form of a direct challenge, or collateral challenge in criminal proceedings.

1 (1992) 16 EHRR 97.
2 *Tre Traktörer Aktiebolag v Sweden* A/159 (1989) 13 EHRR 309.
3 *Axelsson v Sweden* 65 DR 99 (1990).
4 *Benthem v Netherlands* A/97 (1985) 8EHRR 1.
5 *Agrotexim v Greece* (1995) 21 EHRR 250.
6 *Yarrow plc v United Kingdom* 30 DR 155 (1983).

Possible areas for challenge

(1) Over-zealous use of enforcement powers (for example, powers of entry and inspection) in a way that is seen as oppressive or disproportionate. Under present law such challenges have rarely been successful. For a rare example see *Welton v North Cornwall District Council*.[7] The concept of proportionality will be relevant under the case law of the Convention, and will require consideration of whether the authority could have made use of less onerous powers.

(2) Alleged discrimination in the use of enforcement powers. Article 14 prohibits discrimination in enjoyment of Convention rights on grounds such as sex, race, colour, language, religion, political opinion, national or social origin, property, birth or other status. Breach of Art 14 was unsuccessfully argued by the applicant (a gypsy) in *Buckley v United Kingdom*.[8]

(3) Where enforcement action results in someone losing their home, whether proper regard has been paid to their predicament, and whether alternative accommodation has been offered. In *Buckley v United Kingdom* the European Court of Human Rights was satisfied that the planning authorities had not employed disproportionate means to achieve their legitimate aims. 'Article 8 does not necessarily go so far as to allow individuals' preferences as to their place of residence to override the general interest'.[9]

(4) Use of material obtained under compulsion in a prejudicial way in subsequent criminal proceedings. This was the subject of a successful challenge in *Saunders v United Kingdom*.[10] It was argued unsuccessfully before the Court of Appeal in *R v Hertfordshire County Council, ex p Green Environmental Industries Ltd*[11] but that case is due to go to the House of Lords on appeal.

(5) It is not inconceivable that, in due course, someone may allege that an aspect of enforcement action has retrospective effects, contrary to Art 7. In *National and Provincial Building Society v United Kingdom*[12] an unsuccessful challenge was made to retrospective revenue legislation. It should be noted, however, that Art 7 applies only to criminal liability.[13]

(6) People using the highway or other public areas for protests may rely on Arts 10 and 11. The question here will be one of balance between the right to free expression and association and the preservation of public order. In *Steel v United Kingdom*[14] arrests during peaceful protests were found to infringe Arts 5.1 and 10, but other protesters arrested for behaviour likely to cause a breach of the peace failed in their complaint. Concern was expressed in *Huntingdon Life Sciences Ltd v Curtin*[15] about the possibly overwide use of the Protection from Harassment Act

7 [1997] 1 WLR 570.
8 [1996] JPL 1018. See also p 114.
9 [1996] JPL 1018, at 1032.
10 (1996) 23 EHRR 313.
11 [1998] Env LR 153.
12 (1997) 25 EHRR 127.
13 See Application 11408/85 *v Sweden* (1987) 9 EHRR 244.
14 [1998] Crim LR 893.
15 [1998] Env LR D9.

1997 to prevent protest or discussion of matters of public interest by animal rights protesters.

(7) Where a licence is revoked as part of enforcement proceedings, this may possibly be challenged as deprivation of possessions, as in *Fredin v Sweden*.[16] However, there is a distinction between expropriation and control.[17] The authority may be entitled to expropriate on grounds of public interest if it acts lawfully and proportionately, but the issue then arises as to whether compensation should be payable as in *James v United Kingdom*.[18] In general, such compensation must adequately relate to the value of the property taken, unless a different approach is justified by legitimate objectives of economic reform.[19]

The response of local authorities

It is impossible to foresee all of the ingenious and no doubt sometimes unmeritorious uses to which HRA 1998 may be put. In many cases, the question will be one of balancing competing interests and whether a particular enforcement action is proportionate. These are issues which will need to be considered carefully in enforcement procedures and in reports to Committee. A key factor will often be whether the authority can show that it has properly considered the relevant issues. The authority can hardly be said to have taken account of the Convention rights if it has not considered whether any breach may be involved in a particular course of action.[20]

FAIR AND IMPARTIAL HEARINGS

Article 6 of the Convention states: 'In the determination of his civil rights and obligations or of any criminal charge against him, everyone is entitled to a fair and public hearing within a reasonable time by an independent and impartial tribunal established by law'. The term 'civil rights' can cover many areas that local authorities may be involved in, as the case law shows. These include water abstraction, nature conservation, planning control, compulsory purchase and liquor and transport licensing.[21]

In general, the planning, environmental, highways and other relevant functions of local authorities will be subject to appeal processes of various sorts, either to the Secretary of State or to magistrates' courts. There is also the possibility of review on administrative law grounds. The system for appeals against enforcement notices was challenged on the basis of Art 6 in *Bryan v UK*.[22] It was held that the appeal to the Inspector was not of itself 'an independent and impartial tribunal', because the Secretary of State could, at any time, revoke the Inspector's power to determine the appeal. However, the further appeal to the High Court which was

16 (1991) 13 EHRR 784.
17 See *Pine Valley Developments v Ireland* (1991) 14 EHRR 319.
18 [1986] 18 EHRR 123.
19 See also *R v North Lincolnshire Council, ex p Horticultural and Garden Products (Humberside) Ltd* [1998] Env LR 295; *Booker Aquaculture Ltd v Secretary of State for Scotland* [1999] 1 CMLR 35.
20 See *Britton v Secretary of State for the Environment* [1997] JPL 617 at p 632.
21 See generally p 117.
22 [1996] JPL 386.

available, meant that the procedure as a whole did not breach Art 6, notwithstanding that the High Court's grounds for intervening were limited.[23]

The traditional appeal processes against refusal of planning permission, enforcement notices, and so on, are likely, if properly followed, to comply with Art 6. This is particularly so when the normal rules of natural justice are followed. In *R v Secretary of State for the Environment, ex p Slot*[24] the applicant for a diversion order under the Highways Act 1980 claimed that she was entitled to see all written objections to the proposed order. Failure to make these available was held to be breach of natural justice, and the Art 6 point was not considered.

THIRD PARTIES

It is in the area of third-party rights that particular difficulties may arise under Art 6 and under Art 1 of the First Protocol. The grant of planning permission for new development may be a matter which affects the civil rights and the right to peaceful enjoyment of property of existing owners in the vicinity. In *S v France*[25] an eighteenth century house on the River Loire was affected by the building of a nuclear power plant. It was held that noise nuisance and other forms of intrusion could in principle constitute infringement of Art 1 of the First Protocol, the question then being whether a justifiable fair balance had been struck between the general interest and the individual's rights.

As in *Ortenburg v Austria*,[26] such owners may claim interference with their property under Art 1 of the First Protocol and the lack of a fair hearing under Art. In *Ortenburg* the Art 6 claim failed since there was the right of access for the aggrieved owner to both the Administrative Court and the Constitutional Court. However, in the UK, there is no right of third party appeal on the merits against the grant of planning permission, other than judicial review. This may well prove to be a breach of Art 6.

As well as neighbouring owners, there may be third party NGOs who wish to challenge planning permission. However, they will find it difficult to rely on the Convention unless they are a 'victim' in the sense that their Convention rights have been infringed. This may not be the case unless members of the group are actual local residents affected by the decision in question.[27] Such groups may, however, be able to rely in future on the UNECE Convention on Access to Information, Public Participation in Decision Making and Access to Justice in Environmental Matters (*the Aarhuis Convention*). Once ratified, this Convention will have far-reaching implications for local authorities and others involved in environmental decision making.

PLAN AND POLICY MAKING

Another area where difficulties can be anticipated is the plan-making functions of local authorities. The policy outcomes of those plans may have important implications for rights of property. Examples are structure plans, local plans and waste plans. Policies for air quality management and for transport may also be important in future. Those whose health, properties and commercial activities

23 See also *ISKCON v United Kingdom* 76A DR 90 (1994).
24 [1998] JPL 692.
25 65 DR 250 (1990).
26 [1994] 19 EHRR 524.
27 See for example, *Greenpeace Schweiz v Switzerland* (1997) 23 EHRR CD 116.

may be affected by the outcome of such plans may seek to rely on Art 6 to argue for a right to participate fully in those decision-making processes.

The current processes for the hearing and determination of local plan objections may well be found to be in breach of Art 6. The question could then be whether such breach is 'saved' by the right of appeal to the High Court on a point of law. A key factor here will be whether sufficient reasons have been given by the local planning authority for adopting or rejecting the recommendations of the inspector following the inquiry into the plan. If no reasons are given, or inadequate reasons are given, the third party will be unable to ascertain whether or not they have effective grounds for challenge in the High Court or not and accordingly the requirements of Art 6 may not be satisfied. Article 6 requires reasons to be given 'but cannot be understood as requiring a detailed answer to every argument'.[28]

Possible 'problem' areas in relation to development plan making have already given rise in many cases to challenge under English law and may be subject to further challenge in future for incompatibility with Convention rights:

(1) failure on the part of the planning authority to carry out adequate consultation in relation to proposed structure plan policies and to consider representations made;[29]
(2) failure to give adequate reasons in relation to objections to structure plan policies;[30]
(3) there is no right of hearing at examination in public into a structure plan;[31]
(4) the adoption of a selective approach to participation in the EIP process;[32]
(5) failure by the planning authority to carry out adequate consultation in relation to proposed local plan/ UDP policies and to consider objections duly made;[33]
(6) failure to give proper consideration to the recommendations of the inspector after an inquiry into the draft plan, or failure to give adequate reasons for departing from those recommendations;[34]
(7) failure to hold a second public inquiry if changes to the plan are accepted which may prejudice other parties;[35]
(8) pre-judgement of issues and lack of proper consideration of representations generally.

CONCLUSIONS

Many of the requirements of the Convention are already built into existing legislative systems or are provided by the residual rules of natural justice.

28 *Helle v Finland* (1997) 26 EHRR 159 at p 179.
29 See the Town and Country Planning Act 1990, s 33.
30 See for example *Modern Homes (Whitworth) Ltd v Lancashire County Council* [1998] EGCS 73.
31 See the Town and Country Planning Act 1990, s 35B(4).
32 See PPG12 *Development Plans*, Annex A, paras 34-35; Town and Country Planning Act 1990, ss 13 and 40.
33 See *Stirk v Bridgnorth District Council* (1996) 73 P & CR 439; *Miller v Wycombe District Council* [1997] JPL 951.
34 See for example *Drexfine Holdings Ltd v Cherwell District Council* [1998] JPL 361.
35 *R v Teeside District Council, ex p Morrison* [1998] JPL 23; *Alfred McAlpine Homes Northumbria Ltd v Darlington Borough Council* [1999] JPL 53. Compare *Peel Investments Ltd v Bury Metropolitan Borough Council* [1999] JPL 74.

HRA 1998 means, however, that authorities will have to think through the issues raised by Convention rights when carrying out all enforcement, decision-making and policy-making functions. The relevant procedures should be reviewed with these points in mind.

Gypsies and Travellers

INTRODUCTION

A difficult issue for local authorities in recent years has been the scope for challenging the lawfulness of a local authority decision to evict trespassing travellers or gypsies, on the grounds that there was an unreasonable failure to take into account their individual welfare circumstances. It is arguable that after an initial period of vigilance on the part of the English courts against local authority eviction decisions, more recently the tide seems to be turning in favour of a less rigorous scrutiny of those decisions. This section addresses the extent to which the incorporation of the European Convention on Human Rights ("the Convention') under the Human Rights Act 1998 ('HRA 1998') will result in a resurgence of a close scrutiny approach to local authority eviction decisions by the English courts.

THE POSITION BEFORE INCORPORATION OF THE CONVENTION UNDER HRA 1998

Even before the incorporation of the Convention under HRA 1998, the English courts have sought to give some protection to 'the fundamental right to shelter' of gypsies and travellers in the context of local authority decisions to evict them. The impetus for the development of the common law in this way was created by the enactment of the Criminal Justice and Public Order Act 1994 which gave local authorities 'draconian powers' to deal with unauthorised encampments of gypsies and travellers within their area.

Thus, in a judicial review challenge to the decisions of two local authorities to evict travellers using their powers under CJPO 1994 in *R v Lincolnshire County Council, ex p Atkinson*; *R v Wealden District Council, ex p Wales*; *ex p Stratford* ('*Wealden*')[1] Sedley J held that the welfare circumstances of trespassing travellers could not 'be ignored when dealing with one of the most fundamental human needs; the need for shelter with a modicum of security'. Accordingly, it was held that the welfare circumstances of trespassing travellers was a material consideration which had to be taken into account by a local authority before deciding whether or not to evict them using its powers under HRA 1998.

1 [1996] JPLCL Vol 160, 580.

The *Wealden* decision was approved of and applied by the Divisional Court in *R v Wolverhampton MBC, ex p Dunne and Rafferty*.[2] Further, in *R v Kerrier District Council, ex p Uzell*[3] it was held that the same approach was appropriate when considering a challenge to the decision of a planning authority to take enforcement action against a group of travellers unlawfully occupying a site in breach of planning control.

Additionally, and perhaps most significantly, in *R v Brighton and Hove Council, ex p Marmont*[4] Tucker J held that even when a local authority was seeking to exercise its proprietary rights as a landowner by commencing summary possession proceedings against trespassing travellers under Order 113 of the Rules of the Supreme Court, it was still necessary to take into account the welfare needs of the travellers before deciding whether or not to evict them. That said, Tucker J went on to accept the argument of Leading Counsel for the Respondent authority that the extent of the discretion allowed to a local authority when seeking to enforce its proprietary rights as a landowner was a wide one and that on the facts the authority's decision was reasonable.

Most recently, the approach taken in *Marmont* seems to have been taken a stage further in *R v Hillingdon London Borough Council, ex p McDonagh*.[5] This was also a judicial review challenge to a decision of the respondent local authority to commence summary possession proceedings to evict trespassing travellers from its own land. In dismissing the application Carnwath J held that a local authority was not obliged to carry out exhaustive welfare investigations into the circumstances of the trespassing travellers, since this would impede the efficacy of the summary possession procedure.

THE POSITION AFTER INCORPORATION OF THE CONVENTION UNDER HRA 1998

Once HRA 1998 comes into force, the legal landscape in respect of local authority eviction decisions against trespassing travellers or gypsies will be significantly changed by the need to ensure that the actions of local authorities are compatible with Convention rights.[6] Of particular relevance in this context will be Art 8 of the Convention and the right to respect for a person's home provided for therein.

The possible scope of the right to respect for a person's home was considered by the European Court of Human Rights ('ECHR') in *Buckley v United Kingdom*.[7]

Buckley involved a challenge by Mrs Buckley, a gypsy, who had purchased a plot of land and applied for planning permission for three caravans. The local planning authority refused to grant Mrs Buckley planning permission because the caravan development would detract from the rural landscape contrary to the local development plan and would jeopardise road safety. Having refused planning permission, the authority issued an enforcement notice and then instituted criminal proceedings for failure to comply with the enforcement notice. Mrs Buckley alleged that this enforcement action constituted a violation of her rights under Art 8 of the Convention and/or of Art 8 in conjunction with Art 14.

2 (1996) 29 HLR 745.
3 (1995) 71 P & CR 566
4 [1998] 2 PLR 48.
5 (1998) 31 HLR 531.
6 See s 6 of HRA 1998.
7 (1996) 23 EHRR 101.

The ECHR held:

> (1) the right to respect for a person's 'home' provided for in Art 8 of the Convention could be relied on, even where that home had been unlawfully occupied or established;
> (2) the refusal of planning permission, the issuing of an enforcement notice, and the prosecution for failure to comply with the enforcement notice, constituted interference by a public authority with Mrs Buckley's right to respect for her home under Art 8(1);
> (3) the enforcement of planning control had been in pursuit of the legitimate aims of public safety, economic wellbeing, protection of health, and protection of the rights of others as set out in Art 8(2);
> (4) as to the necessity of that interference as required by Art 8(2):
> - the interests of the community had to be balanced against Mrs Buckley's right to respect for her home;
> - there had to be a fair decision-making process;
> - there was a wide margin of appreciation allowed for national authorities in relation to planning matters;
>
> (5) on the facts, the means employed by the planning authority to achieve the legitimate aims pursued could not be regarded as disproportionate, so that the interference with the right to respect for home was justified in accordance with Art 8(2);
> (6) further, that there had been no discrimination contrary to Art 14.

The practical significance of the *Buckley* decision is that local authorities will have to be prepared to justify the proportionality of any decision to evict trespassing travellers or gypsies relative to the legitimate aims being pursued. Of course, a key question when seeking to justify any local authority eviction decision will be the extent to which the English court applies a wide margin of appreciation to any such decision.

The ECHR in *Buckley* held that there was a wide margin of appreciation for national authorities in planning matters because the national authorities are, in principle, better placed than an international court to evaluate local needs and conditions. A similar argument applies in the domestic context, namely that local planning authorities are in principle better placed than a court to evaluate local needs and conditions by virtue of their day-to-day contact with local planning control issues. Accordingly, it is likely that the English courts will also apply a wide margin of appreciation to local authority eviction decisions taken in the planning context.

As to eviction decisions taken by a local authority as a landowner and implemented by way of ordinary possession proceedings, it is strongly arguable that a similarly wide margin of appreciation is appropriate given that the local authority is simply seeking to enforce its proprietary rights as a landowner against persons unlawfully occupying its land.

Nonetheless, even on the assumption that the English courts will apply a margin of appreciation to local authority eviction decisions which will allow significant latitude, it is still the case that the intensity with which decisions are reviewed will be greater than under a *Wednesbury* irrationality principle. As it was put in *R v Lord Saville of Newdigate, ex p A* [8] (the case on the naming of soldiers involved in the 'Bloody Sunday'

8 *The Times*, 29 July 1999 (Court of Appeal).

inquiry), the possible infringement of fundamental rights involves 'anxious scrutiny' and the lowering of the threshold of reasonableness.

When considering the proportionality of any decision to evict trespassing travellers or gypsies, a key consideration is likely to be the extent to which alternative sites are available within any given geographical area. This is underlined by a number of recent cases considered by the European Commission of Human Rights on 4 March 1998.[9] The Commission considered seven applications all on facts similar to those in *Buckley* and complaining, inter alia, of a violation of Art 8. The Commission declared that six of the seven applications were admissible. The single inadmissible application, the *Andrew Smith* case, can be distinguished from the other applications on the basis that there was no clear evidence suggesting a lack of alternative sites.

A further point of practical significance in the context of ordinary civil possession proceedings brought by a local authority is that trespassing travellers or gypsies will be able to seek to rely on their right to respect for their home under Art 8 by way of a defence in the possession proceedings themselves.[10] This will enable the travellers or gypsies to avoid the process of having to apply for the possession proceedings to be adjourned, pending the outcome of separate judicial review proceedings, as currently required by the decision of the Court of Appeal in *Avon County Council v Buscott*.[11]

Moreover, by s 22(4) of HRA 1998, this option will be available to the travellers or gypsies as soon as HRA 1998 comes into force, regardless of whether the decision to commence possession proceedings was taken by the authority before or after the coming into force of HRA 1998. Given the uncertainty about precisely when HRA 1998 will come into force, the practical effect of this is that local authorities should be considering whether eviction decisions are compatible with the Convention as from now.

Finally, even before the coming into force of HRA 1998 there is another reason why local authorities should be careful to consider the particular circumstances of trespassing travellers or gypsies before deciding whether to pursue eviction proceedings against them, namely the terms of the 'Good Practice Guide' on 'Managing Unauthorised Camping' published by the Government in October 1998. Throughout this document there is a heavy emphasis on the need to take account of the needs of travellers and gypsies and to give full consideration to tolerating unauthorised encampments wherever possible. Indeed, the key principle which underlies the Guide is stated to be (at para 5.8) that 'A nomadic way of life is legitimate ... Gypsies and Travellers should be accommodated and "tolerated" wherever practicable, and wherever serious problems do not arise from the encampment'. This represents a tangible shift in approach by central government and is in itself likely to result in local authority decisions to evict travellers or gypsies being subject to closer scrutiny by the English courts.

9 [1998] 25 EHRR (CD) 24, 28, 42, 46, 49, 52, 64.
10 See s 7(1)(b) of HRA 1998.
11 [1988] 1 All ER 841.

Licensing

INTRODUCTION

Local authorities have a miscellany of licensing powers, ranging from theatres and public entertainments to street trading and acupuncture. Local authorities must comply with the principles of natural justice, in addition to any statutory restrictions, when exercising these powers.

There are two Articles of the Convention which are of particular significance to local authority licensing, Art 6(1) which provides for the right to a fair and public hearing and Art 1(1) of the First Protocol which concerns the right to peaceful enjoyment of one's possessions. There are a number of important decisions of the European Court of Human Rights ('ECHR') and European Commission of Human Rights ('the Commission') relating to this area.

Article 6(1) provides that:

> In the determination of his civil rights and obligations or of any criminal charge against him, everyone is entitled to a fair and public hearing within a reasonable time by an independent and impartial tribunal established by law.

THE APPLICATION OF ARTICLE 6(1)

Article 6(1) will apply to the exercise of a licensing power only if it constitutes the 'determination' of a 'civil right'. Both these terms have been given a broad interpretation in ECHR jurisprudence.

The term 'civil right' has an 'autonomous Convention meaning' and is not confined to rights which are classified as private rights in national law. ECHR has recognised the right to engage in commercial activities as a 'civil right' and on this basis has held that Art 6 applies to the licensing of such activities.[1] It is immaterial that the grant or retention of a licence is a matter of discretion rather than an entitlement, and decisions relating both to new and existing licences are covered.[2]

1 See, for example, *Pudas v Sweden* A/125 (1987) 10 EHRR 380 (withdrawal of an interurban transport licence from a private passenger carrier) and *Tre Traktörer Aktiebolag v Sweden* A/159 (1989) 13 EHRR 309 (withdrawal of an alcohol licence from a restaurant).

2 *Benthem v Netherlands* A/97 (1995) 8 EHRR 1 (application for a licence to operate a liquid petroleum gas installation).

A 'determination' requires a 'dispute' or 'contestation' whose outcome is decisive of the applicant's civil rights and obligations.[3] However, ECHR has held that 'contestation' (a term appearing in the French, but not the English, text of Art 6(1)) should be given a 'substantive rather than a formal meaning',[4] and that it extends to administrative measures taken by bodies exercising public authority.[5] It applies equally to questions of law and fact.[6] Disputes concerning the scope of a right, or the manner in which it may be exercised, are covered in addition to those relating to the existence of the right.[7] Once again, it is immaterial that the right in question is discretionary, provided that the applicant can invoke administrative law principles to control the exercise of the discretion.[8] This means that licensing applications, as well as revocations, involve 'determinations', even though local authorities may have a broad discretion in deciding whether or not a licence should be granted or renewed.

WHAT DOES ARTICLE 6(1) REQUIRE?

Article 6(1) requires 'a fair and public hearing by an independent and impartial tribunal established by law'.

There is an extensive jurisprudence as to the elements of a 'fair and public hearing'. The right to a court is fundamental,[9] as is 'equality of arms', the principle that each party should 'be afforded a reasonable opportunity to present his case ... under conditions that do not place him at a substantial disadvantage vis-à-vis his opponent'.[10] ECHR has also held that the right to a 'public hearing' may entail an entitlement to an oral hearing, at least in circumstances where the jurisdiction of a court covers issues both of fact and law.[11] However, on the basis of Convention case law it is immaterial whether local authorities themselves comply with such requirements because an administrative body does not constitute an 'independent and impartial tribunal' for the purposes of Art 6(1).[12]

This does not mean that current licensing procedures will necessarily violate Art 6(1), however. ECHR has held that its requirements may still be satisfied if the proceedings are 'subject to subsequent control by a judicial body that has full jurisdiction and does provide the guarantees of Art 6(1)'.[13]

ARE THE REQUIREMENTS OF ARTICLE 6(1) MET?

The test of subsequent control by a judicial body with full jurisdiction will be met where the decision is subject to appeal in a court which is able to examine the

3 *Ringeisen v Austria* A/13 (1971) 1 EHRR 455, para 94.
4 *Le Compte, Van Leuven and De Meyere v Belgium* A/43 (1981) 4 EHRR 1, para 45.
5 *König v Germany* A/27 (1978) 2 EHRR 170, para 90.
6 *Le Compte* n 4, para 51
7 *Le Compte* para 49.
8 *Pudas* n 1, para 34.
9 *Golder v United Kingdom* A/18 (1975) 1 EHRR 524.
10 *Dombo Beheer BV v Netherlands* [1993] A 274-A 18 EHRR 213, para 33.
11 *Fredin v Sweden (No 2)* (1994) A 283 para 21.
12 Independent means 'independent of the executive and also of the parties': *Ringeisen* n 3, para 95.
13 *Albert and Le Compte v Belgium* A/58 (1983) 5 EHRR 533, para 29.

merits of the case. A much more difficult question is whether it will be satisfied by judicial review proceedings, where the courts are currently confined to examining whether the decision is tainted by illegality, irrationality or procedural impropriety.

Convention jurisprudence suggests that Art 6(1) requires full appellate jurisdiction, at least where the decision does not involve matters of general policy. In *W v United Kingdom* the applicant complained about the denial of access to his children who had been taken into care. ECHR found that Art 6(1) had been violated, notwithstanding that an application for judicial review could be made. There could be no 'determination' in accordance with Art 6(1) in the absence of a tribunal with jurisdiction to examine the merits of the matter.[14]

By contrast, in *Zumbotel v Austria,* a case involving expropriation of land by a government office to build a road, ECHR held that Art 6(1) was complied with even though the jurisdiction of the Austrian Administrative Court was limited to the lawfulness of the administrative action. The Court pointed out that the Administrative Court had, in fact, 'considered ... [the applicant's] submissions on their merits, point by point, without ever having to decline jurisdiction in replying to them or in ascertaining various facts ... *Regard being had to the respect which must be accorded to decisions taken by the administrative authorities on grounds of expediency* (my emphasis) and to the nature of the complaints made by the Zumbotel partnership, the review of the Administrative Court accordingly, in this instance, fulfilled the requirements of Art 6(1)'.[15]

This approach was followed by the Commission in *ISKCON v United Kingdom* when it held that the limitation on the jurisdiction of the High Court to points of law in relation to an enforcement notice in the planning context did not infringe Art 6. The Commission emphasised that it is:

> 'not the role of Art 6 ... to give access to a level of jurisdiction which can substitute ... [the High Court's] opinion for that of the administrative authorities on questions of expediency and where the courts do not refuse to examine any of the points raised ... '.[16]

It seems, therefore, that the question of whether Art 6(1) requires a full investigation of the merits of a local authority licensing decision, or the facts relied on in making that decision, may in turn depend on:

(1) the nature of the applicant's submissions; and
(2) whether the decision involves matters of administrative expediency or whether, for example, it is based on a judgment as to the applicant's suitability for a licence. In the latter case full jurisdiction may be required.

Finally, even if there is no necessity to undertake a full investigation of the merits or facts relied on, Art 6(1) probably requires that a licensing decision should be susceptible to judicial review by reference to the principle of proportionality, which may open it to closer scrutiny than the existing grounds of illegality, irrationality and procedural impropriety.

14 A/121 (1987) 10 EHRR 29 para 82.
15 A/268-A (1993) 17 EHRR 116, para 32.
16 Application 20490/92 76A DR 90 (1994)..

ARTICLE 1 OF PROTOCOL NO 1

Article 1 of Protocol No 1 provides that:

> (1) Every natural or legal person is entitled to the peaceful enjoyment of his possessions. No one shall be deprived of his possessions except in the public interest and subject to the conditions provided for by law and by the general principles of international law.
> (2) The preceding provisions shall not, however, in any way impair the right of a State to enforce such laws as it deems necessary to control the use of property in accordance with the general interest or to secure the payment of taxes or other contributions or penalties.

THE APPLICATION OF ARTICLE 1 OF PROTOCOL NO 1

ECHR has analysed Art 1 as comprising three distinct rules. The first rule, which is expressed in the first sentence, is of a general nature and lays down the principle of peaceful enjoyment of property. The second rule, contained in the second sentence of the first paragraph, covers deprivation of possessions and subjects it to certain conditions. The third rule, stated in the second paragraph, recognises that the states are entitled, among other things, to control the use of property in accordance with the general interest. Before considering whether the first rule has been complied with, the court determines whether either of the last two are applicable.[17]

These rules are not 'distinct' in the sense of being unconnected. The second and third rules concern particular instances of interference with the general right and are to be construed in the light of the principle enunciated in the first rule.[18] In deciding cases under all three rules, ECHR and the Commission have applied a test of 'fair balance' between the demands of the general interest of the community and the protection of the individual's rights.[19]

ARTICLE 1 OF PROTOCOL 1 AND LICENSING PROCEDURES

The term 'possessions' in Art 1 is not confined to physical possessions and extends to other rights and interests which have an economic value. Only existing possessions are included.

In *Tre Trektorer Aktiebolag v Sweden*[20] ECHR held that the economic interests connected with the running of a restaurant were 'possessions' for the purposes of the Article. Withdrawal of the licence to serve alcohol, which had adverse effects on the restaurant's goodwill and value, constituted an interference with the right to the peaceful enjoyment of these possessions. The court did not treat the interference as a 'deprivation', however, although the owners could not continue to operate the property as a restaurant, they retained some economic interests by

17 *Sporrong and Lonnroth v Sweden* A/52, para 61 (1982) 5 EHRR 35.
18 *James v United Kingdom* A/98 (1986) 8 EHRR 123, para 37.
19 In *Sporrong* n 17, the applicants' inability to claim compensation for (or a reduction in the length of) long-term expropriation permits on their property resulted in a finding that the appropriate 'fair balance' had not been struck for the purposes of the general right
20 [1989] A 159 13 EHRR 309.

their leasing of the premises. Rather it treated the withdrawal of the licence as a control over the use of the property.

In circumstances where withdrawal of a licence leaves the former licence-holder with no remaining economic interest in a business, this may be more properly analysed as a 'deprivation'. In practice the category of interference probably matters little. The interference is likely to be seen as justified provided that the authority has acted lawfully and in pursuance of the general or public interest.

The Strasbourg organs have been reluctant to interfere with the judgment of individual states that interference is in the public interest where the conditions for expropriation or the control over the use of property have been enshrined in legislation. It remains to be seen whether domestic courts will take a different view. As in the case of Art 6(1), however, authorities will in any event need to ensure that their decisions can withstand scrutiny by reference to the principle of proportionality.[21]

CONCLUSION

How will local authority reasoning in taking licensing decisions have to change?

Local authorities taking licensing decisions will need to pay specific attention to the proportionality of their actions. It is likely that the introduction of this requirement will bring a greater number of challenges to licensing decisions in the courts.

21 In *Tre Traktörer Aktiebolag* the court found that the withdrawal of the licence, being authorised by the relevant legislation, was lawful, and in the circumstances (inadequate book-keeping and internal controls by the restaurant's owners) did not breach the principle of proportionality.

Chapter 7

Discrimination

INTRODUCTION

There is no general right not to suffer discrimination under the European Convention on Human Rights ('the Convention'). This contrasts, for example, with the broad protection provided by Art 26 of the UN International Covenant on Civil and Political Rights, which places an obligation on contracting states to prohibit, and guarantee effective protection against, discrimination of all kinds. The Convention, and thus the Human Rights Act 1998 ('HRA 1998'), provide a more limited form of protection against discrimination.

Article 14 of the Convention states:

> 'The enjoyment of the rights and freedoms set forth in this Convention shall be secured without discrimination on any ground such as sex, race, colour, language, religion, political or other opinion, national or social origin, association with a national minority, property, birth or any other status.'

Broadly, discrimination under Art 14 consists of differential treatment, on any ground, in relation to the enjoyment of a right which is within the scope of the Convention, involving two or more persons in an analogous situation, in circumstances in which the differential treatment is not shown to be justified.

This chapter considers the principles to be applied when considering each of these various distinct but closely related elements, and some aspects of how those principles apply in the context of local authority functions.

RELATIONSHIP BETWEEN ARTICLE 14 AND OTHER ARTICLES OF THE CONVENTION

Article 14 prohibits the state from discriminating in the way that it secures the enjoyment of Convention rights. It might be thought, in the light of this, that an applicant would have to establish an infringement of another Convention right in order to establish an infringement of Art 14. The European Court of Human Rights ('ECHR') has, however, rejected such a narrow interpretation. In the leading case on Art 14, the *Belgian Linguistics* case,[1] ECHR held that there may be a violation of Art 14, notwithstanding the fact that there has been no

1 (1968) 1 EHRR 252.

infringement of any other Article of the Convention. Equally, where ECHR has found that there has been an infringement of another Convention right, it has shown reluctance to consider the application of Art 14, doing so only where the inequality of treatment in the enjoyment of the particular right is 'a fundamental aspect of the case'.[2]

What is necessary to succeed, however, under Art 14, is to show that the discriminatory act falls within the 'ambit' of one of the other Articles of the convention.[3] What is meant by the 'ambit' of a Convention article? There is no very clear definition of this term in the jurisprudence of ECHR. It is clear, however, that it is not limited to the positive right or obligation conferred or imposed by the Article in question. An Article may secure only limited positive rights for the person, or impose only a negative obligation on the state. Where the state chooses, however, to secure rights which are broader than those immediately protected by a given Article, but which nevertheless fall within its scope, it must do so without discrimination. So, for example, Art 6 of the Convention, which confers a right to a fair trial, does not impose any obligation on the state to provide a right of appeal. If, however, the state chooses to provide such a right, it must ensure that all persons have an equal opportunity to avail themselves of that right. Failure to do so may amount to a violation of Art 6 in conjunction with Art 14.

The application of this principle has important implications for local authorities, expanding the scope for convention claims against them in areas of activity which would otherwise be unlikely to give rise to liability. For example, Art 2 of the First Protocol states 'no person shall be denied the right to education'. This Article confers no positive right to any particular form of education. If the state provides education, however, it must do so in a non-discriminatory way. Failure to do so will amount to a breach of both Art 14 and Art 2 of the First Protocol (see the *Belgian Linguistics* case). Thus, a refusal by an education authority to provide a particular type of schooling in its area would not be a breach of the Convention, but the adoption of an entrance policy to the schools it did provide, which operated in a discriminatory manner would, if not justified, amount to a breach of Art 14 coupled with Art 2 of the First Protocol.

Another example is afforded by Art 8, which enshrines the right to respect for private and family life. This Article confers no obligation on the state to provide a home. Where a local authority as part of its functions provides housing, it should do so in a way which is non-discriminatory. See, for an example of the application of Art 14 in a housing context, *Gillow v United Kingdom*,[4] a case which concerned the requirement in Guernsey to obtain a licence to reside there.

PROHIBITED GROUNDS OF DISCRIMINATION

Domestic law in England and Wales prohibits discrimination on a number of limited grounds, namely race, sex and disability. See, the Race Relations Act 1976, the Sex Discrimination Act 1975 and the Disability Discrimination Act 1995. Under these Acts, if the Respondent can show that the discrimination occurred for a reason other than race, sex, or disability, the claim will fail. The Convention and HRA 1998 is much broader in scope. Discrimination is expressly

2 *Airey v Ireland* A/32 (1979) 2 EHRR 305.
3 See, *Abdulaziz, Cabales and Balkandali v United Kingdom* (1985) 7 EHHR 471.
4 (1986) 11 EHRR 335.

prohibited on a wide range of grounds which include race and sex, but also include language, religion, property and political beliefs. Moreover, the list of grounds set out in Art 14 is open-ended: it includes 'any other status'. ECHR has characterised a large number of other grounds as falling within this category, including sexual orientation, legitimacy, trade union membership and professional status.

It may appear from this, that the ground of discrimination is itself of little importance. This is to overlook, however, the part it plays when the court comes to consider other essential elements of discrimination under Art 14. In particular, the ground can be of importance when seeking to establish that the applicant is in an analogous situation to someone whom he complains has been treated differently in breach of Art 14. Moreover, the ground is of key relevance when the court comes to consider the question of justification. Some types of discrimination are easier to justify than others. Each of these two issues is considered further below.

COMPARATOR

In order to succeed in a claim under Art 14, it is essential to establish that the differential treatment of the applicant and other persons was afforded in an analogous situation. In other words, like must be compared with like. It is at this stage that the ground of discrimination may become of indirect importance. It may be relatively straightforward to establish that, where the ground of discrimination is sex or race, the comparator is in a relevantly similar situation. Where, however, the ground is less 'straightforward', it may be difficult to persuade the court that the situations are analogous. For example, in *Van der Mussele v Belgium*,[5] the court held that a pupil barrister who complained about having to perform work for the state without payment was not in an analogous situation to those in other professions who had no such obligation. This was due to a difference in such matters as the conditions for entry to the professions in question and the functions performed by the professions. Equally, in *DG and DW Lindsay v United Kingdom*[6] the Applicants, who were cohabitees, failed to establish that they were in an analogous situation to a married couple.

DIRECT AND INDIRECT DISCRIMINATION

Domestic discrimination law and European sex discrimination law prohibit both direct and indirect discrimination. Direct discrimination occurs where a person is treated differently to another because of his status. Indirect discrimination occurs when two persons of different status are treated the same, but the nature of the treatment is such as to place persons of one status at a disadvantage compared to the other. For example, a workplace dress code that prohibited the wearing of hats or scarves would, even though applied equally to all employees, discriminate against a Sikh employee whose religion required him to wear a turban.

It is not certain to what extent the principle of indirect discrimination applies under th Convention or under HRA 1998. In the case of *Marckx v Belgium*,[7] ECHR

5 (1983) 6 EHRR 163.
6 Application 11089/84 49 DR 181 (1986).
7 A/31 (1979) 2 EHRR 330.

suggested that rules having a discriminatory effect would be prohibited by the Convention. No case before ECHR, however, has yet been decided on this basis. It may be that domestic courts applying the Convention under HRA 1998, which are familiar with the concept of indirect discrimination under existing domestic law, will be more willing to decide cases based on the principle of indirect discrimination.

This may prove to be the case, for example, in relation to differential treatment on the grounds of religion in an employment context. This is an area in which local authorities may well adopt differential policies. For example, employees are generally given time off to celebrate Christmas, but they are not always given time off to celebrate the Muslim festival of Eid. In the case of *Ahmad v United Kingdom*,[8] European Commission on Human Rights rejected a Muslim teacher's complaint that he had been discriminated against under Art 14, coupled with Art 9, because he was not permitted time off to attend the Mosque on Fridays. In the course of its report, the Commission commented that the religious holidays of the majority of the population tended to be public holidays, which was not true of the religious holidays of minorities. This may make it difficult for an applicant of a religious minority, who wishes to complain that he has been adversely treated in connection with the taking of religious holidays, and perhaps in connection with other religious requirements, by comparison with a member of the religious majority, to establish that the differential treatment occurs in an analogous situation. In these circumstances, however, there may be a potential claim for indirect discrimination. For an example of where such a claim succeeded under the Race Relations Act 1976, see *J H Walker Ltd v Hussain*.[9]

Justification

On its face, Art 14 suggests that the prohibition on discrimination is absolute, that is to say, any act of discrimination, however minor or justified in the circumstances, would constitute a breach. In the *Belgian Linguistics* case, however, ECHR rejected such an inflexible approach. It held that the principle of equality of treatment enshrined in Art 14 is breached only if the distinction has no 'objective and reasonable justification'. The court went on to elaborate on what was required to show an objective and reasonable justification. It said:

> 'A difference in treatment in the exercise of a right laid down in the Convention must not only pursue a legitimate aim: Art 14 is likewise violated when it is clearly established that there is no reasonable relationship of proportionality between the means employed and the aim sought to be realised'.

The test of justification is thus two-fold. The treatment must pursue a legitimate aim and it must be proportionate to that aim.

It is important to note that the defence of justification is available even where the discrimination alleged is 'direct' discrimination. In other words, it may be permissible in certain circumstances to treat men and women, or persons of one ethnic origin and those of another, differently, or even to adopt a policy of positive

8 (1979) 4 EHRR 126.
9 (1982) IRLR 11 (EAT).

discrimination. This contrasts with the position under domestic sex and race discrimination legislation, which, broadly, prohibits all direct discrimination on grounds of sex or race, and provides for the defence of justification only in cases of indirect discrimination.

In determining whether a particular measure is justified, ECHR has recognised that there is a 'margin of appreciation' within which contracting states must be free to choose how they implement Convention rights.[10] The width of the margin of appreciation (that is, the scope of the state's discretion), however, and the degree of cogency of the justification required by the court, vary from case to case depending on the nature of the discrimination in issue. The court has adopted a very strict approach to justification, affording a narrow margin of appreciation in relation to certain types of discrimination, including discrimination on grounds of sex, race, nationality and legitimacy. It has held that such discrimination requires 'very weighty reasons' to be justified.[11] By contrast, the court has been willing to afford states a wide discretion in determining whether discrimination on the ground of 'property' is justified.[12]

The two elements in the test of justification require separate consideration. A measure may pursue a legitimate aim, but nevertheless its application in a particular context may be unjustified because the effect of the discrimination on the individual is disproportionately harmful. In a local authority context, it is likely that it is the proportionality requirement that will, in practice, prove more difficult to establish than the requirement to pursue a legitimate aim. That is because, in many cases, it will be relatively easy to satisfy a court that a particular policy pursues a legitimate aim. For example, the promotion of collective bargaining,[13] the protection of the family,[14] the protection of the health of children,[15] and the giving of preferential treatment in relation to housing to those with strong attachments to an area,[15] have all been held to be legitimate aims. It is these types of policies which are likely to underlie the decisions and acts of many local authorities.[16]

It may be less easy to show, however, that the pursuit of a particular policy is proportionate in the circumstances of an individual case. Difficulties may arise where a policy is applied across the board without reference to the need to do so, or the effect of doing so, in relation to a particular individual. For example, in the case of *Vogt v Germany*,[17] the state was found to have acted in breach of Art 14 coupled with Arts 10 and 11, when it dismissed a teacher because she was a member of the local Communist Party. Although the aim of the state in dismissing her, namely the protection of the German constitution, was held to be legitimate, her sacking was disproportionate in the circumstances because there was no

10 See for example, the case of *Swedish Engine Drivers' Union v Sweden* A/20 (1976) 1 EHRR 617.

11 See, *Schmidt v Germany* A/291-B (1994) 18 EHRR 513 (sex); *East African Asians Cases* (1970) YB 928 (race); *Inze v Austria* A/126 (1987) 10 EHRR 394 (illegitimacy); *Gaygusuz v Austria* Application 17371/90 23 EHRR 365 (nationality); *Hoffman v Austria* [1993] Series A 255-VC (1993) 17 EHRR 293 (religion).

12 See for example, *Gillow v United Kingdom.*

13 *National Union of Belgian Police v Belgium* A/19 (1975) 1 EHRR 578.

14 Application 11716/85 *S v United Kingdom* 47 DR 274 (1986).

15 *Hoffman v Austria.*

16 *Gillow v United Kingdom.*

17 A/323 (1995) 21 EHRR 205.

evidence that she had ever been guilty of any inappropriate behaviour or failure in her duties as a teacher, and because it was difficult in Germany to obtain work as a teacher outside the state system. This case should, however, be contrasted with the case of *Ahmed v United Kingdom*,[18] in which ECHR held that the policy of ensuring political neutrality among local government officers was sufficient justification for placing prohibitions on their political affiliations.

Finally, ECHR has shown reluctance to go behind the reasons advanced by a state for particular treatment to find a discriminatory motivation. Thus in *Abdulaziz, Cabales and Balkandali v United Kingdom*,[19] the court found that the reasons advanced by the Government for a particular immigration policy, namely protecting the labour market and public order, were not a cover for a racially motivated exclusion policy. It is likely that the domestic courts will be equally unsympathetic to claims brought against local authorities which involve accusations of ulterior motivation, at least in the formulation of policy.

18 [1999] IRLR 188
19 (1995) 7 EHRR 471..

Chapter 8

Access to Information

INTRODUCTION

The European Convention on Human Rights ('ECHR') does not endow individuals with any general rights of access to information about them which is being held by public authorities. Thus, for example, the Convention creates no general right of access to police records or to files held by national security agencies. However, under Art 8 of the Convention, which guarantees the individual's right to respect for private or family life, it is possible for individuals to be granted a right of access in certain limited circumstances.

Likewise, while the Convention does not usually confer on individuals a general power to veto decisions by a public authority to hold information about them or to disclose that information to third parties, Art 8 may afford the individual a right to prevent the authority from using information which comes into its possession in a way that is damaging to his private or family life.

Determining the circumstances in which an individual will be able to rely on Art 8 is the key to understanding the limited fashion in which the Convention will assist him to gain control of personal information which is being held by public bodies.

ARTICLE 8

Article 8 of ECHR provides as follows:

> '1. Everyone has the right to respect for his private and family life, his home and his correspondence.
>
> 2. There shall be no interference by a public authority with the exercise of this right except such as is in accordance with the law and is necessary in a democratic society in the interests of national security, public safety or the economic well-being of the country, for the prevention of disorder or crime, for the protection of health or morals or for the protection of rights and freedoms of others'.

That Art 8 can operate as a shield protecting individuals against unwarranted incursions into their private and family lives by public authorities is readily apparent from the wording of that provision. Except in certain limited circumstances, individuals can expect public authorities not to interfere with their private life and this includes expecting that authority not to use information which it has obtained in respect of a particular individual in a way that damages that individual's private life.[1]

However, Art 8 cannot be relied on to create, for the individual, an unfettered right to control the manner in which public authorities use the information which they have obtained, because the right of control which is engendered by Art 8 is restricted in a number of key ways. Most importantly, the individual will not be able to use Art 8 in circumstances where:

(1) the authority is seeking to use information relating to that individual which cannot properly be described as 'private'. Information about an individual will be private if it pertains to the individual's 'private life' as generally defined.[2] Thus, while information contained in an individual's medical records will inevitably be private information, general non-confidential information which is contained in an individual employee's personnel file probably will not;

(2) the particular use of the information does not amount to an 'interference with the individual's private or family life'. In certain circumstances it may be hard for an individual to argue that a public authority has used private information about him in a way that 'interferes with his private life'. Most obviously, if private information comes into the authority's possession and the authority chooses to instantly destroy that information, it is unlikely that that act of destruction would be regarded as a substantive 'interference' with the individual's private life; and/or

(3) the public body can rely on a particular Art 8(2) justification for the use.

JUSTIFYING INTERFERENCE UNDER ARTICLE 8(2)

There have been a number of cases which have considered the question of whether, on the assumption that there has been a *prima facie* breach of Art 8 by reason that the public authority has been holding or disclosing private information about an individual in a way that is damaging to that individual's private life, there is nonetheless a justification for that interference.

The general principle that the interference may be justified where it is in accordance with the domestic law and is necessary in a democratic society has been applied by the court in a number of cases. Thus, for example, in the case of *Leander v Sweden*,[3] the applicant was refused permanent employment as a museum technician with the Swedish Naval Museum on account of certain information held on a secret police register which allegedly identified him as a security risk. The court held that, while holding such information on a secret police register and, moreover, disclosing that information manifestly amounted to a *prima facie* breach of the applicant's Art 8 rights, the acts of holding and disclosing the information were justified on the grounds that they were necessary in a democratic society. After having acknowledged that the interest of the respondent state had

1 See, for example, *Leander v Sweden* (1987) 9 EHRR 433; *TV v Finland* (1994)18 EHRR CD179; *Z v Finland* (1997) 25 EHRR 371; *MS v Sweden* [1998] EHRLR 115 and *Andersson v Sweden* (1997) 25 EHRR 722.

2 See *Costello-Roberts v United Kingdom* (1993) 19 EHRR 112.

3 (1987) 9 EHRR 433.

to be 'balanced against the seriousness of the interference with the applicant's right to respect for family life', the court went on to say that it considered that: 'the margin of appreciation available to the respondent state in assessing the pressing social need in the present case, and in particular in choosing the means for achieving the legitimate aim of protecting national security, was a wide one'.

Similarly, in the case of *TV v Finland*,[4] the applicant who was charged with, inter alia, manslaughter and desecration of a corpse through sexual intercourse, sought to rely on Art 8 in order to avoid a situation in which information relating to his HIV positive status would be disclosed to certain prison and medical staff who were dealing with him. The court held unanimously that no such reliance would be permitted. The interference with his private life was justified in all the circumstances.[5]

In *Z v Finland*,[6] the applicant sought to prevent disclosure of medical records in circumstances where that disclosure was being sought on the grounds that it would assist in the investigation and prosecution of a crime. First, the court held that, in general, the strong interest in maintaining confidentiality could not be overridden except in cases where there was a public interest in defeating it; second, that there would be such an interest in circumstances where disclosure of the confidential information was likely to amount to evidence which was decisive of the prosecution for manslaughter; and third, that the proposed public disclosure of court proceedings after ten years would have been a breach.

It is clear that the court is not generally averse to permitting an authority to use private information in a way that undermines the individual's private life in circumstances where prohibiting that use would be manifestly damaging to the interests of the community. However, if the authority cannot demonstrate that the balance weighs decisively in favour of permitting the proposed use, then the individual ought to be able to rely on Art 8(1) in order to protect against the unwanted (and unwarranted) incursion into his private life.

ACCESS TO PRIVATE INFORMATION

Thus far the analysis has focused on the circumstances in which individuals can rely on Art 8 to prevent the authority from using information about them in a way that undermines their private or family life. However, it is important to recognise that Art 8 can also, in certain circumstances, be relied on by an individual to challenge refusals by a public authority to allow that individual access to private information about him which has come into the authority's possession.

In the case of *Gaskin v United Kingdom*,[7] the applicant who, during his childhood had been placed in the care of a particular local authority, wanted to sue that authority in respect of mistreatment which he allegedly suffered while under the authority's care. For the purpose of advancing his case, the applicant sought access to his social services file. That access was refused by the relevant authority.

4 (1994) 18 EHRR CD179.
5 See further, *MS v Sweden* [1998] EHRLR 115, where disclosure of the applicant's medical records to the benefits authority was held to be justified under Art 8(20); and *Anderssson v Sweden* (1997) 25 EHRR 722, where disclosure of information pertaining to the applicant's mental and physical state by a psychiatrist to social services authorities was justified because of the possible impact on the care of the applicant's son.
6 (1997) 25 EHRR 371.
7 (1989) 12 EHRR 36.

The court held that the refusal to grant the applicant access to the files amounted to a breach of Art 8 by reason that it unjustifiably abrogated the applicant's Art 8 right to be able to know and understand their childhood and early development. (Importantly, the social services file was the only coherent record of the applicant's formative years). Indeed the court held that, irrespective of the authority's refusal to grant access, the mere fact that only those who had contributed to the file had to consent to access and, further, that there was no procedure for allowing access when particular contributors refused consent were sufficient to amount to an (unjustified) breach of the individual's Art 8 right.[8]

Similar principles were applied by the court in the case of *McGinley and Egan v United Kingdom.*[9] In that case, the applicants were stationed on or near Christmas Island at the time of the nuclear tests in 1958. Relying, in particular, on Art 8 of the Convention, they complained that their rights to a fair hearing before the Pensions Appeal Tribunal had been violated by the withholding of medical documents which would have helped them to ascertain whether there was a link between their health problems and exposure to radiation. The court came, inter alia, to the following conclusions. First, 'while the object of Art 8 is essentially that of protecting the individual against arbitrary interference by the public authorities, it does not merely compel the state to abstain from such interference. In addition to this primarily negative undertaking, there may be positive obligations inherent in effective respect for private or family life'.[10] Second, it concluded that, 'Where a Government engages in hazardous activities such as those in issue in the present case, which might have hidden adverse consequences on the health of those involved in such activities, respect for private and family life under Art 8 requires that an effective and accessible procedure be established which enables such persons to seek all relevant and appropriate information'.[11] However, on the facts of the case, there was no breach of Art 8.

The court's readiness to impose a positive obligation on public bodies to allow individuals access to private information held in respect of that individual has, in certain important respects, been mirrored by the British government's readiness to institute statutory rules which similarly oblige the body holding private information to grant rights of access to that information.[12] Of particular importance here are the Access to Personal Files Act 1987 and the Access to Personal Files (Social Services) Regulations (SI 1989, No. 206) which were made under that Act, the Access to Health Records Act 1990, and the Data Protection Act 1998.[13]

Since the enactment of the 1987 Access to Personal Files Act and, further, the Access to Health Records Act 1990, a number of applications have been held to be inadmissible by the Commission. In the case of *Martin v United Kingdom*,[14] an applicant who had been diagnosed as suffering from catatonic schizophrenia, pyschopathy and accelerated intellectual maturity and who had been denied access to his medical records sought to rely on his Art 8 rights in order to gain access to those records. The Commission considered that, on the facts, a fair

8 Paragraph 49.
9 (1998) 27 EHRR 1.
10 Paragraph 98.
11 Paragraph 101.
12 Gaskin itself was decided on the basis of events prior to the coming into force of any of those statutory rules.
13 When the DPA 1998 comes into force an increasing proportion of private material held on file will become amenable to the subject access provisions of the Act.
14 (1996) 21 EHRR CD112.

balance had been struck between the applicant's interest on the one hand and the legitimate aim of protecting the applicant's own mental health on the other. In *Wiltshire v United Kingdom*,[15] the Commission considered that it was not a breach of the applicant's Art 8 rights for the relevant authority to 'edit' the applicant's file in order to protect third parties and/or to refuse to provide certain documents not contained in that file. However, one should not infer from these cases that Art 8 has now been exhaustively applied in the context of access to private information. Article 8 may still have a role to play in pushing back the boundaries of domestic legislation in circumstances where the legislation does not identify the access rules which are to be applied by the relevant public body.[16]

Finally, when assessing the impact of Art 8 on the rights of individuals to gain access to, and have control over, private information held by a public body about them, it is important to bear in mind that, presently at least, there does not appear to be any fundamental mismatch between ECHR jurisprudence and the state of English law on disclosure of confidential information by public bodies. The rights and duties imposed by the common law obligation to maintain confidences would appear, under the existing case law, to be broadly coextensive with the rights and duties imposed by Article. Thus, for example, in the case of *R v Chief Constable of North Wales, ex p Thorpe*,[17] a case where the police revealed to a caravan site owner that the applicant was a sex offender, the court openly referred to the rights and obligations created by Art 8 (although the court found that the rights created by Art 8 were not breached on the facts).

15 (1997) 23 EHRR CD188.

16 See *McMichael v United Kingdom* (1995) 20 EHRR 205, in which the rules relating to access to documents in care proceedings were considered.

17 [1999] QB 396.

Chapter 9

Criminal Prosecutions

INTRODUCTION

At first sight it might be thought that the provisions of the Human Rights Act ('HRA 1998') would have little application to the decisions routinely taken by local authorities which result in magistrates' court prosecutions. On one level the protections which are afforded by Arts 5 and 6 of the Convention (the rights to liberty and security of the person, and to a fair hearing, respectively) could be regarded as matters which will affect only the conduct of actual criminal hearings rather than the steps which have been taken prior to any hearing. That would, however, be too simplistic an approach to the ways in which the application of the Convention rights through the provisions of HRA 1998 will impact in this area.

In practice, the Convention rights will have an importance at each stage of the process prior to the actual prosecution in court, not only in relation to the procedures adopted but also in relation to the substantive decisions which are taken. This latter point is expressly provided for in s 3 of HRA 1998 which requires that, as far as possible, legislation (both primary and secondary) is to be interpreted and applied so as to be consistent with the Convention rights. This means that all the Convention rights are potentially in play, not just those which focus specifically on the criminal process.

For present purposes, this means not only that the legislation relied on as the basis for any prosecution will need to be tested by reference to these standards, but also that the decisions to prosecute in individual cases will be open to scrutiny if the effect of the prosecution is to impinge unlawfully on any other of the Convention rights. In addition the procedures adopted in relation to implementing any decision to prosecute must also be consistent with the more specifically procedural safeguards which exist pursuant to Arts 5 and 6.

This chapter will consider issues relevant both to substantive testing and to procedural testing.

SUBSTANTIVE IMPACT

Local legislation

As indicated already, the substantive impact of Convention rights can be at one of two levels. The first is in relation to the legislative provisions themselves. The second is in relation to the application of those provisions to particular situations and circumstances.

With regard to the first of these levels, in the majority of situations this will be a matter outside the role of local authorities. In a range of situations set out in primary legislation, local authorities are entitled to initiate criminal proceedings in order to enforce compliance with planning, environmental and consumer protection standards. In these situations the role of the local authority is simply to initiate proceedings which can have criminal consequences in accordance with the powers provided by Parliament.

One area in which local authorities do retain a legislative function is in relation to local byelaws. Under s 235(1) of the Local Government Act 1972 ('LGA 1972') local authorities are empowered to 'make byelaws for the good rule and government of the whole or any part of the district or borough … and for the prevention and suppression of nuisances therein'. In fact the s 235(1) power is expressly stated to be in addition to any other specific statutory powers to make byelaws (see s 235(3)). Section 237 of LGA 1972 provides that the byelaws made under s 235 may state that any contravention is punishable by fine after summary conviction.

To date, a local authority's powers to make byelaws are regulated in terms of the procedure which must be followed before any regulation is made, and by reference to the notions developed at common law of reasonableness, certainty and repugancy. For present purposes, little needs to be said with regard to reasonableness beyond noting that the level of scrutiny which this entails is almost indistinguishable from the requirements of *Wednesbury* reasonableness. The requirement of certainty also provides only a minimal level of scrutiny. Following the decision of the Court of Appeal in *Percy v Hall*[1] this is basically a matter of linguistic testing. As long as the words used are not so unclear that it is impossible to give them any sensible meaning, it is more likely than not that the byelaw will be lawful. Repugnancy is also a minimal threshold. The general rule in this regard is that a byelaw will be invalid either if it is inconsistent with the general law of the land or if it regulates an activity which is already regulated under some other regulation or statute. This then merely serves to ensure uniformity and consistency rather than any other matters of substance.

The impact of HRA 1998 will be that a local authority's powers in this respect will be subject to control as to the substance of byelaws. Given the potential scope of the rights protected by the Convention, there is little purpose attempting to identify all the various matters which may require reconsideration for this reason. Perhaps, however, the categories of byelaws which may now be most at risk will be those which impinge on rights of freedom of assembly and association, and of freedom of expression.

Application of statutory powers

Under existing statutory schemes, local authorities are, in many instances, responsible for enforcement issues. Obvious examples of this, in which the enforcement options include magistrates' court prosecutions, are the powers which local authorities have under the Town and Country Planning Act 1990, the Environmental Protection Act 1990, the Control of Pollution Act 1974 and the Consumer Protection Act 1987.

All decisions taken under powers of these types will now be subject to challenge in the course of the proceedings if the effect of the prosecution would be contrary

1 [1997] QB 924.

to any of the Convention rights. Each set of circumstances will have to be considered on its own merits. However, in the majority of these situations it is likely that the substance of decisions which have been lawfully taken under, for example the planning regime, will be consistent with any convention rights.

Nevertheless, particular problems do present themselves. What if a local authority has the power to prosecute a statutory offence which itself infringes a Convention right? Examples of this may arise in connection with the powers of local education authorities under s 444 of the Education Act 1996 ('EA 1996'). That section provides that the parents of a child commit an offence if the child regularly fails to attend the school at which he is registered. This provision can lead to apparently anomalous situations. One such arose in *Bath and North East Somerset District Council v Warman*.[2] In that case, the mother of a girl who had failed to attend school was acquitted by the magistrates in circumstances in which, prior to the beginning of the school term, the girl (aged 15) had left home to live with her boyfriend some distance away from her mother. The mother did not know where her daughter lived, and had objected to her leaving home but had been unable to stop her. The magistrates reached the decision to acquit on the basis that it was a defence if it could be demonstrated that the absence had been on account of 'unavoidable cause'.

The local education authority appealed against the acquittal. The appeal was successful and the case was remitted to the magistrates with a direction to convict the mother. The appeal court accepted that the offence was one of strict liability in the sense that there was no need to demonstrate that the absence of the child was the result of any neglect or default on the part of the parent. On this basis, the fact that the cause of the absence had been beyond the mother's control did not mean that the 'unavoidable cause' defence had any application. Although, when remitting the matter to the magistrates, the appeal court gave a clear indication that the appropriate 'penalty' might be an absolute discharge, this does not avoid the fact that the mother has been convicted of an offence because of the deliberate actions of a third party.

The decision in *Warman* is clearly a hard one on the facts which existed. In the vast majority of other situations the notion of parental responsibility for the actions of the child will not be a difficult one to square with the rights which are afforded by the Convention. However, other broader issues might arise in contexts where the parent has withdrawn the child from school as a result of freedom of expression grounds, or grounds founded on religious conviction. Although in these circumstances, the European case law would not provide a great deal of support for the parental position, the UK courts may take the opportunity to readdress the balancing of these various considerations for themselves.

The example of *Warman*, in the context of s 444 of EA 1996, is simply one example of the additional dimension which HRA 1998 issues will bring, both in relation to decisions by local authorities to commence prosecutions and in relation to the types of points which might be raised in the proceedings themselves. Given the fact that in many instances the prosecutions for which local authorities have responsibility arise out of matters which have a direct effect on their constituents it is possible that HRA 1998 issues will be readily forthcoming, at least in terms of the issues being raised by those facing prosecution. The extent to which any such points will succeed to any real purpose, is, however, altogether more doubtful.

2 [1999] ELR 81.

Nevertheless, local authorities will still need to consider what action they should take if it appears that a decision to initiate a prosecution would infringe a Convention right. The protection given to local authorities by s 6 of HRA 1998 is a limited one. A local authority will only be able to hide behind the argument that it was 'only obeying orders' (that is, merely enforcing primary legislation) if there was no alternative way in which it could have acted. Yet in any situation involving a discretionary power to prosecute, it is unlikely that any argument based on s 6 could succeed. The s 6 defence ought to be confined to situations where the local authority is acting in pursuance of a statutory duty and only then when there was no other course of action open to the authority if it was to fulfil that duty.

Procedural impact

The vast majority of the instances in which local authorities have the power to commence criminal proceedings are already well circumscribed by requirements as to the steps which must be taken prior to the initiation of any prosecution. For example, where a local authority needs to commence proceedings to recover unpaid Council Tax, the contents of the notices which must be served are specifically set out by Statutory Instrument.

However, it should be noted that whether or not a matter is regarded as 'criminal' for the purposes of the application of Convention rights will not necessarily be determined by categorisation as criminal or civil in UK statutes.[3] One example is that matters which go to the Parking Adjudicator could fall within the scope of criminal matters for Convention purposes. Whether or not they do will depend on the nature of the offence and the severity of the penalty which may be imposed. Although parking offences are in general 'low level' matters the fact that the purpose of any such penalty is both punitive and deterrent is a strong indication that the matter is of a criminal character. Thus it is at the least arguable that the Convention will apply to matters going before the Parking Adjudicator.

In most cases the existing statutory requirements as to process and procedure will be sufficient to satisfy the requirement under Art 6(3) of the Convention that any person accused of any criminal charge be informed promptly of the nature and cause of the allegation against him. To date, European case law has not interpreted this requirement as entailing any right to prior notification of the evidence which is to be used in support of the prosecution. In *Brozicek v Italy*[4] it was determined that the substance of what was required was that the information provided should list the offences in question, the date and place (if relevant) where they occurred and the legislative provision that had been breached. It is likely, however, that any person who is accused will be entitled to be provided in advance with any evidence which is relied on by the prosecution pursuant to the requirements of Art 6(3)(b) which provide for any accused to be given adequate time and facilities for the preparation of his defence.

However, the one issue which should be noted is the Art 6 protection of the rule against self-incrimination. In its decision in *Saunders v United Kingdom*,[5] the European Court of Human Rights concluded that there had been a breach of Art

3 See *Engel v Netherlands* A/22 (1976) 1 EHRR 647
4 (1989) 12 EHRR 371.
5 (1996) 23 EHRR 313.

6 of the Convention because information obtained by DTI inspectors from the defendant, acting under their powers pursuant to s 436 of the Companies Act 1985, had then been used against the defendant in subsequent criminal proceedings. Those powers effectively gave the inspectors a power to compel the defendant to provide information. If he refused he was subject to punishment as if he was guilty of contempt of court. For present purposes, the important point is that similar difficulties will arise in connection with planning contravention notices under section 171C of the Town and Country Planning Act 1990. These notices can require owners or occupiers of land to provide information as to various matters (for example the use to which the land is put). In many cases, if not all, the service of such a notice is the precursor to the issue of an enforcement notice under s 172. Under s 171D it is an offence not to comply with the requirements of any contravention notice. In principle there is no reason why the logic of the decision in *Saunders* should not apply equally to this situation. In these circumstances any local authority will have to give careful consideration to the use to which the powers under s 171C are put. In practice, it ought no longer to be possible to use those powers as a means of avoiding the need for the local authority to investigate the situation fully for itself.

Despite the fact that, in the vast majority of instances, by following the procedural rules which already exist, local authorities will avoid any real risk of a challenge based on Convention rights, it is obvious that all prosecution decisions should now be assessed against the framework provided by HRA 1998. Regardless of whether or not it is thought likely that the provisions of HRA 1998 would have any immediate substantive impact, in this area as much in any other, the platform provided by the Convention rights must be regarded as just as important a part of the public law landscape as *Wednesbury* standards.

Appendix

Human Rights Act 1998

1998 CHAPTER 42

An Act to give further effect to rights and freedoms guaranteed under the European Convention on Human Rights; to make provision with respect to holders of certain judicial offices who become judges of the European Court of Human Rights; and for connected purposes. [9 November 1998]

BE IT ENACTED by the Queen's most Excellent Majesty, by and with the advice and consent of the Lords Spiritual and Temporal, and Commons, in this present Parliament assembled, and by the authority of the same, as follows:

INTRODUCTION

1 The Convention Rights

(1) In this Act 'the Convention rights' means the rights and fundamental freedoms set out in–

(a) Articles 2 to 12 and 14 of the Convention,
(b) Articles 1 to 3 of the First Protocol, and
(c) Articles 1 and 2 of the Sixth Protocol,

as read with Arts 16 to 18 of the Convention.

(2) Those Articles are to have effect for the purposes of this Act subject to any designated derogation or reservation (as to which see ss 14 and 15).

(3) The Articles are set out in Sch 1.

(4) The Secretary of State may by order make such amendments to this Act as he considers appropriate to reflect the effect, in relation to the United Kingdom, of a protocol.

(5) In subsection (4) 'protocol' means a protocol to the Convention–

(a) which the United Kingdom has ratified; or
(b) which the United Kingdom has signed with a view to ratification.

(6) No amendment may be made by an order under subsection (4) so as to come into force before the protocol concerned is in force in relation to the United Kingdom.

2 Interpretation of Convention rights

(1) A court or tribunal determining a question which has arisen in connection with a Convention right must take into account any–

(a) judgment, decision, declaration or advisory opinion of the European Court of Human Rights,

(b) opinion of the Commission given in a report adopted under Art 31 of the Convention,

(c) decision of the Commission in connection with Art 26 or 27(2) of the Convention, or

(d) decision of the Committee of Ministers taken under Art 46 of the Convention,

whenever made or given, so far as, in the opinion of the court or tribunal, it is relevant to the proceedings in which that question has arisen.

(2) Evidence of any judgment, decision, declaration or opinion of which account may have to be taken under this section is to be given in proceedings before any court or tribunal in such manner as may be provided by rules.

(3) In this section 'rules' means rules of court or, in the case of proceedings before a tribunal, rules made for the purposes of this section–

(a) by the Lord Chancellor or the Secretary of State, in relation to any proceedings outside Scotland;

(b) by the Secretary of State, in relation to proceedings in Scotland; or

(c) by a Northern Ireland department, in relation to proceedings before a tribunal in Northern Ireland–

(i) which deals with transferred matters; and

(ii) for which no rules made under para (a) are in force.

LEGISLATION

3 Interpretation of legislation

(1) So far as it is possible to do so, primary legislation and subordinate legislation must be read and given effect in a way which is compatible with the Convention rights.

(2) This section–

(a) applies to primary legislation and subordinate legislation whenever enacted;

(b) does not affect the validity, continuing operation or enforcement of any incompatible primary legislation; and

(c) does not affect the validity, continuing operation or enforcement of any incompatible subordinate legislation if (disregarding any possibility of revocation) primary legislation prevents removal of the incompatibility.

4 Declaration of incompatibility

(1) Subsection (2) applies in any proceedings in which a court determines whether a provision of primary legislation is compatible with a Convention right.

(2) If the court is satisfied that the provision is incompatible with a Convention right, it may make a declaration of that incompatibility.

(3) Subsection (4) applies in any proceedings in which a court determines whether a provision of subordinate legislation, made in the exercise of a power conferred by primary legislation, is compatible with a Convention right.

(4) If the court is satisfied–

(a) that the provision is incompatible with a Convention right, and

(b) that (disregarding any possibility of revocation) the primary legislation concerned prevents removal of the incompatibility,

it may make a declaration of that incompatibility.

(5) In this section 'court' means–

(a) the House of Lords;

(b) the Judicial Committee of the Privy Council;

(c) the Courts-Martial Appeal Court;

(d) in Scotland, the High Court of Justiciary sitting otherwise than as a trial court or the Court of Session;

(e) in England and Wales or Northern Ireland, the High Court or the Court of Appeal.

(6) A declaration under this section ('a declaration of incompatibility')–

(a) does not affect the validity, continuing operation or enforcement of the provision in respect of which it is given; and

(b) is not binding on the parties to the proceedings in which it is made.

5 Right of Crown to intervene

(1) Where a court is considering whether to make a declaration of incompatibility, the Crown is entitled to notice in accordance with rules of court.

(2) In any case to which subsection (1) applies–

(a) a Minister of the Crown (or a person nominated by him),

(b) a member of the Scottish Executive,

(c) a Northern Ireland Minister,

(d) a Northern Ireland department,

is entitled, on giving notice in accordance with rules of court, to be joined as a party to the proceedings.

(3) Notice under subsection (2) may be given at any time during the proceedings.

(4) A person who has been made a party to criminal proceedings (other than in Scotland) as the result of a notice under subsection (2) may, with leave, appeal to the House of Lords against any declaration of incompatibility made in the proceedings.

(5) In subsection (4)–

'criminal proceedings' includes all proceedings before the Courts-Martial Appeal Court; and

'leave' means leave granted by the court making the declaration of incompatibility or by the House of Lords.

PUBLIC AUTHORITIES

6 Acts of public authorities

(1) It is unlawful for a public authority to act in a way which is incompatible with a Convention right.

(2) Subsection (1) does not apply to an act if–

(a) as the result of one or more provisions of primary legislation, the authority could not have acted differently; or

(b) in the case of one or more provisions of, or made under, primary legislation which cannot be read or given effect in a way which is compatible with the Convention rights, the authority was acting so as to give effect to or enforce those provisions.

(3) In this section 'public authority' includes–

(a) a court or tribunal, and

(b) any person certain of whose functions are functions of a public nature,

but does not include either House of Parliament or a person exercising functions in connection with proceedings in Parliament.

(4) In subsection (3) 'Parliament' does not include the House of Lords in its judicial capacity.

(5) In relation to a particular act, a person is not a public authority by virtue only of subsection (3)(b) if the nature of the act is private.

(6) 'An act' includes a failure to act but does not include a failure to–

(a) introduce in, or lay before, Parliament a proposal for legislation; or

(b) make any primary legislation or remedial order.

7 Proceedings

(1) A person who claims that a public authority has acted (or proposes to act) in a way which is made unlawful by s 6(1) may–

(a) bring proceedings against the authority under this Act in the appropriate court or tribunal, or

(b) rely on the Convention right or rights concerned in any legal proceedings,

but only if he is (or would be) a victim of the unlawful act.

(2) In subsection (1)(a) 'appropriate court or tribunal' means such court or tribunal as may be determined in accordance with rules; and proceedings against an authority include a counterclaim or similar proceeding.

(3) If the proceedings are brought on an application for judicial review, the applicant is to be taken to have a sufficient interest in relation to the unlawful act only if he is, or would be, a victim of that act.

(4) If the proceedings are made by way of a petition for judicial review in Scotland, the applicant shall be taken to have title and interest to sue in relation to the unlawful act only if he is, or would be, a victim of that act.

(5) Proceedings under subsection (1)(a) must be brought before the end of–

(a) the period of one year beginning with the date on which the act complained of took place; or

(b) such longer period as the court or tribunal considers equitable having regard to all the circumstances,

but that is subject to any rule imposing a stricter time limit in relation to the procedure in question.

(6) In subsection (1)(b) 'legal proceedings' includes–

(a) proceedings brought by or at the instigation of a public authority; and

(b) an appeal against the decision of a court or tribunal.

(7) For the purposes of this section, a person is a victim of an unlawful act only if he would be a victim for the purposes of Art 34 of the Convention if proceedings were brought in the European Court of Human Rights in respect of that act.

(8) Nothing in this Act creates a criminal offence.

(9) In this section 'rules' means–

(a) in relation to proceedings before a court or tribunal outside Scotland, rules made by the Lord Chancellor or the Secretary of State for the purposes of this section or rules of court,

(b) in relation to proceedings before a court or tribunal in Scotland, rules made by the Secretary of State for those purposes,
(c) in relation to proceedings before a tribunal in Northern Ireland–
(i) which deals with transferred matters; and
(ii) for which no rules made under paragraph (a) are in force,
rules made by a Northern Ireland department for those purposes,
and includes provision made by order under s 1 of the Courts and Legal Services Act 1990.
(10) In making rules, regard must be had to s 9.
(11) The Minister who has power to make rules in relation to a particular tribunal may, to the extent he considers it necessary to ensure that the tribunal can provide an appropriate remedy in relation to an act (or proposed act) of a public authority which is (or would be) unlawful as a result of s 6(1), by order add to–
(a) the relief or remedies which the tribunal may grant; or
(b) the grounds on which it may grant any of them.
(12) An order made under subsection (11) may contain such incidental, supplemental, consequential or transitional provision as the Minister making it considers appropriate.
(13) 'The Minister' includes the Northern Ireland department concerned.

8 Judicial remedies

(1) In relation to any act (or proposed act) of a public authority which the court finds is (or would be) unlawful, it may grant such relief or remedy, or make such order, within its powers as it considers just and appropriate.
(2) But damages may be awarded only by a court which has power to award damages, or to order the payment of compensation, in civil proceedings.
(3) No award of damages is to be made unless, taking account of all the circumstances of the case, including–
(a) any other relief or remedy granted, or order made, in relation to the act in question (by that or any other court), and
(b) the consequences of any decision (of that or any other court) in respect of that act,
the court is satisfied that the award is necessary to afford just satisfaction to the person in whose favour it is made.
(4) In determining–
(a) whether to award damages, or
(b) the amount of an award,
the court must take into account the principles applied by the European Court of Human Rights in relation to the award of compensation under Art 41 of the Convention.
(5) A public authority against which damages are awarded is to be treated–
(a) in Scotland, for the purposes of s 3 of the Law Reform (Miscellaneous Provisions) (Scotland) Act 1940 as if the award were made in an action of damages in which the authority has been found liable in respect of loss or damage to the person to whom the award is made;
(b) for the purposes of the Civil Liability (Contribution) Act 1978 as liable in respect of damage suffered by the person to whom the award is made.
(6) In this section–
'court' includes a tribunal;
'damages' means damages for an unlawful act of a public authority; and
'unlawful' means unlawful under s 6(1).

9 Judicial acts

(1) Proceedings under s 7(1)(a) in respect of a judicial act may be brought only–
(a) by exercising a right of appeal;
(b) on an application (in Scotland a petition) for judicial review; or
(c) in such other forum as may be prescribed by rules.
(2) That does not affect any rule of law which prevents a court from being the subject of judicial review.
(3) In proceedings under this Act in respect of a judicial act done in good faith, damages may not be awarded otherwise than to compensate a person to the extent required by Art 5(5) of the Convention.
(4) An award of damages permitted by subsection (3) is to be made against the Crown; but no award may be made unless the appropriate person, if not a party to the proceedings, is joined.
(5) In this section–
'appropriate person' means the Minister responsible for the court concerned, or a person or government department nominated by him;
'court' includes a tribunal;
'judge' includes a member of a tribunal, a justice of the peace and a clerk or other officer entitled to exercise the jurisdiction of a court;
'judicial act' means a judicial act of a court and includes an act done on the instructions, or on behalf, of a judge; and
'rules' has the same meaning as in s 7(9).

REMEDIAL ACTION

10 Power to take remedial action

(1)This section applies if–
(a) a provision of legislation has been declared under s 4 to be incompatible with a Convention right and, if an appeal lies–
(i) all persons who may appeal have stated in writing that they do not intend to do so;
(ii) the time for bringing an appeal has expired and no appeal has been brought within that time; or
(iii) an appeal brought within that time has been determined or abandoned; or
(b) it appears to a Minister of the Crown or Her Majesty in Council that, having regard to a finding of ECHR made after the coming into force of this section in proceedings against the United Kingdom, a provision of legislation is incompatible with an obligation of the United Kingdom arising from the Convention.
(2) If a Minister of the Crown considers that there are compelling reasons for proceeding under this section, he may by order make such amendments to the legislation as he considers necessary to remove the incompatibility.
(3) If, in the case of subordinate legislation, a Minister of the Crown considers–
(a) that it is necessary to amend the primary legislation under which the subordinate legislation in question was made, in order to enable the incompatibility to be removed, and
(b) that there are compelling reasons for proceeding under this section, he may by order make such amendments to the primary legislation as he considers necessary.

(4) This section also applies where the provision in question is in subordinate legislation and has been quashed, or declared invalid, by reason of incompatibility with a Convention right and the Minister proposes to proceed under para 2(b) of Sch 2.
(5) If the legislation is an Order in Council, the power conferred by subsection (2) or (3) is exercisable by Her Majesty in Council.
(6) In this section 'legislation' does not include a Measure of the Church Assembly or of the General Synod of the Church of England.
(7) Schedule 2 makes further provision about remedial orders.

OTHER RIGHTS AND PROCEEDINGS

11 Safeguard for existing human rights

A person's reliance on a Convention right does not restrict–
(a) any other right or freedom conferred on him by or under any law having effect in any part of the United Kingdom; or
(b) his right to make any claim or bring any proceedings which he could make or bring apart from ss 7 to 9.

12 Freedom of expression

(1) This section applies if a court is considering whether to grant any relief which, if granted, might affect the exercise of the Convention right to freedom of expression.
(2) If the person against whom the application for relief is made ('the respondent') is neither present nor represented, no such relief is to be granted unless the court is satisfied–
(a) that the applicant has taken all practicable steps to notify the respondent; or
(b) that there are compelling reasons why the respondent should not be notified.
(3) No such relief is to be granted so as to restrain publication before trial unless the court is satisfied that the applicant is likely to establish that publication should not be allowed.
(4) The court must have particular regard to the importance of the Convention right to freedom of expression and, where the proceedings relate to material which the respondent claims, or which appears to the court, to be journalistic, literary or artistic material (or to conduct connected with such material), to–
(a) the extent to which–
(i) the material has, or is about to, become available to the public; or
(ii) it is, or would be, in the public interest for the material to be published;
(b) any relevant privacy code.
(5) In this section–
'court' includes a tribunal; and
'relief' includes any remedy or order (other than in criminal proceedings).

13 Freedom of thought, conscience and religion

(1) If a court's determination of any question arising under this Act might affect the exercise by a religious organisation (itself or its members collectively) of the

Convention right to freedom of thought, conscience and religion, it must have particular regard to the importance of that right.
(2) In this section 'court' includes a tribunal.

DEROGATIONS AND RESERVATIONS

14 Derogations

(1) In this Act 'designated derogation' means–
(a) the United Kingdom's derogation from Article 5(3) of the Convention; and
(b) any derogation by the United Kingdom from an Article of the Convention, or of any protocol to the Convention, which is designated for the purposes of this Act in an order made by the Secretary of State.
(2) The derogation referred to in subsection (1)(a) is set out in Pt I of Sch 3.
(3) If a designated derogation is amended or replaced it ceases to be a designated derogation.
(4) But subsection (3) does not prevent the Secretary of State from exercising his power under subsection (1)(b) to make a fresh designation order in respect of the Article concerned.
(5) The Secretary of State must by order make such amendments to Sch 3 as he considers appropriate to reflect–
(a) any designation order; or
(b) the effect of subsection (3).
(6) A designation order may be made in anticipation of the making by the United Kingdom of a proposed derogation.

15 Reservations

(1) In this Act 'designated reservation' means–
(a) the United Kingdom's reservation to Art 2 of the First Protocol to the Convention; and
(b) any other reservation by the United Kingdom to an Article of the Convention, or of any protocol to the Convention, which is designated for the purposes of this Act in an order made by the Secretary of State.
(2) The text of the reservation referred to in subsection (1)(a) is set out in Pt II of Sch 3.
(3) If a designated reservation is withdrawn wholly or in part it ceases to be a designated reservation.
(4) But subsection (3) does not prevent the Secretary of State from exercising his power under subsection (1)(b) to make a fresh designation order in respect of the Article concerned.
(5) The Secretary of State must by order make such amendments to this Act as he considers appropriate to reflect–
(a) any designation order; or
(b) the effect of subsection (3).

16 Period for which designated derogations have effect

(1) If it has not already been withdrawn by the United Kingdom, a designated derogation ceases to have effect for the purposes of this Act–

(a) in the case of the derogation referred to in s 14(1)(a), at the end of the period of five years beginning with the date on which s 1(2) came into force;
(b) in the case of any other derogation, at the end of the period of five years beginning with the date on which the order designating it was made.

(2) At any time before the period–
(a) fixed by subsection (1)(a) or (b), or
(b) extended by an order under this subsection,
comes to an end, the Secretary of State may by order extend it by a further period of five years.

(3) An order under s 14(1)(b) ceases to have effect at the end of the period for consideration, unless a resolution has been passed by each House approving the order.

(4) Subsection (3) does not affect–
(a) anything done in reliance on the order; or
(b) the power to make a fresh order under s 14(1)(b).

(5) In subsection (3) 'period for consideration' means the period of forty days beginning with the day on which the order was made.

(6) In calculating the period for consideration, no account is to be taken of any time during which–
(a) Parliament is dissolved or prorogued; or
(b) both Houses are adjourned for more than four days.

(7) If a designated derogation is withdrawn by the United Kingdom, the Secretary of State must by order make such amendments to this Act as he considers are required to reflect that withdrawal.

17 Periodic review of designated reservations

(1) The appropriate Minister must review the designated reservation referred to in s 15(1)(a)–
(a) before the end of the period of five years beginning with the date on which s 1(2) came into force; and
(b) if that designation is still in force, before the end of the period of five years beginning with the date on which the last report relating to it was laid under subsection (3).

(2) The appropriate Minister must review each of the other designated reservations (if any)–
(a) before the end of the period of five years beginning with the date on which the order designating the reservation first came into force; and
(b) if the designation is still in force, before the end of the period of five years beginning with the date on which the last report relating to it was laid under subsection (3).

(3) The Minister conducting a review under this section must prepare a report on the result of the review and lay a copy of it before each House of Parliament.

JUDGES OF THE EUROPEAN COURT OF HUMAN RIGHTS

18 Appointment to European Court of Human Rights

(1) In this section 'judicial office' means the office of–
(a) Lord Justice of Appeal, Justice of the High Court or Circuit judge, in England and Wales;

(b) judge of the Court of Session or sheriff, in Scotland;
(c) Lord Justice of Appeal, judge of the High Court or county court judge, in Northern Ireland.

(2) The holder of a judicial office may become a judge of the European Court of Human Rights ('ECHR') without being required to relinquish his office.

(3) But he is not required to perform the duties of his judicial office while he is a judge of ECHR.

(4) In respect of any period during which he is a judge of ECHR–

(a) a Lord Justice of Appeal or Justice of the High Court is not to count as a judge of the relevant court for the purposes of s 2(1) or 4(1) of the Supreme Court Act 1981 (maximum number of judges) nor as a judge of the Supreme Court for the purposes of s 12(1) to (6) of that Act (salaries etc);
(b) a judge of the Court of Session is not to count as a judge of that court for the purposes of section 1(1) of the Court of Session Act 1988 (maximum number of judges) or of s 9(1)(c) of the Administration of Justice Act 1973 ('the 1973 Act') (salaries etc);
(c) a Lord Justice of Appeal or judge of the High Court in Northern Ireland is not to count as a judge of the relevant court for the purposes of s 2(1) or 3(1) of the Judicature (Northern Ireland) Act 1978 (maximum number of judges) nor as a judge of the Supreme Court of Northern Ireland for the purposes of s 9(1)(d) of the 1973 Act (salaries etc);
(d) a Circuit judge is not to count as such for the purposes of s 18 of the Courts Act 1971 (salaries etc);
(e) a sheriff is not to count as such for the purposes of s 14 of the Sheriff Courts (Scotland) Act 1907 (salaries etc);
(f) a county court judge of Northern Ireland is not to count as such for the purposes of s 106 of the County Courts Act (Northern Ireland) 1959 (salaries etc).

(5) If a sheriff principal is appointed a judge of the Court, s 11(1) of the Sheriff Courts (Scotland) Act 1971 (temporary appointment of sheriff principal) applies, while he holds that appointment, as if his office is vacant.

(6) Schedule 4 makes provision about judicial pensions in relation to the holder of a judicial office who serves as a judge of the Court.

(7) The Lord Chancellor or the Secretary of State may by order make such transitional provision (including, in particular, provision for a temporary increase in the maximum number of judges) as he considers appropriate in relation to any holder of a judicial office who has completed his service as a judge of ECHR.

PARLIAMENTARY PROCEDURE

19 Statements of compatibility

(1) A Minister of the Crown in charge of a Bill in either House of Parliament must, before Second Reading of the Bill–

(a) make a statement to the effect that in his view the provisions of the Bill are compatible with the Convention rights ('a statement of compatibility'); or
(b) make a statement to the effect that although he is unable to make a statement of compatibility the government nevertheless wishes the House to proceed with the Bill.

(2) The statement must be in writing and be published in such manner as the Minister making it considers appropriate.

SUPPLEMENTAL

20 Orders etc under this Act

(1) Any power of a Minister of the Crown to make an order under this Act is exercisable by statutory instrument.
(2) The power of the Lord Chancellor or the Secretary of State to make rules (other than rules of court) under s 2(3) or 7(9) is exercisable by statutory instrument.
(3) Any statutory instrument made under ss 14, 15 or 16(7) must be laid before Parliament.
(4) No order may be made by the Lord Chancellor or the Secretary of State under ss 1(4), 7(11) or 16(2) unless a draft of the order has been laid before, and approved by, each House of Parliament.
(5) Any statutory instrument made under s 18(7) or Sch 4, or to which subsection (2) applies, shall be subject to annulment in pursuance of a resolution of either House of Parliament.
(6) The power of a Northern Ireland department to make–

(a) rules under s 2(3)(c) or 7(9)(c), or
(b) an order under s 7(11),

is exercisable by statutory rule for the purposes of the Statutory Rules (Northern Ireland) Order 1979.
(7) Any rules made under s 2(3)(c) or 7(9)(c) shall be subject to negative resolution; and s 41(6) of the Interpretation Act (Northern Ireland) 1954 (meaning of 'subject to negative resolution') shall apply as if the power to make the rules were conferred by an Act of the Northern Ireland Assembly.
(8) No order may be made by a Northern Ireland department under s 7(11) unless a draft of the order has been laid before, and approved by, the Northern Ireland Assembly.

21 Interpretation, and so on

(1) In this Act–

'amend' includes repeal and apply (with or without modifications);
'the appropriate Minister' means the Minister of the Crown having charge of the appropriate authorised government department (within the meaning of the Crown Proceedings Act 1947);
'the Commission' means the European Commission of Human Rights;
'the Convention' means the Convention for the Protection of Human Rights and Fundamental Freedoms, agreed by the Council of Europe at Rome on 4 November 1950 as it has effect for the time being in relation to the United Kingdom;
'declaration of incompatibility' means a declaration under s 4;
'Minister of the Crown' has the same meaning as in the Ministers of the Crown Act 1975;
'Northern Ireland Minister' includes the First Minister and the deputy First Minister in Northern Ireland;
'primary legislation' means any–
(a) public general Act;
(b) local and personal Act;

(c) private Act;
(d) Measure of the Church Assembly;
(e) Measure of the General Synod of the Church of England;
(f) Order in Council–
(i) made in exercise of Her Majesty's Royal Prerogative;
(ii) made under s 38(1)(a) of the Northern Ireland Constitution Act 1973 or the corresponding provision of the Northern Ireland Act 1998; or
(iii) amending an Act of a kind mentioned in paras (a), (b) or (c);
and includes an order or other instrument made under primary legislation (otherwise than by the National Assembly for Wales, a member of the Scottish Executive, a Northern Ireland Minister or a Northern Ireland department) to the extent to which it operates to bring one or more provisions of that legislation into force or amends any primary legislation;
'the First Protocol' means the protocol to the Convention agreed at Paris on 20 March 1952;
'the Sixth Protocol' means the protocol to the Convention agreed at Strasbourg on 28th April 1983;
'the Eleventh Protocol' means the protocol to the Convention (restructuring the control machinery established by the Convention) agreed at Strasbourg on 11 May 1994;
'remedial order' means an order under s 10;
'subordinate legislation' means any–
(a) Order in Council other than one–
(i) made in exercise of Her Majesty's Royal Prerogative;
(ii) made under section 38(1)(a) of the Northern Ireland Constitution Act 1973 or the corresponding provision of the Northern Ireland Act 1998; or
(iii) amending an Act of a kind mentioned in the definition of primary legislation;
(b) Act of the Scottish Parliament;
(c) Act of the Parliament of Northern Ireland;
(d) Measure of the Assembly established under s 1 of the Northern Ireland Assembly Act 1973;
(e) Act of the Northern Ireland Assembly;
(f) order, rules, regulations, scheme, warrant, byelaw or other instrument made under primary legislation (except to the extent to which it operates to bring one or more provisions of that legislation into force or amends any primary legislation);
(g) order, rules, regulations, scheme, warrant, byelaw or other instrument made under legislation mentioned in paragraph (b), (c), (d) or (e) or made under an Order in Council applying only to Northern Ireland;
(h) order, rules, regulations, scheme, warrant, byelaw or other instrument made by a member of the Scottish Executive, a Northern Ireland Minister or a Northern Ireland department in exercise of prerogative or other executive functions of Her Majesty which are exercisable by such a person on behalf of Her Majesty;

'transferred matters' has the same meaning as in the Northern Ireland Act 1998; and
'tribunal' means any tribunal in which legal proceedings may be brought.

(2) The references in paragraphs (b) and (c) of s 2(1) to Articles are to Articles of the Convention as they had effect immediately before the coming into force of the Eleventh Protocol.

(3) The reference in paragraph (d) of s 2(1) to Art 46 includes a reference to Articles 32 and 54 of the Convention as they had effect immediately before the coming into force of the Eleventh Protocol.
(4) The references in s 2(1) to a report or decision of the Commission or a decision of the Committee of Ministers include references to a report or decision made as provided by paras 3, 4 and 6 of Art 5 of the Eleventh Protocol (transitional provisions).
(5) Any liability under the Army Act 1955, the Air Force Act 1955 or the Naval Discipline Act 1957 to suffer death for an offence is replaced by a liability to imprisonment for life or any less punishment authorised by those Acts; and those Acts shall accordingly have effect with the necessary modifications.

22 Short title, commencement, application and extent

(1) This Act may be cited as the Human Rights Act 1998.
(2) Sections 18, 20 and 21(5) and this section come into force on the passing of this Act.
(3) The other provisions of this Act come into force on such day as the Secretary of State may by order appoint; and different days may be appointed for different purposes.
(4) Paragraph (b) of subsection (1) of s 7 applies to proceedings brought by or at the instigation of a public authority whenever the act in question took place; but otherwise that subsection does not apply to an act taking place before the coming into force of that section.
(5) This Act binds the Crown.
(6) This Act extends to Northern Ireland.
(7) Section 21(5), so far as it relates to any provision contained in the Army Act 1955, the Air Force Act 1955 or the Naval Discipline Act 1957, extends to any place to which that provision extends.

Schedules

SCHEDULE I THE ARTICLES PART I THE CONVENTION

RIGHTS AND FREEDOMS

Article 2
Right to life

1. Everyone's right to life shall be protected by law. No one shall be deprived of his life intentionally save in the execution of a sentence of a court following his conviction of a crime for which this penalty is provided by law.
2. Deprivation of life shall not be regarded as inflicted in contravention of this Article when it results from the use of force which is no more than absolutely necessary:
   (a) in defence of any person from unlawful violence;
   (b) in order to effect a lawful arrest or to prevent the escape of a person lawfully detained;
   (c) in action lawfully taken for the purpose of quelling a riot or insurrection.

Article 3
Prohibition of torture

No one shall be subjected to torture or to inhuman or degrading treatment or punishment.

Article 4
Prohibition of slavery and forced labour

1. No one shall be held in slavery or servitude.
2. No one shall be required to perform forced or compulsory labour.
3. For the purpose of this Article the term 'forced or compulsory labour' shall not include:
   (a) any work required to be done in the ordinary course of detention imposed according to the provisions of Article 5 of this Convention or during conditional release from such detention;
   (b) any service of a military character or, in case of conscientious objectors in countries where they are recognised, service exacted instead of compulsory military service;
   (c) any service exacted in case of an emergency or calamity threatening the life or well-being of the community;
   (d) any work or service which forms part of normal civic obligations.

Article 5
Right to liberty and security

1. Everyone has the right to liberty and security of person. No one shall be deprived of his liberty save in the following cases and in accordance with a procedure prescribed by law:

(a) the lawful detention of a person after conviction by a competent court;
(b) the lawful arrest or detention of a person for non-compliance with the lawful order of a court or in order to secure the fulfilment of any obligation prescribed by law;
(c) the lawful arrest or detention of a person effected for the purpose of bringing him before the competent legal authority on reasonable suspicion of having committed an offence or when it is reasonably considered necessary to prevent his committing an offence or fleeing after having done so;
(d) the detention of a minor by lawful order for the purpose of educational supervision or his lawful detention for the purpose of bringing him before the competent legal authority;
(e) the lawful detention of persons for the prevention of the spreading of infectious diseases, of persons of unsound mind, alcoholics or drug addicts or vagrants;
(f) the lawful arrest or detention of a person to prevent his effecting an unauthorised entry into the country or of a person against whom action is being taken with a view to deportation or extradition.

2. Everyone who is arrested shall be informed promptly, in a language which he understands, of the reasons for his arrest and of any charge against him.
3. Everyone arrested or detained in accordance with the provisions of para 1(c) of this Article shall be brought promptly before a judge or other officer authorised by law to exercise judicial power and shall be entitled to trial within a reasonable time or to release pending trial. Release may be conditioned by guarantees to appear for trial.
4. Everyone who is deprived of his liberty by arrest or detention shall be entitled to take proceedings by which the lawfulness of his detention shall be decided speedily by a court and his release ordered if the detention is not lawful.
5. Everyone who has been the victim of arrest or detention in contravention of the provisions of this Article shall have an enforceable right to compensation.

Article 6
Right to a fair trial

1. In the determination of his civil rights and obligations or of any criminal charge against him, everyone is entitled to a fair and public hearing within a reasonable time by an independent and impartial tribunal established by law. Judgment shall be pronounced publicly but the press and public may be excluded from all or part of the trial in the interest of morals, public order or national security in a democratic society, where the interests of juveniles or the protection of the private life of the parties so require, or to the extent strictly necessary in the opinion of the court in special circumstances where publicity would prejudice the interests of justice.
2. Everyone charged with a criminal offence shall be presumed innocent until proved guilty according to law.
3. Everyone charged with a criminal offence has the following minimum rights:
(a) to be informed promptly, in a language which he understands and in detail, of the nature and cause of the accusation against him;
(b) to have adequate time and facilities for the preparation of his defence;
(c) to defend himself in person or through legal assistance of his own choosing or, if he has not sufficient means to pay for legal assistance, to

be given it free when the interests of justice so require;
(d) to examine or have examined witnesses against him and to obtain the attendance and examination of witnesses on his behalf under the same conditions as witnesses against him;
(e) to have the free assistance of an interpreter if he cannot understand or speak the language used in court.

Article 7
No punishment without law

1. No one shall be held guilty of any criminal offence on account of any act or omission which did not constitute a criminal offence under national or international law at the time when it was committed. Nor shall a heavier penalty be imposed than the one that was applicable at the time the criminal offence was committed.
2. This Article shall not prejudice the trial and punishment of any person for any act or omission which, at the time when it was committed, was criminal according to the general principles of law recognised by civilised nations.

Article 8
Right to respect for private and family life

1. Everyone has the right to respect for his private and family life, his home and his correspondence.
2. There shall be no interference by a public authority with the exercise of this right except such as is in accordance with the law and is necessary in a democratic society in the interests of national security, public safety or the economic well-being of the country, for the prevention of disorder or crime, for the protection of health or morals, or for the protection of the rights and freedoms of others.

Article 9
Freedom of thought, conscience and religion

1. Everyone has the right to freedom of thought, conscience and religion; this right includes freedom to change his religion or belief and freedom, either alone or in community with others and in public or private, to manifest his religion or belief, in worship, teaching, practice and observance.
2. Freedom to manifest one's religion or beliefs shall be subject only to such limitations as are prescribed by law and are necessary in a democratic society in the interests of public safety, for the protection of public order, health or morals, or for the protection of the rights and freedoms of others.

Article 10
Freedom of expression

1. Everyone has the right to freedom of expression. This right shall include freedom to hold opinions and to receive and impart information and ideas without interference by public authority and regardless of frontiers. This Article shall not prevent States from requiring the licensing of broadcasting, television or cinema enterprises.
2. The exercise of these freedoms, since it carries with it duties and responsibilities, may be subject to such formalities, conditions, restrictions or penalties as are prescribed by law and are necessary in a democratic society, in the interests of national security, territorial integrity or public safety, for the prevention of disorder

or crime, for the protection of health or morals, for the protection of the reputation or rights of others, for preventing the disclosure of information received in confidence, or for maintaining the authority and impartiality of the judiciary.

Article 11
Freedom of assembly and association

1. Everyone has the right to freedom of peaceful assembly and to freedom of association with others, including the right to form and to join trade unions for the protection of his interests.
2. No restrictions shall be placed on the exercise of these rights other than such as are prescribed by law and are necessary in a democratic society in the interests of national security or public safety, for the prevention of disorder or crime, for the protection of health or morals or for the protection of the rights and freedoms of others. This Article shall not prevent the imposition of lawful restrictions on the exercise of these rights by members of the armed forces, of the police or of the administration of the state.

Article 12
Right to marry

Men and women of marriageable age have the right to marry and to found a family, according to the national laws governing the exercise of this right.

Article 14
Prohibition of discrimination

The enjoyment of the rights and freedoms set forth in this Convention shall be secured without discrimination on any ground such as sex, race, colour, language, religion, political or other opinion, national or social origin, association with a national minority, property, birth or other status.

Article 16
Restrictions on political activity of aliens

Nothing in Arts 10, 11 and 14 shall be regarded as preventing the High Contracting Parties from imposing restrictions on the political activity of aliens.

Article 17
Prohibition of abuse of rights

Nothing in this Convention may be interpreted as implying for any state, group or person any right to engage in any activity or perform any act aimed at the destruction of any of the rights and freedoms set forth herein or at their limitation to a greater extent than is provided for in the Convention.

Article 18
Limitation on use of restrictions on rights

The restrictions permitted under this Convention to the said rights and freedoms shall not be applied for any purpose other than those for which they have been prescribed.

PART II
THE FIRST PROTOCOL

Article 1
Protection of property

Every natural or legal person is entitled to the peaceful enjoyment of his possessions. No one shall be deprived of his possessions except in the public interest and subject to the conditions provided for by law and by the general principles of international law.

The preceding provisions shall not, however, in any way impair the right of a State to enforce such laws as it deems necessary to control the use of property in accordance with the general interest or to secure the payment of taxes or other contributions or penalties.

Article 2
Right to education

No person shall be denied the right to education. In the exercise of any functions which it assumes in relation to education and to teaching, the State shall respect the right of parents to ensure such education and teaching in conformity with their own religious and philosophical convictions.

Article 3
Right to free elections

The High Contracting Parties undertake to hold free elections at reasonable intervals by secret ballot, under conditions which will ensure the free expression of the opinion of the people in the choice of the legislature.

PART III
THE SIXTH PROTOCOL

Article 1
Abolition of the death penalty

The death penalty shall be abolished. No one shall be condemned to such penalty or executed.

Article 2
Death penalty in time of war

A state may make provision in its law for the death penalty in respect of acts committed in time of war or of imminent threat of war; such penalty shall be applied only in the instances laid down in the law and in accordance with its provisions. The State shall communicate to the Secretary General of the Council of Europe the relevant provisions of that law.

SCHEDULE 2
REMEDIAL ORDERS

Section 10

Orders

1. (1) A remedial order may–

(a) contain such incidental, supplemental, consequential or transitional provision as the person making it considers appropriate;

(b) be made so as to have effect from a date earlier than that on which it is made;

(c) make provision for the delegation of specific functions;

(d) make different provision for different cases.

(2) The power conferred by sub-para (1)(a) includes–

(a) power to amend primary legislation (including primary legislation other than that which contains the incompatible provision); and

(b) power to amend or revoke subordinate legislation (including subordinate legislation other than that which contains the incompatible provision).

(3) A remedial order may be made so as to have the same extent as the legislation which it affects.

(4) No person is to be guilty of an offence solely as a result of the retrospective effect of a remedial order.

Procedure

2. No remedial order may be made unless–

(a) a draft of the order has been approved by a resolution of each House of Parliament made after the end of the period of 60 days beginning with the day on which the draft was laid; or

(b) it is declared in the order that it appears to the person making it that, because of the urgency of the matter, it is necessary to make the order without a draft being so approved.

Orders laid in draft

3. (1) No draft may be laid under para 2(a) unless–

(a) the person proposing to make the order has laid before Parliament a document which contains a draft of the proposed order and the required information; and

(b) the period of 60 days, beginning with the day on which the document required by this sub-paragraph was laid, has ended.

(2) If representations have been made during that period, the draft laid under para 2(a) must be accompanied by a statement containing–

(a) a summary of the representations; and

(b) if, as a result of the representations, the proposed order has been changed, details of the changes.

Urgent cases

4. (1) If a remedial order ('the original order') is made without being approved in draft, the person making it must lay it before Parliament, accompanied by the

required information, after it is made.
(2) If representations have been made during the period of 60 days beginning with the day on which the original order was made, the person making it must (after the end of that period) lay before Parliament a statement containing–
(a) a summary of the representations; and
(b) if, as a result of the representations, he considers it appropriate to make changes to the original order, details of the changes.
(3) If sub-paragraph (2)(b) applies, the person making the statement must–
(a) make a further remedial order replacing the original order; and
(b) lay the replacement order before Parliament.
(4) If, at the end of the period of 120 days beginning with the day on which the original order was made, a resolution has not been passed by each House approving the original or replacement order, the order ceases to have effect (but without that affecting anything previously done under either order or the power to make a fresh remedial order).

Definitions

5. In this Schedule–
'representations' means representations about a remedial order (or proposed remedial order) made to the person making (or proposing to make) it and includes any relevant Parliamentary report or resolution; and
'required information' means–
(a) an explanation of the incompatibility which the order (or proposed order) seeks to remove, including particulars of the relevant declaration, finding or order; and
(b) a statement of the reasons for proceeding under section 10 and for making an order in those terms.

Calculating periods

6. In calculating any period for the purposes of this Schedule, no account is to be taken of any time during which–
(a) Parliament is dissolved or prorogued; or
(b) both Houses are adjourned for more than four days.

SCHEDULE 3
DEROGATION AND RESERVATION

PART I
DEROGATION

The 1988 notification

The United Kingdom Permanent Representative to the Council of Europe presents his compliments to the Secretary General of the Council, and has the honour to convey the following information in order to ensure compliance with the obligations of Her Majesty's Government in the United Kingdom under Art 15(3) of the Convention for the Protection of Human Rights and Fundamental Freedoms signed at Rome on 4 November 1950.

There have been in the United Kingdom in recent years campaigns of organised terrorism connected with the affairs of Northern Ireland which have manifested themselves in activities which have included repeated murder, attempted murder, maiming, intimidation and violent civil disturbance and in bombing and fire raising which have resulted in death, injury and widespread destruction of property. As a result, a public emergency within the meaning of Art 15(1) of the Convention exists in the United Kingdom.

The Government found it necessary in 1974 to introduce and since then, in cases concerning persons reasonably suspected of involvement in terrorism connected with the affairs of Northern Ireland, or of certain offences under the legislation, who have been detained for 48 hours, to exercise powers enabling further detention without charge, for periods of up to five days, on the authority of the Secretary of State. These powers are at present to be found in Section 12 of the Prevention of Terrorism (Temporary Provisions) Act 1984, Art 9 of the Prevention of Terrorism (Supplemental Temporary Provisions) Order 1984 and Art 10 of the Prevention of Terrorism (Supplemental Temporary Provisions) (Northern Ireland) Order 1984.

Section 12 of the Prevention of Terrorism (Temporary Provisions) Act 1984 provides for a person whom a constable has arrested on reasonable grounds of suspecting him to be guilty of an offence under Section 1, 9 or 10 of the Act, or to be or to have been involved in terrorism connected with the affairs of Northern Ireland, to be detained in right of the arrest for up to 48 hours and thereafter, where the Secretary of State extends the detention period, for up to a further five days. Section 12 substantially re-enacted Section 12 of the Prevention of Terrorism (Temporary Provisions) Act 1976 which, in turn, substantially re-enacted s 7 of the Prevention of Terrorism (Temporary Provisions) Act 1974.

Article 10 of the Prevention of Terrorism (Supplemental Temporary Provisions) (Northern Ireland) Order 1984 (SI 1984/417) and Art 9 of the Prevention of Terrorism (Supplemental Temporary Provisions) Order 1984 (SI 1984/418) were both made under ss 13 and 14 of and Sch 3 to the 1984 Act and substantially re-enacted powers of detention in Orders made under the 1974 and 1976 Acts. A person who is being examined under Art 4 of either Order on his arrival in, or on seeking to leave, Northern Ireland or Great Britain for the purpose of determining whether he is or has been involved in terrorism connected with the affairs of Northern Ireland, or whether there are grounds for suspecting that he has committed an offence under s 9 of the 1984 Act, may be detained under Art 9 or 10, as appropriate, pending the conclusion of his examination. The period of this examination may exceed 12 hours if an examining officer has reasonable grounds for suspecting him to be or to have been involved in acts of terrorism connected with the affairs of Northern Ireland.

Where such a person is detained under the said Art 9 or 10 he may be detained for up to 48 hours on the authority of an examining officer and thereafter, where the Secretary of State extends the detention period, for up to a further five days. In its judgment of 29 November 1988 in the Case of Brogan and Others, the European Court of Human Rights held that there had been a violation of Art 5(3) in respect of each of the applicants, all of whom had been detained under s 12 of the 1984 Act. ECHR held that even the shortest of the four periods of detention concerned, namely four days and six hours, fell outside the constraints as to time permitted by the first part of Art 5(3). In addition, ECHR held that there had been a violation of Art 5(5) in the case of each applicant.

Following this judgment, the Secretary of State for the Home Department informed Parliament on 6 December 1988 that, against the background of the terrorist campaign, and the over-riding need to bring terrorists to justice, the Government did not believe that the maximum period of detention should be reduced. He informed Parliament that the Government were examining the matter with a view to responding to the judgment. On 22 December 1988, the Secretary of State further informed Parliament that it remained the Government's wish, if it could be achieved, to find a judicial process under which extended detention might be reviewed and where appropriate authorised by a judge or other judicial officer. But a further period of reflection and consultation was necessary before the Government could bring forward a firm and final view.

Since the judgment of 29 November 1988 as well as previously, the Government have found it necessary to continue to exercise, in relation to terrorism connected with the affairs of Northern Ireland, the powers described above enabling further detention without charge for periods of up to five days, on the authority of the Secretary of State, to the extent strictly required by the exigencies of the situation to enable necessary enquiries and investigations properly to be completed in order to decide whether criminal proceedings should be instituted. To the extent that the exercise of these powers may be inconsistent with the obligations imposed by the Convention the Government has availed itself of the right of derogation conferred by Art 15(1) of the Convention and will continue to do so until further notice.

Dated 23 December 1988.

The 1989 notification

The United Kingdom Permanent Representative to the Council of Europe presents his compliments to the Secretary General of the Council, and has the honour to convey the following information.

In his communication to the Secretary General of 23 December 1988, reference was made to the introduction and exercise of certain powers under section 12 of the Prevention of Terrorism (Temporary Provisions) Act 1984, Article 9 of the Prevention of Terrorism (Supplemental Temporary Provisions) Order 1984 and Article 10 of the Prevention of Terrorism (Supplemental Temporary Provisions) (Northern Ireland) Order 1984.

These provisions have been replaced by s 14 of and para 6 of Sch 5 to the Prevention of Terrorism (Temporary Provisions) Act 1989, which make comparable provision. They came into force on 22 March 1989. A copy of these provisions is enclosed.

The United Kingdom Permanent Representative avails himself of this opportunity to renew to the Secretary General the assurance of his highest consideration.
23 March 1989.

PART II
RESERVATION

At the time of signing the present (First) Protocol, I declare that, in view of certain provisions of the Education Acts in the United Kingdom, the principle affirmed in the second sentence of Art 2 is accepted by the United Kingdom only so far as it is compatible with the provision of efficient instruction and training, and the avoidance of unreasonable public expenditure.

Dated 20 March 1952. Made by the United Kingdom Permanent Representative to the Council of Europe.

SCHEDULE 4
JUDICIAL PENSIONS

Duty to make orders about pensions

1. (1) The appropriate Minister must by order make provision with respect to pensions payable to or in respect of any holder of a judicial office who serves as an ECHR judge.
(2) A pensions order must include such provision as the Minister making it considers is necessary to secure that–
  (a) an ECHR judge who was, immediately before his appointment as an ECHR judge, a member of a judicial pension scheme is entitled to remain as a member of that scheme;
  (b) the terms on which he remains a member of the scheme are those which would have been applicable had he not been appointed as an ECHR judge; and
  (c) entitlement to benefits payable in accordance with the scheme continues to be determined as if, while serving as an ECHR judge, his salary was that which would (but for s 18(4)) have been payable to him in respect of his continuing service as the holder of his judicial office.

Contributions

2. A pensions order may, in particular, make provision–
  (a) for any contributions which are payable by a person who remains a member of a scheme as a result of the order, and which would otherwise be payable by deduction from his salary, to be made otherwise than by deduction from his salary as an ECHR judge; and
  (b) for such contributions to be collected in such manner as may be determined by the administrators of the scheme.

Amendments of other enactments

3. A pensions order may amend any provision of, or made under, a pensions Act in such manner and to such extent as the Minister making the order considers necessary or expedient to ensure the proper administration of any scheme to which it relates.

Definitions

4. In this Schedule–
  'appropriate Minister' means–
    (a) in relation to any judicial office whose jurisdiction is exercisable exclusively in relation to Scotland, the Secretary of State; and
    (b) otherwise, the Lord Chancellor;
  'ECHR judge' means the holder of a judicial office who is serving as a judge of ECHR;
  'judicial pension scheme' means a scheme established by and in accordance with a pensions Act;
  'pensions Act' means–
    (a) the County Courts Act (Northern Ireland) 1959;
    (b) the Sheriffs' Pensions (Scotland) Act 1961;
    (c) the Judicial Pensions Act 1981; or
    (d) the Judicial Pensions and Retirement Act 1993; and
  'pensions order' means an order made under para 1.

Index